CONTENTS

CONTENTS

JAMES JOYCE

THE
ARTIST
AND THE
LABYRINTH

*A Critical
Re-evaluation*

Edited by Augustine Martin

JAMES JOYCE

THE ARTIST
AND THE
LABYRINTH

Edited by Augustine Martin

RYAN PUBLISHING
Independence and Quality

First Edition.

First published in Great Britain 1990 by

Ryan Publishing Co. Ltd.,
62 Frith Street,
London, W1.

British Library Cataloguing in Publication Data

James Joyce : The Artist and the Labyrinth.
1. Fiction in English. (Joyce, James, *1882-1941*)
I. Martin, Augustine.
822'.912

ISBN 1-870805-06-2 (Cased)
ISBN 1-870805-26-7 (Paperback)

Designed in Paris by Franck Marest.
Origination by Wenham Arts.

Printed in England by Clays Ltd, St Ives plc.

EDITOR'S INTRODUCTION

Augustine Martin

This book is shaped to take in the curve of Joyce's development, as befits a volume which has its origin in the first session of the James Joyce Annual Summer School at the author's old University College on St Stephen's Green, Dublin. Within this context it attempts to redress a little the trend of recent post-structuralist Joyce criticism with its tendency to remove Joyce from the world of the ordinary reader. The first article begins with Joyce's student writings and, in a spirit of good-natured pugnacity, proposes a reading of the work which challenges the myth-laden 'hind-sight' of traditional critics. The second, by TP Dolan, is a study of Joyce's language that runs refreshingly counter to the more fashionable linguistic theories which have at once reduced and expanded his fiction to a radio-active field of semiotic correspondences.

To reinforce the sense of a fresh departure, three of the articles are by Irish novelists, Benedict Kiely, John McGahern and John Banville, each from a different post-Joycean generation. Three more diverse responses would be hard to find, Kiely looking upon himself as an inheritor, and Banville as a 'survivor', of the great man's influence. McGahern, on the other hand, prefers to concentrate on the Flaubertian amorality of *Dubliners*.

In dealing with *Portrait of the Artist* the biographer Deirdre Bair explores the interpenetration of the fiction with the life, Colbert Kearney the struggle between artistic and nationalist versions of freedom. The neglected field of Joyce's lyric achievement is explored by a distinguished lyric poet, Eamon Grennan, while the neglected text of *Exiles* is treated as a working script by Vincent Dowling – a former Artistic Director of the Abbey Theatre – who was the first to produce the play professionally on the Irish stage and television screen.

Greatest emphasis falls, understandably, on *Ulysses*, which is variously encountered by three outstanding Joyceans. Clive Hart exposes unexpected narrative structures in the great novel's rhythmic life. Barbara Hardy finds new mythic energies in a strenuous re-reading of both Homer and Joyce. Maud Ellmann brings semiological bell, book and candle to bear on the novel in an essay that is a noble tribute to the memory of her father, that most brilliant and beloved of Joyce's scholars and champions. Petr Skrabanek achieves the impossible by writing an essay on *Finnegans Wake* that serves as an introduction to the book's mysteries for the unseasoned reader, while providing a series of the most original suggestions as to its theme and organising principle.

Joyce's wider affiliations, literary, anthropological and biographical, are rehearsed in different ways by Maureen Murphy, Ulick O'Connor, AN Jeffares and Denis Donoghue. Murphy discovers a folk legacy of betrayal and retribution in the memories that haunted the young Joyce's Ireland. The biographer of Oliver St John Gogarty revisits that curious relationship between the two writers and the Dublin milieu that provided their raw material. Jeffares calls upon his skills as a classicist and literary historian to furnish a revised ancestry for Joyce's metamorphic technique. Denis Donoghue, currently intent on his investigations of modernism, focuses Pound and Joyce within the problematical context of that concern.

Finally, in a luminous gesture of artistic witness, at once analytic and confessional, Brendan Kennelly – poet, novelist and critic – explores Joyce's ambiguous and terrible drives towards personal self-destruction and creative fulfilment.

Augustine Martin
University College Dublin
February 1990.

THE ARTIST
AND THE
LABYRINTH

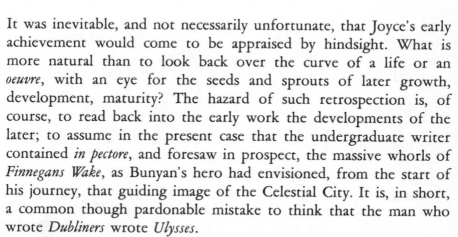

Augustine Martin

It was inevitable, and not necessarily unfortunate, that Joyce's early achievement would come to be appraised by hindsight. What is more natural than to look back over the curve of a life or an *oeuvre*, with an eye for the seeds and sprouts of later growth, development, maturity? The hazard of such retrospection is, of course, to read back into the early work the developments of the later; to assume in the present case that the undergraduate writer contained *in pectore*, and foresaw in prospect, the massive whorls of *Finnegans Wake*, as Bunyan's hero had envisioned, from the start of his journey, that guiding image of the Celestial City. It is, in short, a common though pardonable mistake to think that the man who wrote *Dubliners* wrote *Ulysses*.

This bias of criticism can operate as an unconscious assumption or as a formal heuristic procedure. As far back as 1944 Richard Levin and Charles Shattuck established the latter tendency in their celebrated essay, 'First Flight to Ithaca'[1], finding, often with labour and ingenuity, a prototype for each individual story of *Dubliners* in Homer's *Odyssey*. Though they could find no scrap of external

11

evidence for a theory which might convict Joyce of such repetitious pedantry – this school of commentary received almost universal encouragement, especially from such a critic as Brewster Ghiselin in his influential article, 'The Unity of Joyce's *Dubliners*' in 1956.[2] There he proposed for *Dubliners* an elaborate unity of design rarely, if ever, claimed by a Joycean critic for even the most favoured of the later works. He writes:

> But no constellation, zodiac, or whole celestial sphere of symbols is enough in itself to establish in the fifteen separate narratives, each one in its realistic aspect a completely independent action, the embracing and inviolable order of full structural unity.

The basis of this structural unity is, he claims, *orientation*, a frustrated, unconscious effort on the part of the characters to move eastward, the way of spiritual salvation. [In the following quotation from the same essay I name the relevant stories in parentheses for the reader's convenience:]

> . . . in a sequence of six stories ['The Sisters', 'An Encounter', 'Araby', 'Eveline', 'After the Race', 'Two Gallants'] an impulse and movement eastward to the outskirts of the city and beyond; in a single story ['The Boarding House'] an impulse to fly upward out of a confining situation near the center of Dublin; in a sequence of four stories, ['A Little Cloud', 'Counterparts', 'Clay', 'A Painful Case'] a gradual replacement of the impulse eastward by an impulse and movement westward; in three stories ['Ivy Day in the Committee Room', 'A Mother', 'Grace'] a limited activity confined almost wholly within the central area of Dublin; and in the concluding story ['The Dead'] a movement eastward to the heart of the city, the exact center of arrest, then, in vision only, far westward into death.

Though there are many fine things in Ghiselin's long essay, I have to record my conviction that no reader in his right mind would sense such a design in the most alert first or second reading of the volume. Even when pointed out, all those shufflings to and fro fall well short of basic coherence let alone 'inviolable order of full structural unity'. Having read and taught the book for more than twenty years and lived in the city for much longer, I still find it impossible to visualise such unconscious pedestrian manoeuvres as shaping any literary or geographical pattern. It is, of course, quite sensible to observe that Joyce's characters tend to aimlessness, to getting nowhere, to going round in circles and ending up where they began. But the individual theory is not the real basis of my quarrel.

That quarrel is with the tendency, now long established, to read back into these brilliant, tentative fictions Joyce's later symbolic and mythic structures, often turning good stories into bad allegories. Ghiselin insists, for instance, that Saint Kevin Hydrophilos of *Finnegans Wake* going 'westform' towards a suitable supply of water, and showing his sense of the importance of orientation by genuflecting seven times eastward' is foreshadowed not only in the adventures of the boy in 'Araby' but in the symbolism of water and the east that governs the life of the every character in *Dubliners*. In his final conclusion, Ghiselin salutes *Finnegans Wake* as the culmination of Joyce's achievement – 'a vast epiphany and a communion in which all may share', and goes on to insist:

> *Dubliners* began it, in a single symbolic structure consubstantial with a full-blooded naturalistic narrative defining at once the symbolic method of Joyce's successive masterpieces and the grounds of his mature vision.

The mythic – as well as symbolic – hindsight on *Dubliners* was given new force in a volume edited by Clive Hart in 1969.[3] Including some of the foremost names in Joycean scholarship, this book is a virtual treasure-hunt for proleptic images of Joyce's later mythologies. Nathan Halper, writing on 'The Boarding House', sets out to develop the suggestion by Levin and Shattuck that the piece had its Homeric prototype in 'The interlude of Aphrodite and Ares, the song Demodocus sang in the palace of Alcinous'.

Thus Polly Mooney with 'her light short hair' is Aphrodite, and Bob 'who has not shaved for a few days' – has a red beard like Ares. Mrs Mooney is the smith Haephaestus – 'it does not matter that he is a husband or lame', neither detail being 'germane to the motif'. Jack Mooney, the brother, as Poseidon, the earth-shaking sea-god, because he works in Fleet Street, and as god of fishes, 'he has two bottles of Bass'. It goes on for more than ten pages and is as ludic as the deconstructionists at their best or worse.

Elsewhere in the volume Fritz Senn suggests, rather more cautiously, that the old pervert in 'An Encounter' may be 'a perverted god' while the goal of the boys' quest, the Pigeon House, 'may allude symbolically to the Holy Ghost' because it so alludes – 'C'est le pigeon, Joseph' – in the Proteus episode of Ulysses. In A Walton Litz's essay on 'Two Gallants', Lenehan's meal of peas and ginger beer is 'the Last Supper' and his triple exclamation 'That takes the biscuit!' is a 'reference to the Sacred Host'; Lenehan, after all, 'uses the same phrase in Ulysses. In his essay on 'A Mother' David Hayman identifies the Kearney family leaving the concert room with 'the family of Lot leaving Sodom'. Bernard Benstock in his analysis of 'The Dead' suggests, albeit with much protective irony, that the Morkans' party is a version of the Feast of the Epiphany, and that Gabriel Conroy represents 'all three Magi' – the second syllable of his name suggests the French for king, 'roi'. The coin which he gives Lily – 'though probably not gold' – is the first of the three gifts, the 'cold fragrant air' that escapes from his coat, is the nearest equivalent that can be found to myrrh or frankincense. One senses a certain exegetical desperation creeping in.

The rights and wrongs of these methodologies were debated, but by no means settled, as far back as 1956 by Marvin Magalaner and Richard M Kain.[4] Stanislaus Joyce had objected to Marvin Magalaner's suggestion that Maria, in 'Clay', was both a Halloween witch and the Virgin Mary, accusing the critic of 'exaggeration' and asserting that his brother 'had no such subtleties in mind' at the time of writing. On mature consideration the two critics decided on a compromise, disallowing the virgin and retaining the witch. The fact that the two roles are scarcely compatible was not an issue in their decision. Such incompatibility would not be felt in *Ulysses* or *Finnegans Wake*, but it must surely pose a problem of some kind in a fledgling work like 'The Boarding House' where Joyce is negotiating so delicately between the conventions of nineteenth century Naturalism and that Modernist aesthetic of which he is to become a foremost pioneer.

Myth and symbol remain the Joycean critic's stock-in-trade, and despite the inroads of Postmodernist critical theory, are still the most popular – and the most repetitive and boring – approaches among university students today. The neo-Freudians grope beneath the language for sexual symbolism, the Jungians for archetypes, while Formalists uncover myth beneath myth, folk tale beneath historical fable. The Virgin Mary, the Shan Van Vocht, the Pooka, Finn McCool, Brian Boru, Skin-the-Goat, Queen Victoria, Grania Wail, cavort through the commentaries with Conary Mor, Helen of Troy, Balor of the Evil Eye, Kitty O'Shea, the Goban Saor – 'Dragons out of the water/And witches out of the air'. It is such an easy recipe: to quote a great contemporary, Mrs Beeton, first catch your parallel; then comb the text for supporting evidence, then yoke them together with a flourish of erudition. Those of us who respect and love these Dubliners almost as real people are tempted to exclaim with their creator in an early letter: 'Ah, my poor fledglings, poor Corley, poor Ignatius Gallagher!'.

In a book containing much brilliant research and scholarship, *Backgrounds for Joyce's **Dubliners**,*[5] Donald Torchiana has given the tendency new wind. Writing of 'Clay' he sees Maria as foreshadowing 'what Joyce in *Ulysses* will denominate Gummy Grammy in appearance, a rather grim version of the Shan Van Vocht first noticed by William Tindall'. He goes on to unearth and force into relevance material that no reader of the story, Irish or foreign, could possibly feel the want of. It seems that Drumcondra, where Maria goes visiting, is in the parish 'Clonturk, that is, the Meadow of Swine', which is adjacent to Puckstown, associated with the 'Fomorian Pooka'. This evil creature is 'thoroughly identified' with the Black Pig of Irish mythology. Halloween is the Irish pagan feast of *Samhain*, when the forces of light yield to those of darkness. Consquently:

Unfairly, perhaps, I take Joe Donnelly and family and guests to be the final version of *Samhain* eve's tumultuous triumph of darkness . . . Joe is probably known as a good bloke . . . yet he is also something of a pig.

In his chapter on 'After the Race', Torchiana finds beneath this perfunctory sketch of a Dublin parvenu's heady night on the town the historical 'Races of Castlebar', when, in 1798, a French expeditionary force under General Humbert landed in Mayo and, with the help of a large Irish contingent, scored some initial defeats over the English before being crushed at Ballinamuck. He is, of course, not the first to have taken this brisk anecdote as a parable of Irish political failure. The French drivers, after all, win the Gordon Bennett contest, but the Englishman, Routh, wins the card game in which Jimmy Doyle is the heaviest loser. And Jimmy quarrels with the Englishman over politics. The toasts to their respective countries, England, America, France, Hungary and Ireland emphasise – somehow – that the last is the only one not to have 'achieved a modicum of independence or democracy'. The central and obvious theme of this rather obvious story is thus pushed to the margins, and Joyce is convicted of writing an obscure and floundering political allegory.

Jimmy Doyle is important for being the only example in *Dubliners* of the city's successfully merging Catholic mercantile class – the potential 'merchant princes'. Nor does he cut an altogether hopeless figure in the role; he's learning fast, and his children, given any luck, will complete the upward mobility that his father has set in motion. Polly Mooney might have made it into that milieu had her mother not married a drunkard. A small comedy of manners, this vignette of Dublin 'fashionable life' fills out a certain space on Joyce's canvas of the city's pattern. Slight though it is, 'After the Race', with its vivid opening sentences, may be the most prophetically relevant of all these epicleti to the Ireland of 1992:

The cars came scudding in towards Dublin, running evenly like pellets in the groove of the Naas Road. At the crest of the hill at Inchicore sightseers had gathered in clumps to

watch the cars careering homeward and through this channel of poverty and inaction the Continent sped its wealth
and industry.

I will now look afresh at the early Joyce, excluding as much
hindsight as possible. Our first impression is of a young writer
struggling with certain simple and momentous difficulties. Leaving
aside the distractions of lyric poetry in which he might have set
out to rival Yeats, or drama where he might have followed Ibsen
or Hauptmann, his ambitions in prose fiction, on the evidence,
seem divided between two impulses. These might be named the
self and the city, the artist and the labyrinth, Stephen Dedalus and
his Dubliners. The first version of his first published story, 'The
Sisters', appeared in August 1904 under the pseudonym Stephen
Daedalus. It was the first of what he had planned as

> a series of epicleti, – ten – for a paper. I have written one.
> I call the series *Dubliners* to betray the soul of that
> hemiplegia or paralysis which many consider a city.

The paper is George Russell's *The Irish Homestead*, the 'one' is
'The Sisters' and Joyce has no way of knowing that Russell will
discontinue the arrangement after the publication of two further
stories, 'Eveline' (September) and 'After the Race' (December).
The tension between the self, 'Stephen Dedalus', and the city, i.e.
Mr Cotter and the adult presences in the story, poses a problem.
It is not clear in that first version of the story where the emphasis
falls. Is it on that inquisitive child who had been beaten to the
draw – the knowledge that the priest had died – by Mr Cotter?
Or is it the world of prevarication, caution and half-truth represented by everyone in the story except the boy? In that first version of the story there isn't a mythology in sight. All that symbolic
and mythic implication – Rosicrucian, Eucharistic, oriental, gnomic,
simoniac and paralytic – is built into the story only when Joyce,
four years later, has decided what kind of unity he can cobble for
this handful of experimental and uneven fictions.
It must be significant that the next two stories dispense with

that vigilant first-person narrator, that portrait of the artist as a young boy. Both Eveline and Jimmy Doyle are at a decisive remove from the artistic self; and they mark the upper and lower social parameters of Joyce's city – lower middle class to aspiring merchant prince. (Deconstructionists have thought too little on the social absences from *Dubliners* – no Anglo-Irish gentry, no working class). That significant silence when Lenehan, well down in that pecking order, enters a working-class café in 'Two Gallants' and 'spoke roughly in order to belie his air of gentility'. This tendency away from the self continues in his next story, 'Clay', with a central character even further from the author's own level of consciousness. The impression is surely one of an artist seeking to mark out an imaginary milieu, rather than someone with an elaborate system of mythic correspondence or mystical orientation in his head.

Before returning to the self, Joyce immediately writes 'The Boarding House', 'Counterparts', 'A Painful Case', 'Ivy Day in the Committee Room', all drafted in Trieste by July 1905. Then he is ready to return to childhood self with 'An Encounter' and 'Araby' which he completes before the end of September. That is the month in which he arrives at his *schema* for the volume, conferring on it that celebrated but problematical 'unity' of which there are so many versions real and invented: three stories of childhood, three of adolescence, three of mature life, three of public life. (Later he adds an extra story to adolescence and mature life, and finally that great coping stone, 'The Dead'). The letter to Stanislaus which announces this grand design is suddenly eloquent about Dublin's claims to significance – 'a capital for thousands of years . . . the 'second' city of the British Empire . . . nearly three times as big as Venice . . . it seems strange that no artist has given it to the world'. The city is, for the moment in the ascendant, but the self is still to be assuaged.

Joyce's obsession with the self, or more exactly the artistic consciousness of which his own was the immediate example, antedates the city as an artistic object. When asked in 1904 by the editors of *Dana* for a contribution, he threw himself into the theme most immediate to his concerns, and produced his essay-story 'A Portrait of the Artist' in one day, 7 January, 1904. Containing hardly a reference to the city, it rehearses in headlong, rather turgid prose, the main themes that we later associate with the figure of Stephen Dedalus, as well as the artistic and technical challenges of writing a *Bildungsroman*:

> The features of infancy are not commonly reproduced in the adolescent portrait for, so capricious are we, that we cannot or will not conceive the past in any other than its iron, memorial aspect. Yet the past assuredly implies a fluid succession of presents, the development of an entity of which our actual present is a phase only.[6]

Here, in embryo, are the opening pages of *A Portrait of the Artist as a Young Man*, though it takes Joyce most of ten years and the massive false start of *Stephen Hero* before he can realise this crucial, modernist concept of memory in an answerable style and appropriate form. The piece goes on to establish a sense of the heretic artist, derived in part from the cult of Bruno – whose exaltation of artistic hauteur he had invoked in *The Day of the Rabblement* (1901) to indict Yeats, of all people, for what seemed to Joyce a deplorable egalitarianism. It is all patently early days.

So the young artist 'established himself in the maddest of companies. Joachim Abbas, Bruno the Nolan, Michael Sendivogius, all the hierarchs of initiation cast their spells upon him. He descended into the hells of Swedenborg and abased himself in the gloom of St John of the Cross'.[7]

He will in time distance himself from these heady exemplars, but not before the writing and discarding of *Stephen Hero*. Before the end of 1904 Joyce has left Dublin taking with him the notes, and perhaps some early chapters of this shambling and hybrid narrative. As he proceeds with its composition he is also completing *Dubliners*, all the time describing its contents in terms of satiric realism:

> '. . . I think people might be willing to pay for the special odour of corruption which, I hope, floats over my stories.'
> (*Letters* 15 October 1905)

19

'you will retard the course of civilisation in Ireland by pre-
venting the Irish people from having one good look at
themselves in my nicely polished looking-glass'.
(*Letters* 23 June 1906)

'My intention was to write a chapter in the moral history
of my country and I chose Dublin for the scene because
that city seemed to me the centre of paralysis'.
(*Letters* 5 May 1906)[8]

Meanwhile his brother, Stanislaus, exults in the progress of
Stephen Hero which he describes significantly as a 'lying
autobiography and a raking satire. He is putting nearly all his
acquaintances into it, and the Catholic Church comes in for a bad
quarter of an hour'.[9]

Viewed in the light of this polemic, with its ascription of a
divided purpose, it is easy to see the fatal flaw in *Stephen Hero*.
Apart from the fact that Joyce is not yet ready to write the most
populous novel in modern literature, he confounds and entangles
the two central impulses in his creative vision, the self and the
city. Such long passages as the conversation with the Clonliffe
scholastic in Chapter XIII, the detailed reactions of the students
and the Jesuit President towards the hero's address to the debating
society, the unnecessary line-up of minor characters making one-
off appearances, the fussy narratives of Cranly and the
examinations, even the protracted domestic circumstances surrounding his sister's illness and death, seem to suggest what Yeats
termed 'the will doing the work of the imagination'. It was
obviously an apocalyptic moment when he threw the baggy monster on the flames and turned to a fiction as severely focused and
titled as *A Portrait of the Artist as a Young Man*.

The intensity he achieves in this great book had, of course,
been foreshadowed both in the epicleti of childhood and in the
visionary passages of the failed *Bildungsroman*. In Chapter XXXIII
of *Stephen Hero* is found that feverish sense of destiny, as yet
without ironical mitigation, which had characterised Joyce's first
Portrait of the Artist.

He went through the streets intoning phrases to himself. He repeated to himself the story of 'The Tables of the Law' and the story of 'The Adoration of the Magi'. The atmosphere of these stories were heavy with incense and omens and the figures of the monk-errants, Ahern and Robartes strode through it with great strides. Their speeches were like the enigmas of a disdainful Jesus, their morality was infrahuman or suprahuman; the ritual they laid such store by was so incoherent and heterogeneous, so strange a mixture of trivialities and sacred practices that it could be recognised as the ritual of men who had received from the hands of high priests, anciently guilty of some arrogance of spirit, a confused and dehumanised tradition, a mysterious ordination.

These intimations of an artistic priesthood will soon be purged of Yeatsian and Rosicrucian impurities and reshaped in terms of Joyce's own Catholic liturgy. But not before he has extracted from Yeats the model for his 'mythical method'. Yeats' exquisite prose narrative 'Adoration of the Magi' with its modern re-enactment of the Journey of the Three Wise Men, provided the model for Joyce's one clear, systematic use of a structural myth in *Dubliners*. This is where the plot of Dante's *Divine Comedy* is adopted to the comic action of 'Grace', the only such instance for which there is unequivocal external evidence, that of his brother Stanislaus who declares it 'the first instance of a pattern in my brother's work'.[10]

Indeed the sense of artistic priesthood comes again into play as Joyce sets about the rewriting of 'The Sisters' to constitute it as the key-note and overture to the fourteen fictional orchestrations that make up the rest of *Dubliners*.

The rewritten first paragraph carries the stamp of mature authority; this is the art, elaborate and modern, that will shape the aesthetics of *Portrait* and triumph through the great verbal labyrinths of *Ulysses* and the *Wake*:

He had often said to me: *I am not long for this world*, and I had thought his words idle. Now I knew they were true. Every night as I gazed up at the window I said softly to myself the word *paralysis*. It had always sounded strangely in my ears, like the word *gnomon* in the Euclid and the word *simony* in the Catechism. But now it sounded to me like the name of some maleficent and sinful being. It filled me with fear, and yet I longed to be nearer to it and to look upon its deadly work.

That control of rhythm and cadence; the caress of those mysterious words – their spelling at odds with their sound – which at once define and emphasise the mystery, while somehow holding it at bay; the child's tentative yet implacable will to know. Not only is this definitively the artistic self, but also that self in definitive confrontation with its material challenge, what Yeats was to call its 'body of fate'. That body of fate is initially the old priest's wretched condition, paralytic, physically maimed; gnomonic, mentally stricken (Joyce perversely removed this hint from the original version where old Cotter says "Upper storey" – he tapped an unnecessary hand at his forehead – "gone") and simoniac, spiritually impaired.[11] It is also, by extension, the Irish Catholic Church, lay and clerical. But one is hardly exaggerating to suggest that it is the entire body of 'sluggish matter' that the young priest/artist must redeem, animate and transfigure into 'the radiant body of everliving life'.[12]

This rewritten paragraph, therefore, prepares us for the labyrinth, that majority of Dublin stories which do not concern the presence of the artist figure. A whole 'field of folk' comes to life – Corley, Lenehan, Eveline, Maria, Little Chandler, the Mooneys and their lodgers, Kernan, Power, Farrington, the Morkans and their guests. And it prepares us for the Stephen Dedalus of *Portrait* where the world of Dublin – however vividly glimpsed – serves chiefly as prism and sounding-board for developing artistic sensibility. Joyce has now, by 1914, separated victoriously the two main impulses that had bedevilled his apprenticeship.[13] The next adventure is to bring them together, make them work upon each other, in the counterpoint of his next and greatest work, *Ulysses*.

The mythical method is now in place to meet that challenge.

Stephen/Telemachus awakes in his Sandycove tower while Bloom/ Odysseus begins his day on the city's northside. As the artist moves on the city the allround hero moves warily among its choice and master spirits – Bantam Lyons, Martin Cunningham, Menton, M'Intosh, Nosey Flynn, Ben Dollard, Gertie McDowell, Bella Cohen, Lenehan with awful puns, in comparative security, Corley with his globular head, still assiduously on the touch. Chief among them are the elder Dedalus, based on the author's consubstantial father, and Molly Bloom, based on Nora Barnacle, his wife in whom the word is triumphantly made flesh. Or to put it another way, the Icarus who flew the labyrinth at the end of *Portrait* has returned to transfigure it by the end of *Ulysses*. In *Finnegans Wake* the cycle is completed and renewed: spirit and matter, artist and labyrinth are merged again amid the primal flux in which the whole heroic enterprise had its mysterious source and origin.

NOTES

1 Reprinted in *James Joyce: Two Decades of Criticism*, ed. S Givens (New York: Vanguard Press, 1948), pp. 47-94.

2 Reprinted in *Twentieth Century Interpretations of **Dubliners***, ed. Peter K Garrett (New Jersey: Prentice Hall, 1968), pp. 57-85.

3 Clive Hart, ed *James Joyce's **Dubliners*** (London: Faber and Faber, 1969).

4 Marvin Magalener and Richard M Kain, eds. *Joyce: The Man, The Work, The Reputation* (New York: NYU Press, 1956).

5 Donald T Torchiana, *Backgrounds for Joyce's **Dubliners*** (London: Allen and Unwin, 1986).

6 Printed in the Viking Critical Edition of *A Portrait of the Artist as a Young Man*, ed. Chester G Anderson (New York: Viking Press, 1968), pp. 257-258.

7 ibid., p. 261.

8 Richard Ellmann, ed. *Selected Letters of James Joyce* (London: Faber and Faber, 1975, 79, [7], 83).

9 George Harris Healey, ed. *The Dublin Diary of Stanislaus Joyce* (London: Faber and Faber, 1962), p. 25.

10 Stanislaus Joyce, *My Brother's Keeper* (London: Faber and Faber, 1958), p. 225.

11 Reprinted in Marvin Magalener, *Time of Apprenticeship* (New York: Abelard-Schuman, 1959), pp. 174-180.

12 *Portrait*, p. 221.

13 See Colin MacCabe, *James Joyce and the Revolution of the Word* (London: Macmillan, 1979). I suspect that MacCabe's shrewd discussion of the difference between *Stephen Hero* and *A Portrait* (pp. 63-65), allowing for the differences of terminologies, makes a similar point: '*Stephen Hero* is written at the limit of . . . temporal organisation and *Portrait* inaugurates a new relation between time and meaning'. And again: 'The problem of *Stephen Hero* is that the neutral narrative is time and again interrupted by discourse and these interruptions destroy the possiblity of narrative'. His reading, however, rests – unnecessarily, it seems to me – upon a Freudian insight of Bathes, which insists on an Oedipal source for the narrative dilemma.

THE LANGUAGE OF DUBLINERS

TP Dolan

What Stephen called a 'tundish' the Dean of Studies called a 'funnel', in their celebrated encounter in the Physics Theatre of the Royal University, the very room in which the Annual James Joyce Summer School is held.[1] 'I never heard the word in my life . . . I must look that word up', says the Dean, much to Stephen's chagrin: 'The little word seemed to have turned a rapier point of his sensitiveness against this courteous and vigilant foe'.[2] It led him to reflect 'that the man to whom he was speaking was a countryman of Ben Jonson' and that 'The language in which we are speaking is his before it is mine. How different are the words *home*, *Christ*, *ale*, *master*, on his lips and on mine!' For him, the Dean's language 'will always be . . . an acquired speech'. The incident continues to rankle in his mind. Long afterwards, towards the end of *Portrait*, under the diary entry for April 13, he writes:

That tundish has been on my mind for a long time. I looked it up and find it English and good old blunt English too. Damn the dean of studies and his funnel! What did he come here for to teach us his own language or learn it from us.[3]

The episode is highly suggestive. It concerns matters of history, class, colonialism, and nationalism, all of which were stirred up by Stephen's use of that innocuous, mildly archaic word 'tundish'. Because Joyce employed it so portentously here, the word has become a shibboleth for Irish writers in English, most notably Seamus Heaney, as we shall see. It has been elevated from the humdrum contexts it has inhabited since its first recorded use in a late fourteenth-century Middle English document from Abingdon (see *OED* s.v. 'Tundish'). Shakespeare used it (in *Measure for Measure*; 'For filling a bottle with a tunne-dish'); Jonson, ironically, did not. According to OED it is a local word, not even one of those ordinary English words, once in general use, which have come to have special meanings in Ireland, such as 'hames' or 'yoke'. However, since Joyce's use of it in *Portrait*, it has come to symbolise the cleavage between Standard English and Hiberno-English, with a significance well beyond its original domestic environs.

Seamus Heaney has enhanced the celebrity of the word by using it in a verse towards the end of his great poem, 'Station Island':

. . . Raindrops blew in my face

as I came to. 'Old father, mother's son,
there is a moment in Stephen's diary
for April the thirteenth, a revelation

set among my stars – that one entry
has been a sort of password in my ears,
the collect of a new epiphany,

the Feast of the Holy Tundish.' 'Who cares',
he jeered, 'any more? The English language
belongs to us. You are raking at dead fires,

a waste of time for somebody your age.
That subject people stuff is a cod's game,
infantile, like your peasant pilgrimage.[4]

Here the second speaker challenges the stand taken by the first speaker, who goes along with what Stephen feels: that the English language symbolises the domination of Ireland by the people who spoke it as their native language. The vanquished Irish were compelled to speak it as 'subject people', and it became yet another mark of conquest, with all the rest of the imported cultural baggage. He denies this and claims that 'the English language belongs to us'. So it does, of course, but it should never be forgotten that English is not the native language of Ireland,[5] and we should at this stage examine the implications of those few bitter words: 'the man to whom he was speaking was a countryman of Ben Jonson'.

According to his friend CP Curran, Joyce was very fond of Jonson: 'Harmonies were innate in Joyce, and so word catching was second nature. Ben Jonson was one of his quarries'.[6] This taste is confirmed by Richard Ellmann who writes that when Joyce was in Paris in 1903 he devoted much time to reading major authors, including Shakespeare and Jonson, but he came to prefer the latter: 'Shakespeare having proved too lax [in purely formal terms], he took up Ben Jonson, studying both plays and poems to improve his own technique'.[7] It is possible that Stephen refers to Jonson for another reason, in addition to the obvious one that he was one of Joyce's favourite authors. From a linguistic point of view it is significant that Jonson was writing at the time when the plantations in Ireland were in full swing.[8] They had begun in 1549 with Laois and Offaly, to be followed by Munster in 1586-1592, and then Ulster in 1609. With these plantations came wider exposure to the English language. This was not the first time that the Irish had been exposed to English.

The original invasion of Ireland had taken place in the twelfth century after Henry II had been authorised by the Pope (an Englishman called Nicholas Breakspear, who had taken the name Hadrian IV and reigned from 1154 to 1159) to unite Ireland with England, on supposedly spiritual grounds.[9] The leaders of the invading forces spoke Norman French, and their retainers spoke English. Hence, by the end of that century, there were three languages current in Ireland: the natives continued to use Irish and, depending on their class, the invaders spoke either Norman French or English or both.[10] Within a century or so Norman French declined, and English clung on, but so powerful was the pull of the Irish language that it almost regained linguistic supremacy, in spite of futile legislation, such as the so-called 'Statutes of Kilkenny' (first promulgated in 1366),[11] which attempted, among other things, to deter the ruling elite from going native and using Irish customs, including their language. By the sixteenth century, English retained an uneasy currency in the large towns and a few rural areas. Then came the plantations, which halted the decline of English because the planters who were given land all over the country, except the far west, naturally spoke English and communicated with their tenants, the native Irish, in that language. Thus, for the first time, English became a current vernacular in various settlements throughout most of the country. The important point to note is that it was the language of the people who ran the plantations and symbolised possession and power, whereas those without possession and power spoke Irish. This is what Stephen Dedalus meant: the language spoken by the Dean of Studies was directly descended from the language of the planters; his own dialect of English was descended from the language which the Irish were compelled to learn in order to communicate with those they worked for, to whom (borrowing Heaney's phrase) they were a 'subject people'.

The dialect of English used in Ireland is called 'Hiberno-English', a title which exactly describes its two component parts. It is English, heavily coloured by Irish, in its vocabulary, syntax, idiom, and, of course, its pronunciation. Thus, when an Irish person uses the words 'home, Christ, ale, master', the words are English, but the vowels and consonants are realised as if they were Irish.[12] Not only that, the dialect of English used by Irish people is extremely conservative and retains many features of seventeenth-century English in its pronunciation. Hence Hiberno-English, to adopt another phrase of Heaney's from 'Station Island', fills 'the element with signatures on [its] own frequency',[13] and this frequency clearly differentiates it from Standard English, which causes Stephen so much distress, because it made him feel inferior. This is not surprising in view of the fact that English writers over the centuries have represented the speech of Irish characters in such a way as to make the speakers look silly and dim-witted. Ben Jonson tried to achieve this effect in his *Irish Masque* (1613/1616), with the linguistic absurdities of Dermock, Donnell, Dennish, and Patrick.

Dermock: Wee be Irish men and't pleash tee.

Donnell: Ty good shubshects of Ireland, and pleash ty mayesty.

Dennish: Of Connough, Leynster, Vlster, Munster. I mine one shelfe vash borne in te English payle and pleash ty mayesty.

Patrick: Sacrament o' chreesh, tell ty tale, ty shelfe, be all tree.[14]

Here the Irish are presented as craven subjects, ('shubshects'), with pathetic difficulties in pronouncing 's' and 'th' because these particular sounds did not exist in their own native language of Irish.

The seventeenth century was the formative period for modern Hiberno-English.[15] More and more Irish people learnt English for a variety of reasons, not least for the practical aim of negotiating with the governing class who spread throughout most of the country and set up physical symbols of their rule – the big houses and the estates on which they were built. It was no wonder that the native Irish came gradually to regard English as the language which typified material success, in contrast to Irish, which typified poverty and subservience. This trend continued in the relatively stable eighteenth century as English rule became more and more consolidated and secure. Towards the end of the century, in 1795. St. Patrick's College at Maynooth, Co. Kildare, was founded, and provided a form of education for the Catholic priesthood which could be monitored from the seat of power in England. The Act of Union in 1800 removed the Irish Parliament to Westminster, and this lent further momentum to the perception of English as a desirable medium of intercourse. Then, in the early years of the nineteenth century, great native leaders, such as Daniel O'Connell, chose to use English to communicate with the people at their meetings. In 1831, a system of primary education was introduced. This, too, used English as the medium for instruction. The Great Famine (1845 onwards) had a calamitous effect on the fortunes of the Irish language. Many thousands, maybe a million, died;[16] many had to emigrate. In sheer statistics, the number of people speaking Irish declined, and those who left the country through emigration soon recognised the need to master English.

All these factors were instrumental in determining the supremacy of English at the expense of Irish. By the time of James Joyce's birth in 1882, the English language was in an unassailable position in Ireland but, as we have seen, the Irish language gave a unique flavour to the quality of the dialect of English used by Irish speakers. Hence, the word 'tundish' symbolises the conservative English strain in the dialect, while the pronunciation of the words 'home, Christ, ale, master' symbolises the Irish strain.

Joyce's use of Hiberno-English (henceforth designated 'HE') extends far beyond the matter of pronunciation. In this paper we shall concentrate on two works: *Dubliners*,[17] which first appeared in England in 1914, and *Ulysses* (the Cyclops episode),[18] first published in Paris in 1922. In both books Joyce uses HE[19] judiciously and accurately, with a pronounced fondness for certain features of the dialect, most notably the formation of indirect questions following Irish syntax – that is, with the reversed word-order of subject and verb of the direct question retained in the indirect question, e.g.,

examined the foreign sailors to see had any of them green eyes ('*An Encounter*')

The man asked me how many had I (*ibid*)

the young lady came over and asked me did I wish to buy anything ('*Araby*')

Joe asked would he have another (*Ulysses*, p. 311)

THE ARTIST AND THE LABYRINTH

I wonder did he ever put it out of sight (*U*/336)

Standard English would use 'if' or 'whether', as in this indirect question posed (significantly) by Gabriel in 'The Dead':

Gabriel asked her whether she had had a good crossing.

instead of the normal HE:

Gabriel asked her had she had a good crossing.

The most obvious feature of HE is the presence of Irish words, and Joyce makes regular use of these, e.g.,

deoc an doruis (Ir. *deoch an dorais*, 'drink of the door')
('A Little Cloud')

smahan (Ir. *smeachán*, 'nip, small amount') ('Counterparts')

barmbracks (Ir. *bairín breac*, 'specked cake') ('Clay')

shoneens (Ir. *Seoinín*, 'little John (Bull)') ('Ivy')

Musha, Wisha (Ir. *muise*, 'indeed') (*ibid*)

goster (Ir. *gasrán*, 'conversation') (*ibid*)

omadhauns (Ir. *amadán*, 'fool') ('Grace')

Sha (Ir. *is ea*, 'it is, corresponding to 'yes' (*ibid*)

Beannacht libh ('A blessing with you', 'Goodbye')
('The Dead')

The Cyclops episode in *Ulysses* also contains many Irish words, including *rapparee* (Ir. *ropaire*, 'scoundrel'), *Raimeis*, (Ir. *raiméis*, 'nonsense'), and so forth.

Often an Irish word or idiom is disguised behind the English, often as in the following examples:

Is there any chance of a drink itself? ('Ivy')

Here the word 'itself', representing Ir. *féin*, 'self', 'even/only', looks out of place, but the sentence actually means something like 'Is there any chance of even a drink?'

Show me one here (*ibid*)

It is common practice in Ireland, following the idiom of the Irish language, to use 'show' in place of 'give' or 'hand'.

the dear knows ('Mother')

This expression has a complicated history: in medieval Irish the word for 'God' (*Fiadha*) was very similar in form to the word for 'deer' (fiadh), and so to avoid blasphemy speakers would use the latter word. When the expression was converted into English, as 'the deer knows', which destroys the similarity of the two words in Irish, it became the custom to re-fashion the expression as 'the dear (i.e., the dear one, God) knows'.

I was great with him at the time ('The Dead')

Here 'great' corresponds to Ir. *mór*, which can mean 'friendly'.

he would get his death (*ibid*)

In Irish 'to die' is expressed as *bás a fháil* (lit. 'to get one's death').

Did you call on Grimes?

I did ('Ivy')

There are no words for 'yes' or 'no' in Irish, and speakers

answer simple questions using part of the original interrogatived verb, as here.

The verbal system in Irish is substantially different from that in English, and there are many instances of this dissimilarity in Joyce, sometimes simply represented in expressions such as

it's labour produces everything ('Ivy')

where the 'it's' represents the 'copula' form of the verb 'to be' in Irish which, since it is a Celtic language, has to start every main clause with a verb (hence the development of the 'copula'). This causes the main clause to have the form of a dependent adjective clause. Thus Standard English would have 'labour produces everything', whereas HE has 'it's labour [that] produces everything'.

Irish also has two forms of every verb, one dealing mainly with the tense (time) of an action, and the other dealing with the 'aspect' (the nature) of an action. With the verb 'to be', this feature manifests itself as 'I am', and 'I do be', where the latter form indicates the habitual nature of the verb's meaning. There is a good example of this in 'Grace':

you're a good friend of his not like some of those he does be with.

Here, 'he does be with' indicates the fact that Kernan is habitually in the company of the other people in question. The relative pronouns 'which' or 'that' are often left out in HE, as in the following example

and his eye all bloodshot from the drouth is in it (U/309)

Here, 'is in it' is an adjective clause ('[that] is in it'). The last two words 'in it' are a translation from Irish *ann*, 'there'.

In the matter of subordinate adverbial clauses, Irish has an entirely distinct way of coping with them, based on the use of the conjunction *agus*, 'and', followed by a pronoun and then a non-finite part of the verb. There are many examples of this in Joyce:

> and he swatting all the time (*U*/316)

> and he half smothered in writs (*U*/318)

> and they holding him (*U*/340)

> And he shouting to the bloody dog (*U*/343)

Here the first 'and' means 'even though', the second means 'when', the third and fourth mean 'while'.

Sometimes a subordinating conjunction carries the meaning it has in Irish into HE. A good example of this feature is 'till', representing Irish *go*, which can mean something more than the English temporal 'till', as in

> Wait till I show you (*U*/297)

> Where is he till I murder him? (*U*/341)

Here the two 'till' clauses mean 'and let me show you', and 'and let me murder him', respectively.

There is no verb 'to have' in Irish, and so all those perfect and pluperfect forms of the verb in English which require 'have' in their formation (e.g., 'I have just written a letter') present problems in HE. This results in the well-known form with the verb 'to be' and 'after' (corresponding to the Irish pattern *tá me tar éis* . . ., 'I am after . . .'). Hence we find:

> Sure I'm after seeing him not five minutes ago (*U*/299)

which means 'To be sure, it's only five minutes since I have seen him'.

Where HE uses the 'have' form, there is a slight difference from Standard English because the participle is separated from the verb 'to have', as in Irish, where the participle is separated from the verb 'to be', e.g.,

when he has a drop taken ('Clay')

I've a sup taken ('Ivy')

Here English would have 'has taken' and 'I've taken'.

Statements in Irish are often phrased in the form of a question, and Joyce often uses this form, e.g.,

who should come in but Higgins ('Counterparts')

who should I see dodging along Stony Batter only Joe Hynes (*U*/290)

Here English would have 'Higgins came in' and 'I saw Joe Hynes dodging along . . .' respectively.

Sometimes HE has what looks like bad grammar, but it can be explained from the idiom of Irish. A good example of this is the use of plural subjects with singular verbs. This is due to the fact that in Irish the verb 'to be', for instance, does not change its form (*tá*) from singular (English 'is') to plural (English 'are'). Hence, Irish speakers of English often retain the 'is' form for both singular and plural subjects. Thus we find:

the duties of priesthood was too much ('Sisters')

when sons speaks that way to their father ('Ivy')

the stairs is so dark (*ibid*)

This can happen with nouns, too, again showing the influence of Irish, e.g.,

to buy a waistcoat or a trousers (*ibid*)

Here 'a trousers' corresponds to the Irish *briste*, 'trousers' (pl. *bristí*). Other apparent solecisms include the use of 'them' instead of 'those', again following Irish idiom, e.g.,

them flowers ('Encounter')

them two candlesticks (*ibid*)[21]

Another important feature of HE is the use of archaic vocabulary, such as 'oxter' for 'armpit' ('Grace') and 'codding' for 'joking' (U/298) (cf. 'codology' [U/302]). This is a common form of HE idiom, as is the ubiquitous use of 'so' as a 'clincher' to an argumentative remark, e.g., 'so I would', 'so he would', 'so it is', 'so it would' (U/301/315/319/340) respectively.

An analysis such as this tends by its very nature to underplay the humour that can characterise the skilful use of the HE dialect in fiction. This point is particularly true of the Cyclops episode in *Ulysses* where Joyce's exuberant manoeuvring of his language between Standard English and Hiberno-English usage makes for a level of verbal pleasantry which almost, but not quite, verges on caricature. For instance, the continuous appearance of the 'says I' formula sends up a common Irish idiom (cf. Ir. *ar seisean*, 'says/said he'), e.g.,

Barney mavourneen's be it, says I. (U/291)

Here, apart from the 'says I', the statement itself, with the theatrical 'mavourneen' (Ir. *mo mhúirnín*, 'my darling'), and the 'be', which is abbreviated from the archaic 'let it be', is very whimsical.

Throughout this episode Joyce captures the conversational energy of HE, especially with parenthetic remarks or words such as 'don't be talking', 'gob', 'begob', *a chara*, 'Jesus', 'says I to myself, says I', 'faith', *Moya* (Ir. *mar bh'eadh*, 'as it were').

Often he uses what we may describe as the 'x' of a 'y' formula, which is also a feature of demotic HE, e.g., 'a cracked loodheramaun (Ir. *liudramán*, 'loafer') of a nephew', 'his little concubine of a wife', 'the old prostitute of a mother', etc.

Joyce never fails to give a sense of the linguistic origins of his speakers, even with such light touches as in the following, where the non-standard use of the definite article indicates Irish provenance (Irish has a definite, but no indefinite article – hence a certain confusion, which makes for humour, as to which to use in HE):

And my wife has the typhoid (*U*/320)

Irish people often launch into seemingly unending, breathless strings of clauses loosely linked by 'and', without using formal subordinate clauses, also representing Irish usage, where *agus* often does the work of all other adverbial conjunctions (see, for example, the paragraph beginning 'So then the citizen', *U*/309). Here, again, Joyce faithfully identifies a characteristic feature of HE speech, which is comic when overdone.

Humour is also conveyed by the use of pompous or archaic language (e.g., 'libation', 'lackaday', 'the parliamentary side of your arse', 'varlet', etc.), or with word-play based on malapropism, e.g.,

Who made those allegations? says Alf.
I, says Joe. I'm the alligator *(U*/335)

Such an abundance of HE patterns of speech is contrastively celebrated by Joyce's astute use of a brief passage of low-class English:

God blimey if she aint a clinker, that there bleeding tart. Blimey it makes me kind of bleeding cry, straight, it does, when I sees her cause I thinks of my old mashtub what's waiting for me down Limehouse way (*U*/308-9)

Here 'Blimey', 'aint', 'that there', 'bleeding', 'straight', 'I sees', 'I thinks', 'what's', are solecisms totally foreign to HE, but such accurately observed features of uneducated English speech that one can almost hear them being said.

In this episode in *Ulysses*, Joyce's carefully controlled use of HE idiom creates authentic Dublin dialogue, with all its vitality, wit, and humour. There is nothing patronising about this feature of his art. Unlike some other novelists, such as Somerville and Ross, he is not trying to show up his citizens as child-like figures of fun, worthy of condescending forbearance: he makes them funny, without poking fun at them, because he is organically, linguistically, and racially one of their number.

There are many other examples of HE features in *Dubliners* and the Cyclops episode in *Ulysses*, but this paper has indicated the main categories of the dialect which Joyce used so effectively. Joyce himself was acutely sensitive to the differences between Standard English and Hiberno-English. In natural prose his syntax is grammatically correct Standard English, as is very well demonstrated in his letters, which represent in writing the patterns of ordered speech. When he wishes to make a linguistic point he uses the dialect, for instance in the anecdote about a man in a hotel who says 'For the love o'Jaysus, gintlemin, will ye tell us where's the convaynience' (Letter dated 13 November, 1906).[22] Here 'Jaysus' and 'convaynience' represent the conservative pronunciation of the 'e' vowel preserved in HE; 'gintlemin' represents a common realisation of the 'e' vowel in HE; 'ye' shows the determination in HE, as in Irish, to differentiate between singular and plural 'you'; and the final indirect question preserves the inverted form of a direct question.

In *Dubliners* and the Cyclops episode in *Ulysses* the use of HE is quite restrained, by contrast, for example, with Sean O'Casey's almost extravagant use in *Juno and the Paycock*, *The Shadow of a Gunman*, and *The Plough and the Stars*, in which the characters, who are lower class than most of Joyce's, speak richly dialectal (Dublin) English, thereby proving the linguistic rule that class status is correlated to the variety of language used: the more working class and the less educated the person, the more closely related is their speech to their particular area.[23]

To return finally to the sentiments expressed in Seamus Heaney's poem, it may be claimed that Joyce celebrates and salutes the language of the Feast of the Holy Tundish, not the language of the Feast of the Holy Funnel. Stephen had no reason to feel ashamed of his dialect.

NOTES

1 Still known as 'The Old Physics Theatre' in Newman House (University College), St. Stephen's Green, Dublin.

2 James Joyce, *A Portrait of the Artist as a Young Man* (Harmondsworth, 1964), pp. 188-9.

3 *ibid*, p. 251.

4 Seamus Heaney, *Station Island* (London, Boston, 1984), p. 93.

5 See Alan Bliss, 'Language and Literature', in *The English in Medieval Ireland*, ed. J Lydon (Dublin, 1984), pp. 27-45.

6 CP Curran, *James Joyce Remembered* (London, 1968), p. 24.

7 Richard Ellmann, *James Joyce*, New and Revised Edition (Oxford, New York, Toronto, Melbourne, 1982), p. 120.

8 See Nicholas Canny, 'Early Modern Ireland c. 1500-1700', in *The Oxford Illustrated History of Ireland*, ed. RF Foster (Oxford, New York, 1989), pp. 104-160.

9 See MT Flanagan, *Irish Society Anglo-Norman Settlers Angevin Kingship* (Oxford, 1989), pp. 7-8, 53-4, 277-8.

10 E Curtis, 'The Spoken Languages of Medieval Ireland', *Studies* VIII (1919), pp. 234-54.

11 For the text and translation of these 'Statutes' see *Statutes and Ordinances of the Parliament of Ireland*, I, *King John to Henry V* (Dublin, 1907), pp. 431-69.

12 See Anthony Burgess, *Joysprick: An Introduction to the Language of James Joyce* (London, 1973), p. 28.

13 Op. cit., p. 94.

14 Text edited by Alan Bliss, *Spoken English in Ireland 1600-1740* (Dublin, 1979), p. 93.

15 See RF Foster, 'Ascendancy and the Union', in *The Oxford Illustrated History of Ireland*, op. cit., pp. 161-212.

16 See Cormac O'Gráda, *The Great Irish Famine* (Dublin, 1989), esp. pp. 12-22, 41-50.

17 Quotations are taken from James Joyce, *Dubliners* (London, Glasgow, Toronto, Sydney, Auckland, 1988).

18 Quotations are taken from James Joyce, *Ulysses* (Harmondsworth, 1969).

19 A lucid account of the main features of HE is to be found in PW Joyce, *English as we speak it in Ireland*, Introduction by Terence Dolan, New Edition, Dublin, 1988, ch. 4 'Idioms from the Irish Language', and ch. 7 'Grammar and Pronunciation'.

20 See Richard Wall, *An Anglo-Irish Dialect Glossary for Joyce's Works* (Gerrards Cross, 1986), and JM Clark, *The Vocabulary of Anglo-Irish* (Saint-Gall, 1917).

21 PW Joyce, op. cit., pp. 34-5.

22 *Letters of James Joyce*, ed. Richard Ellmann, II, (New York, 1966), p. 191.

23 See TP Dolan, 'Sean O'Casey's Use of Hiberno-English', in *Irland Gesellschaft und Kultur*, IV, ed. D. Siegmund-Schultze, Halle-Wittenberg, 1985, 108-115. See also Declan Kiberd, *Synge and the Irish Language* (London, 1979), ch. 8, Anglo-Irish as a Literary Dialect: The Contribution of Synge'.

JOYCE'S
LEGACY

Benedict Kiely

In the matter of the legacy that James Joyce left to those of us who came along after him and who, in his formidable shadow, tried to write novels and/or short stories, each writer or would-be writer must speak for himself or herself. So I am not, now and here, going to talk about what Joyce may have done for, or to, other Irish writers, nor of what his influence may have been on Irish writing. Those others, if they were alive and present, might readily stand up to confront my assumptions. Or if they were absent or dead then somebody here present might stand up to do it for them.

Anyway: all that is a matter for elaborate academic consideration, with much quotation and the display of comparisons and contrasts. What I am now attempting is a simple personal statement, and I am entitled to speak on my own behalf and can do so on the best authority.

A novelist I know, a younger man than myself and one whose work I highly respect, once said that Liam O'Flaherty had written as if James Joyce had never existed. He could not have said a truer word. Nor would any man have agreed with him more readily than Liam O'Flaherty himself. For O'Flaherty was very much his own man, as every novelist and every poet, *et cetera*, is entitled to be. And every man and woman. With the qualified exceptions of saints, medical doctors, priests, and those few others who have given up part of themselves either out of the hope of heaven or for the good of mankind, or both combined.

At any rate, O'Flaherty was born in 1897 and his first novel, *Thy Neighbours Wife*, was published by Jonathan Cape in 1923. It might be an interesting exercise for a bright group of students to balance the Dublin of Mr Gilhooley and Gypo Natan with the Dublin of Leopold Bloom.

Kate O'Brien, too, and by way of considerable contrast with O'Flaherty, was very much her own person: something like what a Reverend Mother might have been in the Middle Ages. Not that I was there to find out. But then Reverend Mothers may not have altered so much over the centuries. And other Irish novelists of our time have made their way uninfluenced, for good or ill, by James Joyce. So what?

And one fine novelist, now no longer with us, once said to me that portions of *Ulysses* reminded him of his own 'bad moments', or of the *Encyclopaedia Britannica*. But he was admittedly being facetious, and if he were alive today he would not wish me, in such a context, to mention his name.

What I have to offer, here and now, *my 'umble offering, Mr Copperfield*, are some personal notes about myself and James Joyce. All of us, his readers, have met him. He needs no introduction.

Or, perhaps, what I am trying to offer are the random thoughts of a would-be novelist trying to practice under the shadow of James Joyce. As anyone, with that would-be disposition, round about 1920 and after, must inevitably have been. That is if he, or she, took for want of a better occupation, to the writing of novels.

Here are some notes made over, say, fifty years, about my own reactions to, or feelings about, James Joyce.

In the early 1940s I was living in Dollymount in North Dublin City and attempting to write my first novel. If you stood on the roof of the garage of the house in which I then and there lived you had a clear view, even on a misty day, of the long and level strand of Dollymount on which Stephen Dedalus cried out to his heavenly gods when he saw the young woman with skirts kilted up and wading in the salt water:

> She was alone and still, gazing out to sea; and when she felt his presence and the worship of his eyes her eyes turned to him in quiet sufferance of his gaze, without shame or wantonness. Long, long she suffered his gaze and then quietly withdrew her eyes from his and bent them towards the stream, gently stirring the water with her foot hither and thither. The first faint noise of gently moving water broke the silence, low and faint and whispering, faint as the bells of sleep; hither and thither: and a faint flame trembled on her cheek.
> – Heavenly God! cried Stephen's soul, in an outburst of profane joy.

There below me was the broad seaside road from central Dublin to the Hill of Howth. Beyond that road a narrow run of water where two tides meet, and beyond that the dunes and seabirds and the long strand and the bathers and courting couples and golf-clubs of the Bull Island: which, as we all know, would not be there at all if it had not been for that much maligned man, Captain Bligh of The Bounty. The story is that Bligh, before he moved on to better things, had an admiralty post in Dublin and drew up a plan to protect the port from silting. The plan which included the building of the Bull Wall was put into effect even if that was not until after Bligh's departure: and the sand that would have blocked the harbour piled up behind the wall and out of the North Bull sandbank, and with the aid of the immortal sea, created the Bull Island. So that had it not been for the Captain, Stephen Dedalus could not have walked on the place to be enraptured by life and the wading sea-bird of a girl.

The influence of Captain Bligh on the work of Joyce is something that has not yet been considered by scholars of Joyce: at any rate, not Joycean scholars who might be too much like Buck Mulligan and the Jesuit Kinch.

Nor, without Bligh, could Stephen on his way to that vision have seen the young Irish Christian Brothers pounding in their big rural boots over the planks of the Bull Bridge:

> He turned seawards from the road at Dollymount and as he passed on to the thin wooden bridge he felt the planks shaking with the tramp of heavily shod feet. A squad of christian brothers was on its way back from the Bull and had begun to pass, two by two, across the bridge. Soon the whole bridge was trembling and resounding. The uncouth faces passed him two by two, stained yellow or red or livid by the sea, and as he strove to look at them with ease and indifference, a faint stain of personal shame and commiseration rose to his own face. Angry with himself he tried to hide his face from their eyes by gazing down sideways into the shallow swirling water under the bridge but he still saw a reflection therein of their topheavy silk hats, and humble tapelike collars and loosely hanging clerical clothes . . . .

> Their piety would be like their names, like their faces, like their clothes; and it was idle for him to tell himself that their humble and contrite hearts, it might be, paid a far richer tribute of devotion than his had ever been, a gift tenfold more acceptable than his elaborate adoration.

He might perhaps have tried a little harder. Yet he did give us honestly the reactions of a Jesuit-educated young man who had been stepping perilously and shamefacedly on the boundaries of the religious life, and who is just now about to make his declaration of escape; who is also and unavoidably affected by the snobbery of his father; who dreads that failing fortunes, for which the father is responsible, might lead downwards, no other way, to the pit of humiliation in which the son of a gentleman might have to go to school, not to Clongowes Wood College and the Jesuits, nor even to the city–surrounded Belvedere college, but to the Christian Brothers:

– I never liked the idea of sending him to the christian brothers myself, said Mrs Dedalus.

– Christian brothers, be dammed! said Mr Dedalus. Is it with Paddy Stink and Mickey Mud? No, let him stick to the jesuits in God's name since he began with them. They'll be of service to him in after years. Those are the fellows that can get you a position.

– And they're a very rich order, aren't they, Simon?

– Rather. They live well, I tell you. You saw their table at Clongowes. Fed up, by God, like gamecocks.

With high comedy Joyce allows Simon to give us the common or backyard idea both of the sons of Ignatius of Loyola and of Edmund Ignatius Rice of Waterford.

It is a curious thing . . .

Brinsley McNamara, novelist and early Abbey theatre playwright who wrote the novel, *The Valley of the Squinting Windows*, and a lot more besides, and the privilege of whose friendship I was to have in the forties and fifties, prefaced most of his statements with those five words. That was the way he saw the world. He even entitled a collection of his short stories, *Some Curious People*. For his autobiography, unfortunately never finished, he picked a title out of Goldsmith: *The Long Vexation*. They were both men from the Irish midlands:

I still had hopes, the long vexation passed
Here to return and die at home at last

Brinsley could be a rancorous man and was much involved in con troversy around the theatre and elsewhere. But since we were of different generations we had nothing to quarrel about, and we had also, I flatter myself, a natural compatibility: and there will be much to say about him in the future. For the moment I salute his noble, most impressive shade, and borrow a phrase. So, it is a curious thing that the first good apologia for James Joyce that I ever encountered was spoken in class in secondary school by an

Irish Christian Brother. It is also a curious thing that his name was Rice. He was, I think, some sort of a relation of the heroic founder. That Brother Rice, the one I knew, was a learned man and could have taught anything, as in the course of a few years I found out, but he elected to teach mathematics to a class of dullards in mathematics, and of all the dullards, I was the dullest. Years afterwards when I had come to know him as a great human being, I dared to ask him if he had done it for a penance and with his eye on the world to come. He laughed, really laughed, in a way that may or may not have answered my question.

John Desmond Sheridan, a good humorous writer, once said that at school he suffered a lot from and for trigonometry and then, when he left school, he found out that all the lighthouses were measured. So much did I suffer that if it had not been for RL Stevenson's father or grandfather having had something to do with lighthouses I would have loathed the things for the rest of my life.   Then one day in the thick of a shower of sines and cosines Rice threw his head back and shook his mane and said: 'James Joyce'. Just the two words and just like that. As if he had seen somebody on the ceiling. We did not know who he was talking to, or about. There was nobody of the name in the class. We looked up and saw nothing and nobody. We were, as I afterwards worked out, about to get the side or fringe benefit of something he had recently read. This was what it was all about.

Somewhere in the south of Ireland, or the Free State, a thundering and puritanical professor had made an attack on the morals of a poet, as evidenced by a new collection of the poet's poems. The poet was FR Higgins. Was the collection *The Dark Breed* or *The Gap of Brightness*? I can't recall. The professor roundly condemned passages which he considered lascivious. Lascivious, to us, sounded fine. A definite improvement on sines and cosines. Out of a book Rice read three poems. We listened hopefully but ended up little the wiser. Any evening going home from school through Fountain Lane you could hear better from some of the girls who went with the soldiers. Then in Irish and English he read out more-or-less parallel passages from Douglas Hyde's *The Love Songs of Connacht*. Surely to God nobody could accuse the great scholar

Douglas Hyde, who was to become the first president of the Irish Republic, of lasciviousness. So the professor was a fool. Years afterwards I met the man, not in the halls of academia but in connection with a weekly newspaper, and I realised that Rice had been right.

That day, from the defence of Fred Higgins he sailed on to his defence of Joyce, giving us his life and times and literary merit in a splendid speech: as good an introduction to the man as anything I have encountered since. It was the best trigonometry lesson I ever sat through.

Where the sea flows over the full fresh water
My love I saw, under still boughs.

'Isolation is the soul of art', James Joyce decided when he was writing that remarkable manuscript, portion of which was published as *Stephen Hero* and out of which was to emerge the perfect shape of *A Portrait of the Artist as a Young Man*. His artistic isolation, this deliberate choice of exile, silence and cunning, in the original sense of the word, his building around himself of a house of silence in which to await his eucharist and forge the uncreated conscience of his race, his final lamentation, 'poor aches? of Ailing', by the waters of Babalong, will all be familiar coin to careful readers of what he has written. His *Non Serviam* applied to Irish nationalism as well as to the Catholic Church. Stephen Dedalus said in *A Portrait of the Artist as a Young Man*, 'I will not serve that in which I no longer believe, whether it call itself my home, my fatherland or my church . . . '

Yet in spite of the finality of that denial, a great deal of the varied furniture of the mind that produced three of the most remarkable novels of modern times was shaped by various manifestations of Irish nationalism; from the hard pride of Parnell down to the loud-mouthed intolerance of the Citizen (Polyphemus Cusack) in Barney Kiernan's pub. With a mind instinctively sceptical Joyce naturally could not accept, as Daniel Corkery accepted, the enthusiasms of an Ireland on the road to revolution. An extreme nationalist voicing his opinions in a tavern would have passed through Corkery's mind to become hard, dignified, sombre, as elemental as the hard rocks on the coast of West Cork. In Joyce's Citizen there is no escaping the note of mockery; pleasant mockery, with none of the bitterness that he reserved for the denial of the religious faith of his childhood; but with a Rabelaisian detachment that showed how he saw extreme nationalism as a most remarkable example of the tomfoolery of pantomiming man. It was (when I first read it) impossible to avoid laughing with Joyce and hearing a score of nationalist orators and seeing a myriad of letters to the Dublin papers, when the Citizen shatters the argument of Leopold Bloom, the tolerant and wandering Jew!

> Where are our missing twenty millions of Irish should be here today instead of four, our lost tribes? And our potteries and textiles, the finest in the whole world! And our wool that was sold in Rome in the time of Juvenal and our flax and our damask from the looms of Antrim and our Limerick lace, our tanneries and our white flint glass down there by Ballybough and our Huguenot poplin that we have since Jacquard de Lyon and our woven silk and our Foxford tweeds and ivory raised point from the Carmelite convent in New Ross, nothing like it in the whole wide world! . . . What do the yellow johns of Anglia owe us for our ruined trade and our ruined hearths? And the beds of the Barrow and Shannon that won't deepen with millions of acres of marsh and bog to make us all die of consumption.

For Joyce, time ended and infinity began in pre-1916 Dublin. When the revolution came he was living outside Ireland, reading about it in the papers, reading, for instance, how his fellow-student Clancy, who had been the Davin of *Portrait* had been murdered by British soldiers. Daniel Corkery once wrote, very simply and weakly and inadequately, to put it mildly, that James Joyce went astray: only a very partial explanation, you might well say, for the phenomena of *Ulysses* and *Finnegans Wake*. Joyce was divided bitterly within himself because he was too great a man and an artist to carry scepticism to a chilly negation of everything that had made him as he was. The result was that he dramatised himself, most notably in *Finnegans Wake* as the poor exile of Erin, as the national apostate, rejected, as Shem the Penman was rejected. Frank Budgen, the painter, in his *James Joyce and the Making of Ulysses*, reported a conversation he had with Joyce as they walked along the Bahnhofstrasse in Zurich one evening. Joyce had read to Budgen the passage from *Ulysses*, portion of which I have already quoted, in which, Budgen wrote, 'the Fenian giant, representative of the most one-eyed nationalism, denounces the bloody and brutal Sassenach'. Joyce wondered suddenly what his own countrymen would think of his work. His English friend held that they would not like it because they were men of violent beliefs and *Ulysses* was the book of a sceptic. Joyce said he knew it was the work of a sceptic but that he did not want it to appear the work of a cynic, because he did not want to hurt or offend those of his countrymen who were 'devoting their lives to a cause they feel to be necessary and just.'

The sceptic living in Zurich in self-chosen exile and in his self-built house of silence could draw gigantic fun out of the nationalist ideals that precluded and formed a part of the 1916-22 revolution. But he could also see the necessity and justice of that revolution as it appeared to the eyes of men who might have regarded *Ulysses*, if they had looked at it at all, as the work of a man demented by a devil. From his boyhood days at Clongowes, Joyce had shown himself as an instinctive protester against injustice, even if his instinct could end in eccentricity. In this connection a passage written by Budgen on the politics of Leopold Bloom is well worth quotation. While the young arrogance of Stephen Dedalus was the wall that Joyce built to fortify his house of silence against the world, behind that was the wise humility of Leopold Bloom, not completely apart from the Ignatian third degree of humility; Budgen wrote:

Bloom's politics are as little spectacular as are his good deeds and yet I fear that they are of the kind that in the days that are with us and near us lead to the dungeon and the firing squad.

Budgen was writing, it must be remembered, before 1934, before
the totalitarian state had fully developed the furnace and the gas-
chamber. 1930 – the Age of Innocence. He went on about the
politics of Leopold Bloom:

> To the conservative they are revolutionary; to the
> revolutionary they are menshevik, social reformist; to the
> ardent nationalist they are pacifist, defeatist; to the facist
> they are anarchist. And for all his prudence, there is in
> Bloom a strain of impulsive simplicity, as there certainly
> was in Ulysses, that would probably lead him to speak up
> just when he ought for his own good to lie low.

In the writings of Daniel Corkery (by way of violent contrast)
there was no evident internal division, no heart-scalding contradiction, as there was in the writings of James Joyce. Corkery had seen
his people and accepted them, their lives and their beliefs and, on
occasion, even their petty meannesses: and the mountains and the
city that make up the background to their lives. But his acceptance
of the people who move through his stories and of the revolution
that for a few years gave a new tempo to their lives implied also a
definite denial of much of the past and present of the life of
Ireland. In literature it meant that Corkery denied Lever and
Lover, Francis Sylvester Mahony, Somerville and Ross, Jane
Barlow, Liam O'Flaherty, Sean O'Casey and others. And since their
connection with Ireland was too obvious to be denied it meant the
infinite splitting of hairs to decide what was Irish and what was
Anglo-Irish. In his later years, Corkery, who had written so finely
in English, had, because of his absorption in the Gaelic Revival,
almost denied the possibility of an Irishman properly expressing
himself in or producing literature in English. It seemed to me then
that Irish writers, and perhaps Irish politicians, might learn
something from the politics of Leopold Bloom.

At an early date James Joyce had made that famous statement:

> I do not think that any writer has yet presented Dublin to
> the world. It has been a capital of Europe for thousands of

years, it is supposed to be the second city of the British Empire and it is nearly three times as big as Venice. Moreover, on account of many circumstances which I cannot detail here, the expression 'Dubliner' seems to me to have some meaning and I doubt whether the same can be said for such words as 'Londoner' and 'Parisian' both of which have been used by writers as titles. From time to time I see in publishers' lists announcements of books on Irish subjects, so that I think people might be willing to pay for the special odour of corruption which, I hope, floats over my stories.

The book that Joyce then offered to the publisher, Grant Richards, appeared, as did the *Portrait*, before 1918. The major portion of *Ulysses* was written before that date. Yet it is necessary to go back to that correspondence between Irish writer and English publisher in any consideration of the relationship between modern Irish fiction and the life of the cities and large towns of Ireland. Joyce was the first Irish writer to feel about the streets as Carleton and others had felt about the fields, as Maria Edgeworth had felt about the great houses of the landed gentry.

Joyce had already had an unfortunate contact with the publisher, Grant Richards, in which the manuscript of a book of verse had been mislaid, and now Richards was further trying his patience by passing on to him the amazing objections of the moral British printer to the manuscript of *Dubliners*. Consequently, the tone of his letters moves from the sceptical tolerance of a man trying to reason with the obtuse, to the downright anger of a man whose arguments have been blunted against dunderheads. He had, he claimed, tried to present Dublin to an indifferent public under the aspects of childhood, adolescence, maturity and public life. If the moral printer denounced the stories 'Two Gallants' and 'Counterparts', a Dubliner, Joyce thought, would denounce 'Ivy Day in the Commitee Room'. The 'more subtle inquisitor', would denouce 'An Encounter', 'the enormity of which the printer cannot see because he is, as I said, a plain blunt man'. An Irish priest might denounce 'The Sisters' and an Irish boarding-house keeper might denounce 'The Boarding House'. But Joyce had written what he had written and there was an end on it. 'My intention', he said, 'was to write a chapter in the moral history of my country and I chose Dublin for the scene because that city seemed to me the centre of paralysis'.

In all that there could have been a foretelling of the Censorship of Publications Act: a harelipped child that came to us along with our national independence, or partial independence. In these days of a flourishing Arts Council and bursaries and grants, and the existence of the admirable institution of *Aosdana*,[1] it may seem a long way back to the time when the only award an Irish novelist was liable to get in his own country was to have his book banned from circulation for being 'in general tendency indecent and/or obscene'. Yet that time is well within the living memory of younger writers than myself (say Edna O'Brien and John McGahern) and I myself received this honour for three novels that by drugstore standards today would be considered pretty harmless reading.

The sad but comical truth was that the censorship business had advanced, or retrogressed, to such a stage of ludricosity that you were practically disgraced if you were not banned. Everybody, or nearly everybody, native or foreign was banned. A few good Irish writers escaped by the sheer accident that they did not emphasise the fact that young women might have, at least, two legs. To some foreign writers, Mauriac and others, a sort of fool's pardon or ecclesiastical benison was granted. The censors, I feel, were in two minds about Graham Greene because he was supposed to be some class of a Roman Catholic: a convert, by God! But there were lesser aliens than Graham Greene who were allowed in because they also were supposed to be Catholic writers. And the best I can do for them now is not to mention their names and to forget that they were acceptable in Dublin bookshops in the days of my own indecency. And/or Obscenity.

Joyce chose Dublin for its paralysis. But he chose it for a more sensible and a more fruitful reason also. Because the city was in his bones as no other part of Ireland or of the world could possibly be. The artist began by writing a chapter from the moral history of the city, 'in a style of scrupulous meanness'. He went on to write down the history of his own struggle to break all the bonds that bound him to a city, a church, a country: went on then to remember one day out of the life of that city, a day symbolising all days and hinting at eternity. The final solution of the struggle between the artist and the city was something very like victory for the city, seen dimly through the mists and shadows of *Finnegans Wake*, a city standing for all cities, a river meaning all rivers and carrying on its waters the burden of a universal mythology, a river flowing from the mountains to the sea, as is generally the way with rivers, and the rainclouds to burst on the mountains, a circle symbolising the cyclic history of man: 'riverrun, past Eve and Adam's, from swerve of shore to bend of bay, brings us by a commodius views of recirculation back to Howth Castle and Environs'.

This may not be the place for considering the validity or the lack of validity in the odd idea that Joyce dug out of Giambattista Vico, nor the exact significance of Joyce's attempt to reject the city, the church and the country. My concern at the moment is with his inability to forget the city, with the fact also that he was the first Irish writer to see the corporate life of a city or a town as something with a universal meaning. Harry Levin in his study of Joyce brought out well the positions held with regard to each other by the artist and the city. And Frank Budgen in his *James Joyce and the Making of Ulysses* indicated with a certain amount of truth that Joyce was more a Dubliner than an Irishman:

> His form of patriotism is that of a citizen of a free town in the Middle Ages. He has told me that he would rather be burgomaster of a city like Amsterdam than emperor of any empire, for a burgomaster is somebody among people he knows, while an emperor rules over unknowable people in unknown territories.

Cyril Connolly, long ago in *Horizon*, pointed out that the attitude of Joyce to Dublin had nothing to do with the 'provincial quality of Irish patriotism', but much to do with 'the pagan sentiment of birthplace', with the *dulcis moriens reminiscitur Argos* of Virgil and Theocritus, with the feelings of Sophocles for Colonus and

Odysseus for Ithaca. Louis Golding, the novelist, in a little book on Joyce, once disputed the reality of Joyce's connection with the pagan sentiment of birthplace, yet it is possible that, when one very important reservation has been made, Cyril Connolly was close to the truth. Nothing less than that strong pagan sentiment could explain the dominance of one city in the work of a man who had lived in four cities, a dominance that grew more powerful until in *Ulysses* the writer assumed in the reader an impossible familiarity with the city, until in *Finnegans Wake* the city is seen through mists, a strange symbol as old as Nineveh and as new as San Francisco.

The pagan sentiment of birthplace was in Joyce the rich red heart of his celebration of the city, but it was a wounded heart cut by the thin black knife of the Joyce denial, the 'something sinister' that Buck Mulligan noted in Stephen Dedalus: denial of his parents, his home, his friends, his city, his country, the faith of his childhood. Stephen Dedalus cried out: 'But I say: Let my country die for me'. And out of the death that the knife of denial was to bring to all things, the living work of art should grow, the flight of the winged man who rejected the earth and flew upwards fatally towards the burning heart of the sun. He wrote in Stephen Hero:

> He got down off the tram at Amiens Street instead of going on to the Pillar because he wished to partake in the morning life of the city. The morning walk was pleasant for him and there was no face that passed him on the way to its commercial prison but he strove to pierce to the motive centre of its ugliness.

Now, in the history of modern Dublin thousands of young men must have walked that same walk in the morning: over the bridge over the Liffey, between shining shop-windows and a disturbingly large number of pretty girls in Grafton Street, and between the coloured rows of flowers in Stephen's Green. But, at odd moments, Stephen Hero seems to go with a knife in his hand, killing that he might find life, probing bitterly to find everywhere the ugliness of mortality. That breath of the Manichee is one of the things that Joyce and Mr Graham Greene have in common. It is interesting, too, that in the case of the great English novelist the urban thing seems not any longer to be a corporate life but a scab that has covered Europe from Piccadilly to Stamboul, that can follow men even to the borders of the primitive in Mexico or Liberia.

The relations between James Joyce and the fantasist, ancient Gaelic or modern European, and the various techniques he employed, from the 'scrupulous meanness' of *Dubliners* to the ether-dream swirl of *Finnegans Wake*, have already provided matter for books and will, unless something extraordinary happens, provide matter for many more. Back in 1948 the novelist Francis MacManus drew attention to the light that a reading of Professor Macalister's *Secret Languages of Ireland* could throw on the underground racial origins of *Finnegans Wake*. Macalister dealt with ancient private languages, with the many kinds of *Ogham* for example, each based on alphabets that took their letters from divisions of nature, or history, or geography. Tree-*Ogham* would base its letters on Ash, Beech, Cedar, Elm, Fir and so on; Food-*Ogham* on Apple, Bread, Celery, Dumpling. 'Talking in riddles', concluded that very learned man, 'had been at all times a favourite amusement among the Celtic peoples'.

Frank Budgen argued that Joyce would no more be bound down by the dogmas of one artistic school than by the dogmas of one church. The analogy is not exact; but it is true to say that Joyce was the most insatiable experimenter in the history of the novel. The various techniques used in *Ulysses* have already been examined and re-examined from the quite normal opening on top of the Martello Tower, through the cross-headed paragraphs of the newspaper office, or cave of the winds, the birth and growth and death of language in the House of Horne, the Freudian fantasy of the *Walpurgisnacht* in darkest Dublin, to the wide stream of the night thoughts of Marion Bloom. After that there could only be *Finnegans Wake*, which to most readers, and perhaps pardonably so, is inexplicable folly; and after *Finnegans Wake* there was nothing, except the partially successful efforts of studious men and women to find the path through the maze.

JAMES JOYCE

There is a possibility that in *Finnegans Wake* James Joyce wrote the book that Giovanni Papini vaingloriously promised to write. Writing an annoying little preface to the volume of essays called, in English, *Labourers in the Vineyard*, (published by Sheed and Ward in a translation made by Alice Curtayne) Papini begged the forgiveness of his dear reader for presenting a group of portraits instead of the great universal portrait which had not yet come to light. He wrote:

> Perhaps you were expecting *Adam* or *The Record of Mankind*, which I have been promising since I was a young man. The truth is that I have been thinking out this book and working on it for fully twenty years. But with the passage of time and a correspondingly wider range of observation and deeper reflection, the work becomes continually longer and, for me, continually more difficult. It will be a book such as is rarely seen to-day; I mean as regards its dimensions: three hundred chapters in three large volumes. However I set about it, I can hardly concede less to the human species . . . I can keep within the limits of two thousand pages simply because I have been terse, but more than that I cannot grant. If even three men out of the whole world read the book, I shall not hold these years to have been wasted.

In the portion of *Finnegans Wake* that outlines the significance of Shem the Penman, who absorbed what the coherent and intelligible daylight of *Ulysses* and *A Portrait of the Artist as a Young Man* had revealed as Stephen Dedalus, there is this passage:

> Then, pious Eneas, conformant to the fulminant firman which enjoins on the tremylose terrian that, when the call comes, he shall produce nichthemerically from his unheavenly body a no uncertain quantity of obscene matter not protected by copiright in the United States of Ourania or bedeed and bedood and bedang and bedung to him, with this double dye, brought to blood heat, gallic acid on iron ore, through the bowels of his misery, flashy, faithly, nastily, appropriately, this Esuan Menschavik and the first till

last alschemist wrote over every square inch of the only foolscap available, his own body, till by its corrosive sublimation one continuous present tense integument slowly unfolded all marryvoising moodmoulded cycle wheeling history (thereby, he said, reflecting from his own individual person life unlivable, transaccidentated through the slow fires of consciousness into a dividual chaos, perilous, potent, common to allflesh, human only, mortal but with each word that would not pass away the squidself which he had squirt-screened from the crystalline world waned chagreenold and doriangrayer in its dudhud.

The reader who is not hardened by a certain acquaintance with the eccentricities of the later Joyce may not find that passage particularly revealing. Balanced against the previous quotation from Papini it really does reveal that Giovanni Papini and Shem the Penman – or Stephen Dedalus or James Joyce – had, at least, an intention in common: to write the story of man. It reveals also, and this time even to the most sceptical regarder of both the aims and methods of Joyce, that Papini and Joyce had very different ways of putting their intentions into practice. One trivial difference was that Joyce managed to condense his narration into one volume, even if it was a volume of more than six hundred very large pages, even if that one volume, like Giambattista Vico's theory of history, or like the Buddhist snake eating its own tail, was a rigid symbol of the truth that the story of man comes out of mystery and goes again into mystery.

A more important difference between the methods of Joyce and Papini can be indicated by quoting another passage from another writer – a Frenchman. Fortunately it is possible to translate the language of the French nation as it is never satisfactorily possible to translate the language of *Finnegans Wake*. Jean-Richard Bloch said that the art of writing was the struggle of Jacob with the angel, of the artist with his double:

But this duel must be carried on in the presence of seconds, of a referee. The reader constitutes the seconds or the referee. As soon as we pass from sleep to waking, from dream to formulation, from mental language to artistic creation, an unseen interlocutor arrives. The endeavour to make our thoughts clear and precise is always the search for a communication. The readers, be they five or five thousand, or fifty thousand, are there before you when you work and it is their silent presence which gives you courage.

It is one part of the truth about *Finnegans Wake* to say that James Joyce dispensed with the referee and the rules, and ordered the seconds out of the ring. The poor exile of Erin wailing by the waters of babalong; the writer who had mastered the English language until it was no longer for him a sufficient medium; the man with weak eyes, and ears sensitive to music; the scholar in myth writing at a time when comparative mythology had been brought further than ever before; the searcher into the things behind consciousness in a time when the science of the sub-conscious (a very doubtful term) had become a cant; the reader of obscure authors, accepting from a little-known Italian historian a very probably false philosophy of history; the man who had already shown that for him one river could symbolise every river and one city represent all cities, who had written of the father (Bloom-Ulysses) searching for the son (Stephen-Telemachus), wrote in *Finnegans Wake* of the city as the father and the river as the mother, of himself as the two contesting sons, of . . . the list could go on and on, aspect adding to aspect, definition to definition, until the picture of the writer became as complex and cloudy as the book that he named by the name of a ballad of the Dublin streets.

Complex and cloudy, because only the very devoted reader of James Joyce will arrive at *Finnegans Wake* with the enthusiasm excited by the melodies and meditations in *A Portrait of the Artist as a Young Man*. Mr Louis Golding, going all the way with Joyce in seeing Bloom-Ulysses as the complete man, was still inclined to think that Shem and Shaun emerging in instalments in *Work in Progress* were lost up a side-alley and separated from the main line of Joycean development. But Joyce is one of those writers who must be followed all the way, even if the pursuit into the labyrinth

of *Finnegans Wake* only leads back 'by a commodius vicus of recirculation' to the small boy on the first page of *Dubliners* repeating
to himself the words 'gnomon' and 'paralysis' as if they were
enchanted symbols.

As somebody discovered somewhere in Milton, it is not an easy
matter to cross chaos, with or without a guide. It is even more
difficult to attempt to guide others across chaos, and the commentators who have up to the present tried to trace the thread of
meaning through *Finnegans Wake* can never expect more than a few
select companions for their journey. The two Americans, Campbell
and Robinson, who had the first, as far as I know, determined
attempt at explanation, had also as their major weakness the pro-
fundity of their new world reverence for James Joyce. When
allowances have been made for the uncritical things that can always
come from too much fervour – and I suggest as an admirable corrective an essay by Andrew Cass, '*Sprakin Sea DJoytsch*', published in
The Irish Times for 26 April 1947 – the Campbell and Robinson
book was and is valuable. For those two commentators and for a
few other people *Finnegans Wake* is:

> running riddles and fluid answer . . . a mighty allegory of
> the fall and resurrection of mankind . . . a strange book, a
> compound of fable, symphony and nightmare – a mon-
> strous enigma beckoning imperiously from the shadowy pits
> of sleep. Its mechanics resemble those of a dream, a dream
> which has freed the author from the necessities of common
> logic and has enabled him to compress all periods of his-
> tory, all phases of individual and racial development, into a
> circular design, of which every part is beginning, middle
> and end.

Balance against those high words some of the many sound
arguments that can be advanced against *Finnegans Wake*: that Giambattista Vico's work *La Scienza Nuova* and the whole notion of history passing through recurrent phases, theocratic, aristocratic,
democratic and chaotic, was just an insane eighteenth century simplification on which no valid, universal view of man's origin and

destiny could be based; that Joyce was a pedant and a punster and, at some awful moments, both together; that his mythology is the exiled and apostate Irishman's ingrowing toenail, not the voyage down the wide river of common fable and poem and legend that, more than anything else, makes all men brothers. The argument that the difficulty facing the reader of *Finnegans Wake* invalidates it as a channel for ideas has, in the course of the years that have passed since publication, more or less disproved itself. The guileless arguments that Joyce was either a practical joker or slightly deranged were never worth consideration at any time, for they usually sprang from utter ignorance of everything Joyce had written. Granted there are moments when his application to the mystical significance of numbers makes even the sympathetic reader doubtfully shake his head.

But will all its oddities, obscure symbolism, associative words, melting into character, and of all characters into mist and nothingness, with its extreme adherence to doubtful philosophical and historical theories, *Finnegans Wake* is one of the most remarkable works of genius in modern literature. Papini was probably right in his estimation of the extent of work to be called *Adam* or *The Record of Mankind*. Joyce pressed the work into one volume by an unprecedented feat of condensation, by making an attempt to join together a hundred words so as to make not another word but an all-significant harmony. As a record of mankind the book is very likely a failure, because of that doubtful cyclic theory of history, because Joyce, being a great laugher and not a philosophic historian, being also a pedant, buried his meaning under a million pedantries and a million puns. It may be that Joyce was the erudite author who, as Milton and Goethe did not, lost control of his erudition and hid forever the lonely road his mind followed in a forest of reference and cross-reference.

Stephen Dedalus boasted bitterly that he was not afraid to make a mistake, 'even a great mistake, a life-long mistake and perhaps as long as eternity, too'. It may be that *Finnegans Wake* was in the art the terrible mistake of James Joyce, because it offered neither to himself nor to younger writers any outlet from the circle, charmed but vicious, like the snake eating its own tail.

NOTES

1 A government-sponsored, self-perpetuating community of Irish artists, each receiving an annual pension or **cnuas** which pronounces from time to time on matters of cultural concern.

DUBLINERS

John McGahern

Dubliners has often been compared to *The Untilled Field*; Moore's stories are seen to have foreshadowed Joyce's, and they are linked in trying to establish a tradition for that dubious enterprise, The Irish Short Story. I do not use 'dubious' in the pejorative sense, other than the absurdity of trying to tout one race or literary form above any other. Remarkable work in the short story has come continually out of Ireland, but it is likely that its very strength is due to the absence of a strong central tradition. Stanislaus Joyce is most persuasive in his articulation of this problem for the Irish writer, if problem it be; for to live here is to come into daily contact with a rampant individualism and localism dominating a vague, fragmented, often purely time-serving, national identity. James Joyce's remark about the citizens of Trieste – 'They are all for the country when they know which country it is' –could be equally true of his own countrymen. Moore expressed this rowdy individualism, and in some respects he personified it, as did Patrick Kavanagh later, but it is not applicable to Joyce.

The author of *The Lake, Drama in Muslin, Hail and Farewell* was a writer of genius. The stories in *The Untilled Field* are as fresh on the page today as when Moore wrote them to be translated into Irish in 1900. That he wrote them for translation may have much to do with their freshness and energy. Moore's artistic insecurity was as great as Kavanagh's. That he was writing the stories for translation probably freed him from a crippling responsibility: he did not have to protect himself with an imposed formality; above all, he did not feel called upon to ruin them with 'style'. In his forthright way Joyce described these stories as 'stupid', but the social inaccuracy he pinpointed we do not notice today. Moore was not so scathing about *Dubliners*, though his reaction was almost as unsympathetic. Given the disparity in temperaments, backgrounds, and upbringings, it could hardly have been otherwise, and it makes the attempt to force the two books into the same tradition extraordinarily misplaced. Moore's genius was erratic and individualistic. Joyce's temperament was essentially classical, and he knew exactly what he was attempting in *Dubliners*.

> As for my part and share in the book I have already told all I have to tell. My intention was to write a chapter of the moral history of my country and I chose Dublin for the scene because that city seemed to me the centre of paralysis. I have tried to present it to the indifferent public under four of its aspects: childhood, adolescence, maturity and public life. The stories are arranged in this order. I have written it for the most part in a style of scrupulous meanness and with the conviction that he is a very bold man who dares to alter in the presentment, still more to deform, whatever he has seen and heard. I cannot do any more than this. I cannot alter what I have written. All these objections of which the printer is now the mouthpiece arose in my mind when I was writing the book, both as to the themes of the stories and their manner of treatment. Had I listened to them I would not have written the book.[1]

The authority and plain sense suggest that Joyce was well aware that he was working within a clearly defined tradition. To look towards Moore for any tradition is not useful. All of Moore is self-expression: he constantly substitutes candour for truth. In *Dubliners* there is no self-expression; its truth is in every phrase. 'The author is like God in nature, present everywhere but nowhere visible'.

I do not think we have to look further than Flaubert and the group of writers close to him who wrote in France at the height of the nineteenth century. The early Joyce, aesthetically at least, would have fitted perfectly into this portrait of the group Henry James wrote to William Dean Howells:

> What was discussed in that little smoke-clouded room was chiefly questions of taste, questions of art and form, and the speakers, for the most part, were in aesthetic matter, radicals of the deepest dye. It would have been late in the day to propose among them any discussion of the relation of art to morality, any question as to the degree in which a novel might or might not concern itself with the teaching of a lesson. They had settled these preliminaries long ago, and it would have been primitive and incongruous to recur to them. The conviction that held them together was the conviction that art and morality are two perfectly different things, and that the former has no more to do with the latter than it has with astronomy or embryology. The only duty of a novel was to be well written; that merit included every other of which it was capable.[2]

The first reactions to *Dubliners* were not unlike the criticism Flaubert had to confront until the end of his life: that the work was depressing, with no uplifting message, too withdrawn and cold; and, though all too accurate, lacking in feeling and compassion.

In the light of Joyce's statement – 'I have written it for the most part in a style of scrupulous meanness and with the conviction that he is a very bold man who dares to alter in the presentment, still more to deform whatever he has seen or heard'. – it is interesting to look at the following paragraph from a letter George Sand wrote to Flaubert in 1876:

This wish to portray things as they are, the adventures of life as they present themselves to the eye, is not well thought out, in my opinion. It's all the same to me whether one depicts inert things as a realist or as a poet; but when one touches on the emotions of the human heart, it's a different matter. You cannot detach yourself from this consideration; for you are a human being, and your readers are mankind. Your story is inevitably a conversation between you and the reader. If you show him evil coldly, without ever showing him good, he's angry. He wonders whether he is the villain, or you. What you wanted to do, however, was to rouse him and maintain his interest; and you will never succeed if you are not roused yourself, or if you conceal your emotion so effectively that he thinks you indifferent. He's right: supreme impartiality is antihuman, and a novel must above all be human. If it isn't, the public cares nothing for its being well written, well composed and well observed in every detail. The essential quality – interest – is lacking.[3]

In the same letter she also writes:

I have already challenged your favourite heresy, which is that one writes for twenty intelligent people and doesn't care a fig for the rest. That is not true, since you yourself are irritated and troubled by lack of success. . . . One must write for all those who have a thirst to read and can profit from good reading. Then the writer must exhibit his own highest moral principles, and not make a mystery of the moral and beneficent meaning of his book. In *Madame Bovary*, people perceived what that was. If one part of the public cried scandal, the healthier and more numerous part saw in it a severe lesson given to a woman without conscience or faith – a striking lesson to vanity, to ambition, to irrationality. They pitied her: art required that; but the lesson was clear, and it would have been more so, it would have been for *everybody*, if you had wished it to be, if you had shown more clearly the opinion that you held, and that the public should have held, about the heroine, her husband, and her lovers.[4]

In all of Flaubert's long and rich correspondence, nowhere is his position stated more lucidly than in his reply; despite his obvious affection for George Sand, he is uncompromising:

And now, chère maître – and this is in reply to your last letter – here, I think, is the essential difference between us. You, always, in whatever you do, begin with a great leap toward heaven, and then you return to earth. You start from the *a priori* from theory, from the ideal. Hence your forbearing attitude toward life, your serenity, your – to use the only word for it – your greatness. I, poor wretch, remain glued to the earth, as though the soles of my shoes were made of lead: everything moves me, everything lacerates and ravages me, and I make every effort to soar. If I tried to assume your way of looking at the world as a whole, I'd become a mere laughing-stock. For no matter what you preach to me, I can have no temperament other than my own. Nor any aesthetic other than the one that proceeds from it. You accuse me of 'not letting myself go' naturally. But what about discipline? What about excellence? What do we do with those? I admire Monsieur de Buffon for putting on lace cuffs before sitting down to write. That bit of elegance is a symbol. And, lastly, I try, naively, to have the widest possible sympathies. What more can be asked of anyone?

As for revealing my private opinion of the people I bring on stage, no, no! a thousand times no! I do not recognize my *right* to do so. If the reader doesn't draw from a book the moral it implies, either the reader is an imbecile or the book is false because it lacks exactitude. For the moment a thing is True, it is good. Even obscene books are immoral only if they lack truth . . .

And please note that I execrate what is commonly called 'realism', even though I'm regarded as one of its high priests. Make what you can of all that.

To try to please readers seems to me absolutely chimerical. I defy anyone to tell me how one 'pleases'. Success is a result; it must not be a goal. I have never sought it (though I desire it), and I seek it less and less.[5]

In reply George Sand wrote:

You no longer look for anything but the well-turned sentence. That is something, but only something – it isn't the whole of art, it isn't even half of it; it's a quarter at most, and when the three other quarters are fine one does without the one that is not.[6]

He is, if anything, even more forthright:.

You make me a little sad, chère maître, when you ascribe to me aesthetic opinions that are not mine. I think that rounding out a sentence is nothing. But that *to write well* is everything. Because: 'Good writing implies strong feeling, accurate thinking, and effective expression'. (Buffon.)

The last term is thus dependent on the two others, since it is necessary to feel strongly in order to think, and to think in order to express. Every bourgeois can have heart and delicacy, be full of the best feelings and the greatest virtues, without for that reason becoming an artist. And finally, I believe Form and Matter to be two abstractions, two entities, neither of which ever exist without the other.

The concern for external Beauty you reproach in me is for me a *method*. When I come upon a bad assonance or a repetition in one of my sentences, I'm sure I'm floundering in the False. By dint of searching, I find the proper expression, which was always the *only* one, and which is, at the same time, harmonious. The word is never lacking when one possesses the idea.

'The concern for external beauty you reproach me with is for me a method'. The method in *Dubliners* is that people, events, and places invariably find their true expression. This is so self-evident that comment becomes superfluous. Everything is important in *Dubliners* because it is there and everything there is held in equal importance.

In 'The Sisters', a priest's madness is toned down to the banal, to social sanity and acceptance:

> – Wide-awake and laughing-like to himself. . . . So then, of course, when they saw that, that made them think that there was something gone wrong with him . . .

A simple walk through Westmoreland Street in 'Counterparts' is seen through a vain and weak man raising himself in his own eyes:

> He came out of the pawn-office joyfully, making a little cylinder of the coins between his thumb and fingers. In Westmoreland Street the footpaths were crowded with young men and women returning from business and ragged urchins ran here and there yelling out the names of the evening editions. The man passed through the crowd, look-ing on the spectacle generally with proud satisfaction and staring masterfully at the office-girls. His head was full of the noises of tram-gongs and swishing trolleys and his nose already sniffed the curling fumes of punch.

The whole of the Roman Church in the figure of the silenced priest is completely redeemed into the company of the little Dubliners engaged with themselves and the ward elections in 'Ivy Day in the Committee Room':

> – Tell me, John, said Mr O'Connor, lighting his cigarette with another pasteboard card.
> – Hm?
> – What is he exactly?
> – Ask me an easier one, said Mr Henchy.
> – Fanning and himself seem to me very thick. They're often in Kavanagh's together. Is he a priest at all?
> – 'Mmmyes, I believe so. . . . I think he's what you call a

black sheep. We haven't many of them, thank God! but we have a few. . . . He's an unfortunate man of some kind. . . .
– And how does he knock it out? asked Mr O'Connor.
– That's another mystery.
– Is he attached to any chapel or church or institution or –
– No, said Mr Henchy, I think he's travelling on his own account. . . . God forgive me, he added, I thought he was the dozen of stout.

The rich local humour is never allowed to stray out of character. It generally consists of badly digested scraps of misinformation which are adhered to like articles of faith once they are possessed, and used like weapons to advance their owner's sense of self-importance, or to belabour that of others. It could have been a happy evening in 'Grace' but they 'vituperated' one another:

– Pope Leo XIII., said Mr Cunningham, was one of the lights of the age. His great idea, you know, was the union of the Latin and Greek Churches. That was the aim of his life.
– I often heard he was one of the most intellectual men in Europe, said Mr Power. I mean apart from his being Pope.
– So he was, said Mr Cunningham, if not *the* most so. His motto, you know, as Pope, was *Lux upon Lux* – *Light upon Light*.
– No, no, said Mr Fogarty eagerly. I think you're wrong there. It was *Lux in Tenebris*, I think – *Light in Darkness*.
– O yes, said Mr M'Coy, *Tenebrae*.
– Allow me, said Mr Cunningham positively, it was *Lux upon Lux*. And Pius IX. his predecessor's motto was *Crux upon Crux* – that is, *Cross upon Cross* – to show the difference between their two pontificates.
The inference was allowed. Mr Cunningham continued.
– Pope Leo, you know, was a great scholar and a poet.
– He had a strong face, said Mr Kernan.
– Yes, said Mr Cunningham. He wrote Latin poetry.
– Is that so? said Mr Fogarty.
Mr M'Coy tasted his whisky contentedly and shook his head with a double intention, saying:

– That's no joke, I can tell you.

While Maria in 'Clay' is disturbed and confused and sings the first verse of her song twice over, the prose is never any of these things and remains wonderfully alert and balanced:

> But no one tried to show her her mistake; and when she had ended her song Joe was very much moved. He said that there was no time like the long ago and no music for him like poor old Balfe, whatever other people might say; and his eyes filled up so much with tears that he could not find what he was looking for and in the end he had to ask his wife to tell him where the corkscrew was.

Particularly in 'The Boarding House', 'Grace', and 'The Dead', pun, coincidence, and echo are used as a writer of verse would use the formality of rhyme, deepening the sense of the lives of these mortal-immortal Dubliners, drawing together the related instincts of the religious, the poetic, and the superstitious.

The prose never draws attention to itself except at the end of 'The Dead', and by then it has been earned: throughout, it enters our imaginations as stealthily as the evening invading the avenue in 'Eveline'. Its classical balance allows no room for self-expression: all the seas of the world may be tumbling in Eveline's heart, but her eyes give no sign of love or farewell or recognition.

Joyce does not judge. His characters live within the human constraints in space and time and within their own city. The quality of the language is more important than any system of ethics or aesthetics. Material and form are inseparable. So happy is the union of subject and object that they never become statements of any kind, but in their richness and truth are representations of particular lives – and all of life.

I do not see *Dubliners* as a book of separate stories. The whole work has more the unity and completeness of a novel. Only in the great passages of *Ulysses* was Joyce able to surpass the art of *Dubliners*. In many of these, like the Hades episode, his imagination returns again and again to his first characters, his original material.

71

NOTES

1 Richard Ellmann, ed. *Selected Letters of James Joyce* (London: Faber and Faber, 1975), p. 83.

2 Francis Steegmaller, ed. *The Letters of Gustave Flaubert* (Harvard University Press: Volume II), pp. 224-225.

3 ibid. p. 229.

4 ibid. p. 229.

5 ibid. pp. 230-231.

6 ibid. p. 231.

7 ibid. p. 231.

SURVIVORS
OF
JOYCE

John Banville

I begin with a quotation from Nietzsche:

> Every great phenomenon is succeeded by degeneration,
> especially in the domain of art. The example of greatness
> incites all vainer natures to extreme imitation or attempts
> to outdo; in addition to which, all great talents have the
> fatal property of suppressing many weaker shoots and for-
> ces, and as it were laying nature waste all around them. The
> most fortunate thing that can happen in the evolution of
> an art is that several geniuses appear together and keep one
> another in bounds; in the course of this struggle the
> weaker and tenderer natures too will usually be granted
> light and air.

The figure of Joyce towers behind us, a great looming Easter
Island effigy of the Father. In the old days it was considered fitting
that children should honour the parent, and I could, indeed, spend
the next fifteen or twenty minutes paying tribute to that stone

Nobodaddy at my shoulder. But when I think of Joyce I am split in two. To one side there falls the reader, kneeling speechless in filial admiration, and love; to the other side, however, the writer stands, gnawing his knuckles, not a son, but a survivor.

There are artists whom one can use, from whom one can learn one's trade. I am thinking of, let us say, Catullus, Piero della Francesca, Beethoven, Henry James; they are the strugglers, the self-conscious ones, the *sentimental*, in Schiller's sense of the word. Their work is to some extent exoskeletal, in that one can see, or at least glimpse here and there on the surface, the processes by which the work was produced. Such glimpses are invaluable for the apprentice. This is how we learn – and not the least part of the lesson is the manner by which the struggle, the visible labour, is welded into the work, to become another *aspect* of the work, so that form is constantly *trans*formed into content. This generative and transfiguring process is a large part of the greatness of the *Carmine Catulli*, of Piero's frescoes, of the String Quartet Opus 131, of *The Golden Bowl*.

And then, there are the artists who are of no use to the tyro, from whom one learns nothing. Let us pick another four at random: Virgil, Vermeer, Mozart, James Joyce. In the work of artists such as these, the methods of production are well-nigh invisible, buried so deeply inside the work that we cannot get at them without dismantling the parts, as a schoolboy with a Swiss watch. The greatness, or part of the greatness, of an *Aeneid*, of a *View of Delft*, of a *Don Giovanni*, of a *Ulysses*, rests in the fact that they are, in an essential way, *closed*. By this I do not mean to say that these works of art are difficult, or obscure – what could be more limpid than the light that hovers over Delft? – but that they are *mysterious at their core*. There is something uncanny about such art. It does not seem to have been produced by human hands, but to have created itself out of nothing by some secret, unknowable means. And so the work stands before us, light and lightsome, glossy as an apple, full of chat – and utterly impenetrable. Such art is not to be known except in its surface – but of course, as we know, the surface of a work of art can be as deep as the deepest depths.

I think, myself, that the truly great works of art, the ones before which we fall silent, and simply stand and gape, all have this quality of reticence, of being somehow turned away from us, gazing off, like nature itself, into another sphere of things, another reality. I want to emphasise this. For the most part we think the 'best', the most 'successful' art is that which is most accommodating to us, which exists on the same scale as ours, which *gives* itself to us: 'Shatter me, Music!' Rilke cries, but Music hears him not, Music is too busy singing to itself. The gaze which great art gives us back is utterly vacant; the sirens are silent.

I am conscious that, to many, Joyce will seem more aptly set among my first quartet of masters than my second. Who, you will say, could have been more self-conscious, more one of Schiller's sentimentalists, than he? And it will be no good my pointing out that Joyce himself held that the artist should stand disengaged from his art, off in the background somewhere, paring his nails – no one pays much attention any more to *that* piece of piety. And further, you will say, where in literature can the *process* have been more a part of the work itself than in *Portrait*, or *Ulysses*, or *Finnegans Wake*?

For the most part, of course, I must bow to these objections. Nothing is simple. But I would invite you to consider the evidence. What is it in *Ulysses*, in *Finnegans Wake* (I leave aside the problematical *Portrait*) that compels our awed attention? Is it, in the former, the sense of 'real life' that is conveyed through Bloom and Stephen and Molly and the myriad other characters, so that we seem to look at ourselves, as it were, through the wrong end of a telescope, dainty, loveable, and wonderfully clear – is this what brings us back, over and over, to *Ulysses*? Permit me, once again, to quote Nietzsche, at somewhat more length this time:

Created people. – When we say the dramatist (and the artist in general) actually *creates* characters, this is a nice piece of deception and exaggeration in the existence and dissemination of which art celebrates one of its unintentional and as it were superfluous triumphs. In reality we understand very little of an actual living person and generalize very superficially when we attibute to him this or that character: well, the poet adopts the same *very imperfect* posture towards man as we do, in that his sketches of men are just as *superficial* as is our knowledge of men. There is much illusion involved in these created characters of the artists; they are in no way living products of nature, but, like painted people, a little too thin, they cannot endure inspection from close to. And if one should even venture to say that the character of the ordinary living man is often self-contradictory and that created by the dramatist the ideal that hovered dimly before the eye of nature, this would be quite wrong. An actual human being is something altogether *necessary* (even in those so-called contradictions), but we do not always recognize this necessity. The invented human being, the phantasm, desires to signify something necessary, but only in the eyes of those who comprehend even an actual human being only in a crude, unnatural simplification: so that a couple of striking, often repeated characteristics, with a great deal of light on them and a great deal of shadow and twilight around them, suffice to meet all their demands. They are thus quite ready to treat phantasms as actual, necessary human beings because they are accustomed when dealing with actual human beings to take a phantasm, a silhouette, an arbitrary abridgement for the whole. – That the painter and the sculptor, of all people, give expression to the 'idea' of the human being is mere fantasizing and sense-deception: one is being tyrannized over by the eye when one says such a thing, since this sees even of the human body only the surface, the skin; the inner body, however, is just as much part of the idea. Plastic art wants to make characters visible on the outside; the art of speech employs the word to the same end, it delineates the character in sounds. Art begins from the natural *ignorance* of mankind as to his interior (both bodily and as regards character): it does not exist for physicists or philosophers.

So much for the 'people' in *Ulysses*.

In *Finnegans Wake*, is it the element of the crossword puzzle that attracts us? Much has been made of the mephistophelian pact between Joyce's work and academe, and it is true that without the attentions of the academics, much in Joyce would have gone unexplained. (The corollary of this is that without the surety of an academic posterity, Joyce might have done things differently; but that is another lecture). What the burners of midnight oil glean from the *Wake*, however are mere *facts*. They are *interesting* facts, they are sometimes *beautiful* facts, but still, they are only facts. Edmund Wilson shrewdly pointed out that, in the case of *The Waste Land*, the more widely we read in other works, the more references we spot, and the more references we spot, the more *The Waste Land* diminishes. Something the same is true of *Finnegans Wake*. The more of it we decipher, the more we 'use it up'. Of course, it is not serious diminishment; but anyone who has ever completed a crossword knows that curious, ashen sense of futility, of nausea, almost, that comes along with the 'solution'.

I hasten to add that I am not suggesting that understanding of a work of art makes one feel sick; I do believe, however, that what we come to know about a work is simply that: *a knowing about*, a peripheral knowledge. Knowing a thing, however intimately, however deeply, is not always the same as *understanding* it. We are back to the boy with the dismantled Swiss watch.

We are asking: what is it fascinates us about *Ulysses* and *Finnegans Wake*? – what quality is it in such works that prompts us to set them up as canonical? Wallace Stevens believed, or professed to believe, that in our post-religious age, poetry could be the supreme, sustaining fiction without which Man would perish. Works such as *The Waste Land* and *Ulysses* have taken on, or have been conferred with, a biblical quality: they have become the Psalms, they have become the Book. Why? What constitutes the quality of the numinous in them? What is it that speaks to our need for texts, for Holy Writ?

I believe it is the quality of *closure*.

To repeat: great art, I am convinced, does not 'reveal' itself to us, does not open outward to our needs; on the contrary, it is great precisely because it is closed against us. This, I realise, is not a comfortable formulation. Art, as I have said, is supposed to be accommodating, 'all-embracing', as one might say. It is supposed to let us know things – morals, psychology, the world of nature, ourselves. I don't believe this is so – or, I should say, I believe the matter is more complicated, more circuitous than we ordinarily imagine. Far from allowing us to know things with any immediacy, art, I believe, *makes things strange*. This it does by illuminating things, literally: the making of art is a process in which the artist concentrates on the object with such force, with such ferocity of attention, that the object takes on an unearthly – no, an *earthly* glow. As Rilke has it:

> Perhaps we are *here* only to say: house, bridge, fountain, gate, jug, fruit-tree, window – at most: column, tower . . .
> but to *say*, that is, oh, to say them *more* intensely than the things themselves ever dreamed of existing.

And later, in the same Elegy:

> And these things, that live by perishing, know you are praising them; fleeting, they look to us for deliverance: us, the most fleeting of all. They want us to change them, utterly, in our invisible heart, within – oh, endlessly – within us. Whoever we may be at last.
> Earth, isn't this what you want: to arise within us, *invisible*? Is it not your dream to be wholly invisible someday? – O Earth, invisible!

This is not such a mystical, not such a high-falutin process as it may seem, this interiorisation of things, this taking into us of the world, of all that stuff out there which is not ourselves. It happens all the time, continuously, in art. And its result is a different order of understanding, which *allows* the thing its thereness, its outsideness, its absolute otherness. Such understanding is wholly individualistic, yet profoundly democratic. Every thing has its own place, its own space, which it inhabits utterly.

This process of incorporation, I hold, is a process of *style*. Has North America ever existed so intensely – if a great deal more economically – as it does in the pages of *Lolita*? Has the light of day ever fallen on a patch of wall with such heartbreaking tenderness as it does in certain pictures by Vermeer? Has Dublin ever *spoken* so vividly as it does in *Ulysses*, in the *Wake*? And yet, from such works, what do we *know*, that we have not always known? Nothing, except style. Here is Henry James:

> In literature we move through a blest world in which we know nothing except by style, but in which also everything is saved by it.

Style. Does Joyce *have* a style? – does he have *a* style, as distinct from styles, in the plural? Eliot thought not (and Eliot was always good when it came to Joyce, mainly, I think, because the poet did not quite trust the novelist, and was definitely not in awe of him, as so many of us are). Certainly there *had been* a style, or the makings of one, in *Dubliners* and *Portrait* and the first forty or fifty pages of *Ulysses*. It was a curious, ambiguous style – how, for instance, are we to take the closing pages of *Portrait*, which read like the gushing of a poetic adolescent: is it irony, or not? It was a style which Joyce thought better of – or worse, depending on your opinion of the rest of *Ulysses*, and the *Wake*. It is one of the great mysteries of Modernism, this transformation of a Nineties aesthete into the Rabelaisian author of *Ulysses* and the *Wake*. I speak, of course, not of the transformation of a soul, but of a style. The movement is, surprisingly, a movement not from impurity to purity, but vice versa; it is a movement from Flaubert to Balzac, contrasted here by Proust:

> In Flaubert's style, every aspect of reality is converted into a similar substance, a vast surface glistening monotonously. No impurities remain. Every surface has become reflective. Everything is depicted there, but by a process of reflection, without altering its homogeneous nature. All that was different has been converted and absorbed. In Balzac, on the other hand, exist side by side all the undigested, as yet unconverted elements of a future style which is not yet in existence.

'. . . a future style which is not yet in existence': could there be a better characterisation of the methods of the *Wake?*

It is, I believe, the absence of, or the concealment of, a unified, recognisable style, that gives to Joyce's work its peculiar, impregnable, *frightening* authority. He is one of those writers . . . or should I say, *he is a writer* (for he is probably unique) whose work is utterly free of solecisms, of errors of judgement, of mistakes: for such things, should they seem to appear, are immediately transformed, by a sort of continuous chain reaction, into *inventions*. I happen to think that a formulation such as 'The heaventree of stars hung with humid nightblue fruit' is pretty ghastly, yet when one comes across it in its context, the surprise of it, the –possible– humour of it, the *ambiguity* of it, leave one breathless.

Joyce was never silent, but he was certainly cunning. He was the supreme escape-artist, a Houdini of the word, who used every possible rhetorical device in order to bury himself – the living, breathing self – so deep inside the work that when we knock we get back only the faintest response, and even that may be, for all we know, merely an echo of our knuckles on the wood. Under the guise of an all-accepting humanism, Joyce created an impenetrable fortress, an edifice like that in which Maggie Verver finds herself immured in *The Golden Bowl*:

> . . . it had reared itself there like some strange, tall tower of ivory, or perhaps rather some wonderful, beautiful, but outlandish pagoda, a structure plated with hard, bright porcelain, coloured and figured and adorned, at the overhanging eaves, with silver bells that tinkled, ever so charmingly, when stirred by chance airs.

One might pause over the ever so charming silver bells, but the hard, bright porcelain, that's the stuff, all right.

Do not mistake me; I am not criticising. I believe the trick that Joyce pulled in creating at least two great, closed works of art out of an aesthetic that *seemed* to descend from the ethereal to the earthly, is the true mark of his genius. As a reader, I can only applaud. As a writer, I feel, to paraphrase Simon Dedalus, that I have been left where Jesus left the Jews. Nor is *this* a criticism: it's no business of Joyce to haul the rest of us on to the raft, nor even to give us a peek inside the pagoda. It's just that it is cold out here, and, half the time, it feels like drowning.

A PORTRAIT OF THE ARTIST AS A YOUNG MAN

Deirdre Bair

'A Background for Myself': The Evolution of *Stephen Hero* to Stephen Dedalus in *A Portrait of the Artist as a Young Man*.

James Joyce described himself as an autobiographical novelist, believing his life and work to be one and the same, 'interwoven in the same fabric'.[1] In the years since he said this, much critical ink has been expended on its interpretation. Stephen Dedalus' remark, made in *Stephen Hero*, might serve as the best commentary on it: 'Oh, the world of professors whom he helps to feed!'[2] Joyce's biographer, Richard Ellmann, described this fusion of life and work as 'the mixture of self-recrimination and self-justification which the great writer, like lesser men and women, has made the subject of his life-long conversation with himself'.[3] Joyce's erstwhile friend, Gogarty, said Joyce made his friends and family into 'accessories before the fact', by showing the book as he wrote it to those whom he wanted to influence, indirectly threatening that if their behaviour did not meet with his approval, they were likely to find themselves cast unflatteringly as characters within its pages.

'All immortals had relatives and next-door-neighbors', the American writer Diane Johnson wrote, and in Joyce's case, they served to fuel his inner drives as well as to illuminate the social and intellectual pressures of the Ireland of his age, which rightly or wrongly, he believed were put upon him.[4]

But first, as we see in *Portrait of the Artist as a Young Man*, we must deal with the question of the author James Joyce, as we consider his interpretation of that complex man known to relatives, friends and lovers (depending on who speaks of him) as 'Jim' or 'Joyce' or 'My brother', as he interprets and portrays this complex amalgamation of himself through the character of Stephen Dedalus. Ellmann describes this as follows:

> At the age of twenty-one, Joyce had found he could become an artist by writing about the process of becoming an artist, his life legitimizing his portrait by supplying the sitter, while the portrait vindicated the sitter by its evident admiration for him.[5]

A number of other writers have also addressed this question of the role of self and place within their own fiction, and these offer interesting possiblities to think about when reading Joyce.

Frederick Barthelme speaks of autobiography as

> ubiquitous, first novel or last – it's the data stream, so it's there in inflections, images, gestures, incidents, in the set decoration and in the mouths of babes. This is true whether you write work that appears to be from life but isn't, or you write remarkable new prose that seems to want to have come from the planet Zombia.[6]

A critic commenting upon Philip Roth's *Zuckerman* novels, says that Roth

> has made his own life and vocation the subject of his art, reinventing his autobiography and giving it the resonance of literary myth.[7]

Roth himself believes that 'It's language and moral sensibility that transform raw experience into fiction. The experience is the ground that you set your feet on'.[8] Roth is unknowingly echoing Jung here, who called his own autobiographical writing 'symbolic memory', and who said of it:

> The years when I was pursuing my inner images were the most important of my life. In them everything essential was decided. It was the *prima materia* for a lifetime's work.[9]

Joyce, too, 'plunged back into his own past' for his *prima materia* when he wrote *A Portrait of the Artist as a Young Man*. Ellmann believes that he did so 'mainly to justify it, but also to expose it'. As Joyce explained to Stanislaus:

> We are what we were: our maturity is an extension of our childhood, and the courageous boy is father of the arrogant young man.[10]

I conduct my own literary research through biography, and in recent years, this idea of Joyce's has been one of the governing theories of biographical inquiry. In fact, in the book I am just now finishing, the biography of Simone de Beauvoir,[11] I have taken great pains to explain the childhood in detail for non-French readers because it does indeed pre-figure and in many ways form the mature woman.

Some eighty years after Joyce, however, another Irish writer, Edna O'Brien, spoke of this very same thing:

> One's autobiography is vast. The mother that one knew at eight is not the mother that one knew at sixteen. What I do is a form of imaginative and extensive and ruminative autobiography. There are many more things to be dug out of that quarry. And I find it's the place and the people and it's the emotion, of course, above all else, that inspires me most, and that draws from me the greatest particularity. I'm very obsessed with detail and particularity, what Rilke calls "the divine detail".[12]

This is very much what Joyce does. In the first draft of *Stephen Hero*, the work that later became *Portrait of the Artist as a Young Man*, Joyce insists that:

> 'the features of infancy' belong to a portrait as much as the features of adolescence. The past has no 'iron memorial aspect,' but implies 'a fluid succession of presents.' What we are to look for is not a fixed character but the development of an entity of which our actual present is a phase only.[13]

He goes on in this same vein to describe his conception of personality as a river rather than a statue – and this of course is a premonition of what his later view of consciousness became. And, of course, it is also an extremely Jungian position.

But in drawing upon his own past as a series of continuing presents for his fiction, Joyce has done so much more than simply to create a kind of crypto-autobiography. He has allowed the political, the surreal, the mythic and the grimly realistic to intrude upon his embellished and reimagined life. John Cheever described how he wrote fiction, and his description could well have been uttered by Joyce before him:

> I have been a storyteller since the beginning of my life, rearranging facts in order to make them more interesting and sometimes more significant. I have improvised a background for myself – genteel, traditional – and it is generally accepted.[14]

Let us look now, at how *Portrait of the Artist as a Young Man* came to be the work we have before us today.

In January, 1904, the twenty-two year old Joyce was living in a chaotic household at 7 St Peter's Terrace. His mother had died the previous August, his penniless father had run out of things to mortgage when he commuted his pension and had just been reduced to selling the piano, infuriating Joyce and leaving him, his two brothers and six sisters not only without money for food but also without any means of distraction from their poverty through entertainment. Each of the siblings, in his or her own way, was plotting a withdrawal from the household's hunger, violence and despair; Joyce was plotting his through ambition. 'I want to be famous while I am alive', he had written to his aunt Josephine Murray. Now he was about to make his first concerted effort to do so.

He heard that John Eglinton and Fred Ryan were planning to begin a new intellectual journal to be called *Dana*, after the Irish earth-goddess, and were seeking submissions. He sat down on January 7th, and in one day wrote an autobiographical story that, as Ellmann describes it, 'mixed admiration for himself with irony'.[15]

When he read the story, Eglinton was confused by it, saying 'I can't print what I don't understand', and he and Ryan rejected it at once, citing (according to Stanislaus) 'the sexual experiences narrated in it'. Also according to Stanislaus, Joyce had his own opinion: 'Jim thinks they rejected it because it is all about himself, though they professed great admiration for the style of the paper'. To which Stannie couldn't help adding 'They always admire his style'.

From this rejected story came the genesis of Joyce's mature fiction. The late William York Tindall believes that 'Joyce wrote one great big novel in four great big parts',[16] and if we accept this description, then we see Joyce, for the next ten years labouring on part one, first as *Stephen Hero*, and later, converting it into, give-or-take an odd hundred or so, the 250-plus pages that became the final, printed version of the book.

In the process, he turned autobiography into memoir. By melding his own political, religious, social and sexual history, he was able to show different gradations of the lived life. Ultimately he created a work of fiction that incorporated differing degrees of reality – his own, his family's, and the Ireland in which he could not live, but without which he could not live either.

Throughout his life, whenever anyone asked if he would ever return to Ireland, Joyce's standard reply was 'Have I ever left it?'. Overall, this is certainly true, but with *Portrait of the Artist as a*

Young Man, the most interesting aspect of the work (to me at least) is what he left out (and thus left behind) and why. I propose to view this book first in terms of what isn't there, and to do this, we will first have to examine *Stephen Hero*.

We can do so by starting with Stanislaus' explanation for Joyce's development of the character, Stephen Dedalus, trying to come to terms with the problems he encounters throughout his young life:

> The idea he [meaning Joyce] had in mind was that a man's character, like his body, develops from an embryo with constant traits. The accentuation of these traits, their reactions to hereditary influences and environment, were the main psychological lines he intended to follow.[17]

To begin with, let us start by listing some of what he includes in the massive *Stephen Hero* and excises from *Portrait of the Artist as a Young Man*: The first book is filled with detail. Incidents and people are described at length. The Dedalus family is fleshed out much more fully, giving 'a richly sordid background to the arrogant growth of Stephen's mental independence'.[18] Maurice (the Stanislaus character) especially takes up many pages, and the illness and death of the sister Isabel is told in sad, funereal plentitude. All this is missing in *Portrait*. There is a sort of godfather, Mr Wilkinson, whose house is described in detail in the manuscript, and he is entirely absent from the finished book. In *Stephen Hero*, Stephen takes great pains to convince his family to share his admiration for Ibsen's plays, and there is none of this in *Portrait*. Joyce also omitted the long passage in which Stephen meditates about what an Epiphany actually is in an interesting and highly revealing passage which seems central to an understanding of the artist Joyce later became. He eliminates it entirely in *Portrait*, preferring instead to show rather than tell. Emma Cleary, the girl of whom Stephen dreams, is a dramatic part of *Stephen Hero*; she is reduced to her initials, EC in *Portrait*.

Joyce's friends, Cranley, Lynch and the rest, are introduced to the reader in *Stephen Hero* as real flesh and blood people. They are clearly identified by their appearance and points of view, and have an independent reality apart from Stephen's. In *Portrait*, Joyce allows them to enter into the text only as facets of Stephen's mind, only as points of reference for Stephen to bounce his ideas upon, as the necessary extension of his thought. He pontificates to them and they are there only to listen, to serve as features in his mental landscape who need be given no further space upon these pages than their names and what they have to say in reply to Stephen. But he, however, in both versions fits the description given to him in a recent letter to the editor of the New York Times, written by a disgruntled professor upset with the debate over the *Ulysses* text, who calls Stephen 'narrow, priggish, cruel and venomously disputatious'.[19] She has a good point in many crucial instances in both *Stephen Hero* and *Portrait*.

But one of the most striking differences of both texts is the way Stephen himself is described. In the first, he is rougher, cruder, more emotionally and intellectually immature and, in many ways, a much more sympathetic fellow because of it. He is proud and arrogant and does a lot of foolish things, but his rages are more those of a callow adolescent than a nasty twit. When he rebels against church and family, his rebellion seems more the ordinary sophomoric coming of age that most of us have gone through at one time or another as we assert our independence and adulthood. In *Stephen Hero*, Stephen Dedalus seems to be someone the reader identifies with rather than reacts against. We feel for this callow youth, a kind of romantic sympathy, an *engagement* that obviously dissatisfied Joyce because he took such pains to eliminate it in *Portrait*. It is as if Stephen, as the hero, is an adolescent who contains much that is universal in his development and subsequent rebellion, while Stephen, as the artist, is the young adult who has honed his vision, sharpened and refined it, and now declares his credo, saying to his reader

Take it or leave it. This is what I am. And what I am is 'non serviam.' I'll tell you what it is and how it got to be this way, and then, dear reader – take it or leave it.

Joyce's intention was to refine his central character, his fictional persona, to 'assume his isolation'.[20] At the same time as this young artist is deliberately choosing isolation and doing everything he can to alienate everyone around him, he is busy collecting friends and family so that he can tell them he's doing it. I think the important thing to note here is that he is at the very same time telling everyone what he is doing so that he can measure their response to it. He courts disciples to share his opinions and points of view, demanding of them more and greater demonstrations of allegiance: however, when he brings them to the point where they say 'no further', beyond that point they will not follow him, then he says 'aha, I knew you would do this, I knew you would forsake me. I was ready for it, so now I can forsake you, too'. – He is setting himself up to be set up. I like Ellmann's description:

> He buys his own ticket for Holyhead, but claims to have been deported. . . . Of this young man it may be safely predicted that he will write letters home.[21]

So Joyce came to abandon page after lyrical page of *Stephen Hero*. Portraits of people who are charming, foolish, wicked, or sad were jettisoned; descriptions of places, houses, gardens, and things were cast aside or else kept and sharpened, made to do double and triple descriptive and symbolic work. But it is Stephen's ideas that undergo the most radical refinement, and this finally becomes the vehicle for restructuring a shapeless mass into what many critics agree is a novel that represents perfection of structure, the ultimate unity of content, where characer and idea are united in seamless, streamlined form.

We can see what Joyce did with this novel if we look at some of his views of the creative process. In his essay on James Clarence Mangan, published in the UCD literary magazine *St Stephen's* in 1902, Joyce said that every poet must incorporate into himself 'the life that surrounds it, flinging it abroad again amid planetary image'. He used this same phrase in *Stephen Hero* and he retained it in *Portrait*, where he developed it more fully.

In the novel, he describes literature as 'the phenomenon of artistic conception, artistic gestation and artistic reproduction'. Then he goes on to describe the progression from lyrical to epical and then dramatic art. It is a longish quote, but like the Chinese box within a box, or the little wooden Russian doll with many smaller versions of the same within, it is a capsule commentary within the larger explanation, i.e. Stephen's theory of aesthetics, which is the focal point of the novel, and which becomes point of departure if not governing vision for the next novel and then, with further refinements, the one that marks completion and finality:

> The simplest epical form is seen emerging out of lyrical literature when the artist prolongs and broods upon himself as the centre of an epical event and this form progresses till the centre of emotional gravity is equidistant from the artist himself and from others. The narrative is no longer purely from the artist himself and from others. . . . The narrative is no longer purely personal. The personality of the artist passes into the narration itself, flowing round and round the persons and the action like a vital sea. . . . The dramatic form is reached when the vitality which has flowed and eddied round each person fills every person with such vital force that he or she assumes a proper and intangible esthetic life. . . . The mystery of esthetic like that of material creation is accomplished. The artist, like the God of the creation, remains within or behind or beyond or above his handiwork, invisible, refined out of existence, indifferent, paring his fingernails.[22]

So how then did he compose this novel, he who wished to remain within or behind or beyond or above his handiwork? Many critics believe the style lies somewhere between Joseph Conrad and *Madame Bovary*. Many others see it as a *Bildungsroman*, the novel of adolescent development, which had been popular for about one hundred years before Joyce wrote his and which remained even more popular after, setting it in the tradition that ranges from Goethe's *Wilhelm Meister* through Meredith's *Richard Feveral*,

JAMES JOYCE

Butler's *The Way of All Flesh* to Thomas Mann's *Magic Mountain* and *Tonio Kroger*, to Lawrence's *Sons and Lovers*, Maugham's *Of Human Bondage* and Thomas Wolfe's *Look Homeward Angel*.

Joyce intended his hero to represent Vico's theory that we project and reveal our deepest selves through our heroes, as in our myths and our dreams. What makes this view especially interesting is that his projections include alienation and exile, two concepts which we now consider crucial to the depiction and description of the age in which we live, and which we identify much more closely with the anti-hero than with the hero. We no longer see ourselves capable of living heroically, so perhaps what makes Joyce's novel so popular today is that we can legitimately view Stephen Dedalus as the outsider, the anti-hero who fulfils our deepest fears and wishes, and thus stands for our chosen image of ourselves. It is this double view of hero vs anti-hero that we can bring to a reading of this almost 85-year old novel, that enhances the inherent irony of Joyce the creator, paring his fingernails with ironic indifference over this sometimes pompous young fellow, that makes us want to take his side and sympathise with him. When he says 'non serviam', we reply 'you are right to do so'.

It is, however, a novel of beautiful imagery, of wonderfully vivid language, of impressionistic scenes and sudden, startling moments of understanding. It is a novel of moral positions and social ideas. When one considers all this, it is truly astonishing to realise the economy and precision with which Joyce inserts them into the text at key, crucial moments. Nothing is there unless it works to enhance Joyce's development of Stephen; everything there contributes to the idea of Stephen, the development of Stephen, the character of Stephen. What this all adds up to finally is a novel of the development of character, but with such refinement of technique that it seldom comes through upon first reading. This novel crackles with energy and intellectual vitality, all of which coalesces, merges, melds and finally explodes. Every sentence is important and must not be skimmed or hurried over, for each one builds upon the others until finally in the experience of reading it, there is wholeness, harmony and radiance in all aspects of this text.

Let me talk about some of the techniques and then cite just the high points within each episode of the novel. Embryonic growth underlies part of the imagery during Stephen's youth. Stanislaus notes that in the first draft of *Portrait*, Joyce describes a man's character as developing 'from an embryo' when he spoke of the 'constant traits', as in the section I quoted earlier. Ellmann ties this in with the gestation of Nora's pregnancy, which coincided with Joyce's decision to rewrite *Stephen Hero* just after Lucia's birth. Certainly there is embryonic imagery tied in with Stephen's growth from a little boy to a youth, and we see this in the many liquids which inform this part of the text. We have water, urine, slime, amniotic tides, drops of water, in many different ramifications.

This leads into his fascination with words, and with the way he allows language to determine the age of his hero – from the childlike beginning to the deepening understanding and consciousness. Then this is related to sensory experiences. We can mention the word 'suck' which is the sound of the lavatory in the hotel, and the related water images of the two 'cocks' you turn to get hot or cold water. These passages convey foetal imagery of the liquid which corresponds exactly with Stephen's young age, and his fascination and puzzlement with words, but there are sexual overtones in these passages which both underline his innocence at this stage of his development and prefigure his preoccupations to come at a later date.

These sorts of passages do something else as well – they allow Joyce to switch from one subject to another by a continuous stream of association. Think only of the beginning, where 'Baby Tuckoo' hears a political argument but does not understand it, where Dante's brushes are linked to Davitt and Parnell.

Part one is also the section in which the major themes are set out and which then change and develop throughout the rest of the novel. These are his parents, the mother whom he loves and the father for whom he first feels admiration that becomes shame if not hatred. The church is here, rigid, inflexible, certain of itself as the one sure truth. The politics of Dante's brushes becomes the collision of the Church with the politics of Stephen's father, who refuses to accept the Church's betrayal of Parnell. And of course there is art – Stephen sings the song of the wild rose blooms and he dances. But all of these – every one of them – become the support mechanisms for Stephen's central consciousness. All this detailed attention to family and friends is not to develop their personalities in and of themselves; rather it is only to enhance the development of Stephen's perception, his apprehension of himself within the family that surrounds him.

The infant Stephen's consciousness grows gradually, mostly in terms of perception and sense-experiences of state, church and family. The chapter ends with his first clash with authority, prefiguring all those to come. It takes place in an educational institution, but it is education in the religious context, so the moral victory of his first 'non serviam' that follows his visit to the rector prefigures the final 'non serviam' which comes after University College, the ultimate educational experience within the religious setting.

In Part II, he is beginning to set himself apart and his pride is now developing. He is an ordinary little boy for all intents and purposes, but he believes himself to be an exception – another instance of Joycean irony. The situations here vary: from school to family scenes, to his romantic visions, and awakening sexual awareness – which terrifies him. He is upset by his 'monstrous reveries', and when he finds the word 'foetus' carved into his father's old college desk, he loathes himself, not the one who carved it. Rather than being reassured that he is just the same as other boys and now has the generational evidence to prove it, he is shocked by what he considers 'a brutish and individual malady of his own mind'. This chapter ends with his visit to Nighttown and his encounter with the prostitute, so we see the importance, not only of sex, but also of secular life.

Chapter III becomes of crucial importance in terms of where it is placed within the novel, just as Scylla and Charybdis and Anna Livia Plurabelle will be in the two novels that follow. Here we have the gripping, frightening sermon on death, judgement, hell and heaven. It certainly confirms Samuel Beckett's comment that Joyce's writing is not about something, but is that something itself,[23] for this sermon provokes absolute terror from which

Stephen can only escape through a temporary religious frenzy almost as frightening as the fear which inspired it. And the Joycean irony here is that this is not conversion to religious conviction, but is instead refuge, temporary relief gained through confession. The intensity of his relief and happiness is so artificial that it cannot last. His exaltation cannot hide the real problem lurking behind it within this young man's life. For, when the priest in confession implores him to 'give up that sin', Stephen comes to the decision that he would rather give up religion instead.

In Part IV, he is asked about a vocation because this earlier religious zeal has so impressed the Director. All this is described in beautiful imagery, scenes of waning light and death. The Director is 'slowly dangling and looping the cord of the other blind', and this makes Stephen realise that his 'destiny was to be elusive of social or religious orders – the snares of the world were its ways of sin. He would fall. He had not fallen yet, but he would fall silently, in an instant'. Here we have a beautiful combination of images of sin with images of myth, of Stephen the schoolboy with Dedalus, the mythical fabulous artificer.

So he realises the prophecy of his name, and the image of the 'fabulous artificer', will become the symbol within this novel of 'the artist forging anew in his workshop out of the sluggish matter of the earth a new soaring impalpable imperishable being'. This statement not only becomes his manifesto of his future as an artist, but a statement about the material he would incorporate into his fiction. His essay on Ibsen, *Drama and Life*, which he wrote in 1900, is worth a second look in connection with this – I only just mention it here in passing.

And when Stephen denies the church and becomes aware of his vocation as an artist, Joyce is drawing attention to the fact that art will become his substitute for religion. 'This was the call of life to his soul, not the dull gross voice of the world of duties and despair, not the inhuman voice that had called him to the service of the altar'.

Directly after this he encounters the wading girl – a kind of secularisation of the Virgin Mary which echoes the secularisation of his religious beliefs, and which Stephen accepts as such: 'her

95

image had passed into his soul forever and no words had broken the silence of his ecstacy'.

Part V strengthens his image of the artist and allows him to become preoccupied with his aesthetic theory. Here, he is trying to cut himself loose from the fatal bonds of Dublin to prepare for his exile. What is striking about this section is that Epiphany as a technique is absent, and instead we have the notions and terminology of Thomas Aquinas contrasted with those of Aristotle. There is the sublime vs the beautiful, the moral vs the material beauty. He talks about the 'Quidditas', the whatness of a thing, the 'immediate perception . . . followed by the analysis of apprehension'.

He works this out carefully through a conversation with Lynch, who serves as the often comic and sometimes grotesque counterpoint to Stephen's point. Stephen moves from the discussion of the static, the tragic emotion which looks toward feelings of pity and terror; to the kinetic, dramatic emotion which urges the perceiver toward desire and loathing; to the æsthetic emotion, which must be static because the mind is arrested and above kinetic desire and loathing. What must be evoked is æsthetic stasis, the ideal pity or terror, which is 'called forth and prolonged and at last dissolved by what I call the rhythm of beauty'.

Lynch asks: 'What is art? What is the beauty it expresses?' Stephen replies that 'Art is the human disposition of sensible or intelligent matter for an æsthetic end'. From Aquinas he argues that 'That is beautiful which pleases' – and leads to truth, i.e. a combination of Plato, Aristotle and Aquinas, which all lead him back to ponder perceptions of beauty, such as the differences between the classic (Goethe) and the Romantic (Lessing).

From this, he goes into *integritas*, *consonantia* and *claritas* – wholeness, harmony and radiance. And from that, he decides that art will divide itself into three forms, with each one leading to the next: in the first, the lyric, the artist presents the work in relation to himself; in the epic, he presents the work in relation to himself and others; in the dramatic he presents the work in relation to others – and is nonetheless forced to admit that even in literature, which he calls the 'highest and most spiritual art', the forms are often confused.

Then he ends with God paring his fingernails. And he, Stephen, has been entirely serious and humourless throughout this discussion. Joyce gives us relief from his unceasing pedantry by allowing Lynch to be amusing – or pausing to allow a noisy carriage to pass by, or some other aspect of Dublin life to intrude – because he is the supreme craftsman, the writer who knows his reader must be given some sort of respite from Stephen's unrelenting intellectual argument.

One difference between this part of *Stephen Hero* and *Portrait* is that the earlier work is all unrelieved theory while the published novel has these moments of real life intruding upon Stephen's conception of art.

And an important point to realise is that in this chapter, in which we have Stephen's æsthetic theory in its final development –at least within this novel – we have it in an incomplete form in which it is fairly easy to punch some major holes. It is the portrait of a *very young artist*, with some thoughts and actions which show lack of insight and experience and also, because of arrogance and pride, which show lack of full moral or spiritual scope.

But Stephen is counting on Aquinas to carry him along this line until he comes to phenomena of artistic conception, gestation, and reproduction for which he will require an entirely new terminology and personal experience. And when he gets there, he is ready to pay the price to move on.

Thus, he has to break with the old life in order to continue to develop as an artist, and the alienation, so eagerly and callowly embraced as a young man in, of and for itself, has now become an absolute necessity for the serious and committed further development of the still brash-but-definitely-wiser young artist.

As the book ends, he is not yet the mature artist, but he is one step further along the road to becoming one. His mother prays that he will learn what his heart is and what it feels while he is away from his family, and he does not disagree with her.

But as he goes forth to encounter the reality of experience and to forge in the smithy of his soul the uncreated conscience of his race, we have come to the end of part one of Stephen Dedalus' ongoing quest. The forging of heart and brain, separate until this point, becomes the further quest that leads us into *Ulysses*.

NOTES

1 Louis Gillet, *Claybook for James Joyce*, trans. Georges Markow-Totevy, (London and New York: Abelard-Schuman, 1958), p. 133.

2 James Joyce, *Stephen Hero* (New York: New Directions, 1963), p.97.

3 Richard Ellmann, 'That's Life', *The New York Review of Books*, June 17, 1971, pp. 3-7.

4 Diane Johnson, 'Austin and Mabel: the Amherst affair and love letters of Austin Dickinson and Mabel Loomis Todd', ed. Pilly Longsworth (New York: Farrar Straus and Giroux, 1984), *The New York Times Book Review*, March 4, 1984, p. 3.

5 Ellmann, *James Joyce (revised)*, (New York and London: Oxford University Press, 1983), p. 144-45.

6 Frederick Barthelme, 'Writing the Second Novel: A symposium', *The New York Times Book Review*, 17 March, 1985, p. 1 and 40.

7 Michiko Kakutani, 'Is Roth Really Writing About Roth?', *The New York Times*, Monday, May 11, 1981, p. C17.

8 *Ibid.*

9 Jung, 'Memories', p. 199/191, in James Olney, *Metaphors of Self: The Meaning of Autobiography* (Princeton: Princeton University Press, 1981), p. 92.

10 Ellmann, p. 295.

11 *Simone de Beauvoir: A Biography* (New York: Summit Books; London: Jonathon Cape, *et. al.*, 1989).

12 Maureen Howard, 'Edna O'Brien', *Voque*, April, 1985, p. 199.

13 Ellmann, p. 145.

14 Michiko Kakutani, 'Separating the Real Cheever from the Invented', review of *John Cheever: A Biography* by Scott Donaldson, *The New York Times*, Wednesday, June 22, 1988, p. xx.

15 Ellmann, *JJ (revised)*, p. 144.

16 Professor Tindall relished this remark and said it frequently to his doctoral seminar at Columbia University in 1970-71.

17 Scholes and Kain, 'The Workshop of Dedalus', (Evanston, Northwestern U. Press, 1965), p. 60.

18 *Stephen Hero*, introduction, p. 11.

19 Marianne DeKoven, 'Letters to the Editor', *The New York Times*, 4 July, 1988, p. 22.

20 Ellmann, *JJ (revised)*, p. 292.

21 Ellmann, *JJ (revised)*, P. 292.

22 Ellmann, p. 296, PAYM 214, 215.

23 Samuel Beckett, 'Dante ... Bruno ... Vico ... Joyce', *An Examination of James Joyce: Analyses of the 'Work in Progress'* (Norfolk, Conn.: New Directions, 1969).

STEPHEN'S GREEN -
THE IMAGE OF IRELAND
IN JOYCE'S PORTRAIT

Colbert Kearney

The fourth section of *A Portrait of the Artist as a Young Man* is concerned with Stephen's vocation. The ordered piety of Stephen's life has drawn the attention of the Director of Vocations at Belvedere College and Stephen is summoned to an interview.

> – In a college like this, he [*the Director*] said at length, there is one boy or perhaps two or three boys whom God calls to the religious life. Such a boy is marked off from his companions by his piety, by the good example he shows to others. He is looked up to by them; he is chosen perhaps as prefect by his fellow sodalists. And you, Stephen, have been such a boy in this college, prefect of Our Blessed Lady's sodality. Perhaps you are the boy in this college whom God designs to call to Himself.

Stephen decides that the celibate life of the priest is too cold for him and he smiles when he realises that he is rejecting the power and status attached to the Jesuit House in favour of 'the misrule and confusion of his father's house and the stagnation of vegetable life' [148].

In the next episode Stephen walks out along the Bull Wall and onto Dollymount Strand, thoughts of his mythological namesake, Daedalus, swirling in his mind:

> Now, at the name of the fabulous artificer, he seemed to hear the noise of dim waves and to see a winged form flying above the waves and slowly climbing the air. What did it mean? Was it a quaint device opening a page of some medieval book of prophecies and symbols, a hawklike man flying sunwards above the sea, a phrophecy of the end he had been born to serve and had been following through the mists of childhood and boyhood, a symbol of the artist forging anew in his workshop out of the sluggish matter of the earth a new soaring impalpable imperishable being? [154f]

In this excited sense of 'a new wild life' he takes off his canvas shoes and socks, climbs down from the Bull Wall and wades up a long rivulet which flows down the strand into the sea.

> A girl stood before him in midstream, alone and still, gazing out to sea. She seemed like one whom magic had changed into the likeness of a strange and beautiful seabird. Her long slender bare legs were delicate as a crane's and pure save where an emerald trail of seaweed had fashioned itself as a sign upon the flesh. Her thighs, fuller and softhued as ivory, were bared almost to the hips where the white fringes of her drawers were like feathering of soft white down. Her slateblue skirts were kilted boldy about her waist and dovetailed behind her. Her bosom was as a bird's, soft and slight, slight and soft as the breast of some darkplumaged dove. But her long fair hair was girlish: and girlish, and touched with the wonder of mortal beauty, her face.

> She was alone and still, gazing out to sea; and when she felt his presence and the worship of his eyes her eyes turned to him in quiet sufference of his gaze, without shame or

wantonness . . .

> – Heavenly God! cried Stephen's soul, in an outburst of
> profane joy . . .

> Her image had passed into his soul for ever and no word
> had broken the holy silence of his ecstacy. Her eyes had
> called him and his soul had leaped at the call. To live, to
> err, to fall, to triumph, to recreate life out of life! A wild
> angel had appeared to him . . . [171f.]

Much has been written about Stephen's ecstacy and how the
vision of the girl is an image of the life he feels called to, a symbol
which resolves his previously conflicting desires – Blessed Virgin
and Fallen Woman, immortal and mortal, ideal and actual, soul and
body. But there is one minor point which has been – as far as I
know – overlooked: the seaweed on the girl's skin.

Before looking more closely at the seaweed we must remind
ourselves that when reading this sequence we are always aware that
what Stephen sees is at least partly a product of his imagination.
We must presume that the other seasiders on Dollymount Strand
did not react to the wading girl as Stephen did because they did
not see what Stephen saw. For Stephen alone it was as if the Angel
of the Lord appeared unto him and he conceived of the Holy
Spirit. For the others it must have been less apocalyptic; if they
noticed a girl wading through the rivulet, it is most unlikely that
she seemed to them to be a mysterious mixture of woman and
bird or that she inspired in them thoughts of the soul, baptism,
the Blessed Virgin, the Holy Spirit in the form of a dove and so
forth.

The more perceptive of the young males probably noticed that
there was a slick of seaweed on one of the girl's legs and probably
assumed that it had accidentally become attached to it. It is most
improbable that any of them would have seen and explained that
seaweed as Stephen does:

> an emerald trail of seaweed had fashioned itself as a sign
> upon the flesh.

The entire passage is so famous, so familiar, that we need to remind ourselves just how extraordinary this description is. Stephen is suggesting that the seaweed had intentionally placed itself and shaped itself on the girl's leg in order to effect a certain communication. In earlier cultures it was not unknown for divine agencies to leave such messages in order to test the intelligence of mortals but there can be no such attribution here. The implication here is that there is in (at least) some natural phenomena a significance or meaning which is only available to individuals such as Stephen Dedalus who tend to ask what such phenomena mean. Earlier, when Stephen *seemed* to hear waves and *seemed* to see Daedelus in flight, he asked himself what it meant: was it a prophecy or a symbol?

We are not dealing here with common sense but with a most uncommon set of senses. Those familiar with *Ulysses* are at an advantage when reading this part of *Portrait*. In *Proteus* the same Stephen is walking along a beach – albeit on the other side of the bay – musing on the nature of visual perception:

> Ineluctable modality of the visible: at least that if no more, thought through my eyes. Signatures of all things I am here to read, seaspawn and seawrack, the nearing tide, that rusty boot. Snotgreen, bluesilver, rust: coloured signs.[31]

Of even more interest to my present purpose is the arrival of the old woman with the milk in Telemachus. We cannot say for certain how Mulligan and Haines see this old woman but we feel sure that they do not see her as Stephen sees her:

> He watched her pour into the measure and thence into the jug rich white milk, not hers. Old shrunken paps. She poured again a measureful and a tilly. Old and secret she had entered from a morning world, maybe a messenger. She praised the goodness of the milk, pouring it out. Crouching by a patient cow at daybreak in the lush field, a witch on her toadstool, her wrinkled fingers quick at the squirting dugs. They lowed about her whom they knew, dewsilky cattle. Silk of the kine and poor old woman, names given

her in old times. A wandering crone, lowly form of an immortal serving her conqueror and her gay betrayer, their common cuckquean, a messenger from the secret morning. To serve or to upbraid, whether he could not tell: but scorned to beg her favour.[12]

The process here is only initially surprising. While Mulligan indulges in condescending banter with the woman, Stephen observes her in the context of his own thoughts. He wonders if she is a messenger – or in its Greek form, an angel – from another world beyond the confines of common sense and he wonders what her message is. He imagines her milking her own cattle at daybreak. At first he sees her as a witch but the image of the flanks of the cattle shining with dew generates the phrase *dewsilky cattle*, and that in turn identifies the old woman as Ireland, two of whose many names were *Sioda na mBo* and *An tSeanbhean Bhocht*. It is not entirely unreasonable to see this old woman as the goddess Ireland because she, like the country, is here serving her conqueror, Haines the Englishman, and her betrayer, Mulligan the Irishman. There does not seem to be any message, merely the confirmation for Stephen that Ireland is – as it always was – the prey to internal treachery and external oppression.

The process on Dollymount is similar if less obvious. Stephen sees the girl as a messenger – he actually calls her a 'wild angel' – who reveals his vocation to him. Most of the imagery is traditional, a combination of the Venus Anadyomene and the Holy Spirit in the form of a dove.

But what of the 'emerald trail of seaweed'? A sign of what? Joyce does not tell us: perhaps he felt it was too obvious to need pointing, perhaps he wanted us to work it out for ourselves.

Notice the colour: the ineluctable modality of the visible. Stephen had noticed four shades in 'the endless drift of seaweed. Emerald and black and russet and olive'. [155]. The shade of the seaweed which fashions itself significantly on the girl's leg is emerald, bright green, the national colour of Ireland which is sometimes known as the Emerald Isle. Therefore green is a sign of Irishness, not only in common usage, but in the *Portrait* where on the opening page 'the wild rose blossoms/On the little green place' and green is the colour associated with the nationalist leader, Parnell. The green seaweed hallmarks this traditional image as Irish. The implication is that the art which Stephen aspires to and which this girl represents will have a national dimension. This seems to be at odds with Stephen's later dismissal of Irish nationalism and indeed it is; but though Stephen – like his creator – disagreed with the popular nationalism of the Gaelic League and Sinn Fein, he himself had what might be called national ambitions. When, just before he leaves Ireland, he meets Davin, he tells him that 'the shortest route to Tara was *via* Holyhead', which suggests that his destination was Tara or the soul of Ireland. And he is more explicit in the final lines of the book when he announces his ambition as being 'to forge in the smithy of my soul the uncreated conscience of my race'.

The idea of supernatural beings appearing on earth in human form in order to communicate with human beings is as old as literature or folklore. It is a feature of classical European literature. Perhaps the most famous version is that in Book One of the *Aeneid* where Aeneas encounters his divine mother Venus disguised as a Carthaginian maiden. Aeneas suspects that this is no ordinary maiden but it is only as she departs that he knows for sure:

> Venus finished speaking and as she turned away her beauty shimmered, a rosetint glowed about her neck and her sacred hair exuded a divine perfume. Her gown trailed down to her feet and it was her walk which revealed that she was indeed a goddess. [11.402ff.]

In 1902 Joyce would have recognised the influence of Virgil in the close of Yeats' play *Cathleen Ni Houlihan*. Yeats had brought the passions of his nationalist audience to a frenzy by having Ireland represented by an old woman who on leaving the stage is transformed into 'a young girl . . . with the walk of a queen'. Two traditions fuse in Yeats' play, the classical and the native Irish. *Cathleen Ni Houlihan* was but one of many names for Ireland imaged as a beautiful maiden. Two others names have already been mentioned – *Silk of the Kine* and *The Poor Old Woman* – but generally Ireland was imaged as a young female. In Yeats' play the old woman represents the oppression of the country under foreign rule while the royal maiden – never seen on stage – suggests the noble energy of the country fighting for independence.

The image of Ireland as a female goes back to the earliest times but in the eighteenth and nineteenth centuries it found new forms of creative expression in poetry, in which subversive political passions were disguised as romance. It is now disputed whether some of the most famous of these poems were originally intended to be anything other than simple love poems, but what is beyond dispute is, firstly, that there was an ancient tradition of presenting Ireland in the form of a woman and, secondly, that there was a more recent tendency in Gaelic poetry to suggest the oppression of the Gaelic nation by describing the plight of a beautiful maiden kept in bondage by a cruel tyrant. Poems of the eighteenth century and earlier which were capable of being read as political allegories were highly prized and frequently translated into English by Irish nationalists of the nineteenth century. One of the most famous translators was James Clarence Mangan, a strange Dublin bohemian whose career fascinated Joyce. Mangan's best known translation is *My Dark Rosaleen*, a free rhetorical fantasy which is closer to the spirit of contemporary nationalism than to the relatively simple *Roisin Dubh*.

Roisin Dubh may well be one of those poems which was originally written as a love poem, but which evolved a political allegory. The original context of another famous Gaelic poem which Mangan translated – *Gile na Gile* by the astonishing virtuoso, Aogan O Rathaille – is undeniable. Here is the first stanza:

The Brightest of the Bright met me on my path so lonely;
The Crystal of all Crystals was her flashing dark-blue eye;
Melodious more than music was her spoken language only;
And glories were her cheeks, of a briliant crimson dye.

This visionary woman is about to be married to a boor when

the poet reminds her that a nobleman – the Stuart Pretender – is waiting to be united with her. The poet goes away sorrowing, knowing that nothing can be done until warriors come across the sea to save the woman.

Gile na Gile may well be the first *aisling*, a species of visionary poem with a clear political allegory which was extremely popular in the eighteenth century, especially in Munster. The word *aisling* suggests a vision, a dream or an hallucination. In a typical *aisling*, the poet is lost in mist or twilight when he is confronted by a woman of superhuman beauty. He asks if she is one of the fairy spirits or one of the classical goddesses or one of the legendary beauties. She replies – directly or allegorically or both – that she is Ireland and that she is imprisoned by a brutal tyrant and will remain so until her true love comes from overseas and liberates her. The poet pledges himself to her and promises to do all in his power to expedite her liberation. Poetry and politics merge.

Before going any further let me make one thing clear: I am not suggesting that the sequence with the girl on Dollymount Strand was intended by Joyce to be an *aisling*, nor do I think that the reader should read it as an *aisling*. Obviously it is not. I wish to suggest that there is a national element in the Dollymount vision. In presenting the crucial moment of Stephen's self-discovery as an encounter with a beautiful young woman, Joyce was following a European tradition in which the Ideal – Divine Truth or Eternal Beauty – is incarnated in a young maiden. Joyce was also aware that there was in the Irish tradition a distinct species of this genus of visionary literature which we may call 'the national allegory'. The key element of this literature – and of the more specialist *aisling* – was the identification of the female as a symbol of Ireland: when the poet declares his allegience to her he dedicates himself to the service of his country. Stephen identifies the bird-girl not as Eire or Cathleen Ni Houlihan or any related Gael but as an angel, 'an envoy from the fair courts of life'. I may seem to be attaching excessive importance to a slick of seaweed but nobody can doubt that Joyce placed it there because he attached great importance to it. Whether young Joyce ever actually saw such a girl in such circumstances with or without a slick of seaweed is neither here nor there; the meaning of the seaweed sign will emerge in the context of Joyce's writings rather than in his history.

The *Portrait* is set at a time of great nationalistic fervour in Ireland and the prominence of Davin in the university chapter reflects that fervour. Stephen seems more attracted to Davin than to any of his other fellow students and allows him a unique casual intimacy. And this despite the fact that Davin is, in Stephen's eyes, an unsophisticated peasant who represents the kind of nationalism which he himself finds so repellent. Stephen reserves some of his bitterest barbs for Davin and yet he sees him as his friend. Why is he 'won over to sympathy by the speaker's simple accent?' [181f.] Perhaps some clue lies in Stephen's memory of Davin's narrative.

Davin's adventure occurred when he was on his way home from a fierce game of hurling – the most traditional of Gaelic sports. Walking alone in the Ballyhoura Hills in almost total darkness, he realised he was lost. Coming on a cottage, he knocked at the door and asked for a glass of water. His own narrative continues in a pronounced Munster accent:

After a while a young woman opened the door and brought me out a big mug of milk. She was half undressed as if she was going to bed when I knocked and she had her hair hanging; and I thought by her figure and by something in the look of her eyes that she must be carrying a child. She kept me in talk a long while at the door and I thought it strange because her breast and her shoulders were bare. She asked me was I tired and would I like to stop the night there. She said she was all alone in the house and that her husband had gone that morning to Queenstown with his sister to see her off. And all the time she was talking, Stevie, she had her eyes fixed on my face and she stood so close to me that I could hear her breathing. When I handed her back the mug at last she took my hand to draw me in over the threshold and said. *'Come in and stay the night here. You've no call to be frightened. There's no-one in but ourselves. . . .'* I didn't go in, Stevie. I thanked her and went on my way again, all in a fever. [182f].

It is important to bear in mind that, as in the case of the old milkwoman in *Ulysses*, Stephen's perception of the affair in the aptly named Ballyhoura Hills is very different from that of his companion. For Davin it was an occasion of sexual sin: Stephen had spoken freely to him of his sexual experiences and now Davin was being equally confidential. As far as Davin is conerned, the woman of the cottage was impelled by some lust to make her outrageous suggestion which Davin did well to refuse. This is not at all how Stephen understands it:

> The last words of Davin's story sang in his memory and the figure of the woman in the story stood forth, reflected in other figures of the peasant women whom he had seen standing in the doorways at Clane as the college cars drove by, *as a type of her race and of his own*, a batlike soul waking to the consciousness of itself in darkness and secrecy and loneliness and, through the eyes and voice and gesture of a woman without guile, calling the stranger to her bed. (*my italics*) [183].

In Stephen's imagination the woman is emblematic of the Irish race, a people who have yet to achieve their own soul or identity but who are stumbling towards it. (This train of thought becomes easier to follow if we skip ahead to Stephen's final ambition: *to forge in the smithy of my soul the uncreated conscience of my race*). Inasmuch as she is *a type of her race*, the peasant woman is the soul of Ireland, the national goddess in human form. Her appearance and behaviour are strikingly different from those associated with her in the popular mind: instead of a beautiful maiden who has been raped and imprisoned by a foreign tyrant, we have a rather slovenly figure who takes advantage of her husband's absence by attempting to seduce a passing stranger.

Stephen would not be surprised at Davin's imaginative failure:

> [Davin] the young peasant worshipped the sorrowful legend of Ireland. The gossip of his fellow students which strove to render the flat life of the college significant at any cost loved to think of him as a young fenian. His nurse had taught him Irish and shaped his rude imagination by the broken lights of Irish myth. He stood towards the myth

upon which no individual mind had ever drawn out a line of beauty and to its unwieldy tales that divided themselves as they moved down the cycles in the same attitude as towards the Roman catholic religion, the attitude of a dullwitted loyal serf. [181]

Davin's sense of the soul of Ireland has evolved through the medium of what Stephen sees as a flawed nationalism, the false outmoded cult of the Poor Old Woman. Davin's immersion in a rude shapeless mythology has hampered his imaginative development. How could Davin recognise the soul or the true identity of Ireland when, like so many other nationalists and Gaelic revivalists, he had sacrificed his own intellectual freedom to the repressive demands of the Irish Roman Catholic Church? Davin's cult of the sorrowful legend of Eire – as sanctioned by the Catholic Church – placed a powerful taboo on the sexuality offered by the woman of the Ballyhoura Hills.

The vision on Dollymount Strand was more liberating: the recognition of the godhead is productive of joy rather than sorrow.

– Heavenly God! cried Stephen's soul, in an outburst of profane joy. [171]

The female who excites this joy is neither an idealised damsel in Pre-Raphaelite distress nor a crude peasant from the hidden Ireland. She is essentially an ordinary Dublin girl; far from representing the coy prudery which later politicians had attached to the image of Ireland, the Dollymount girl exudes a balanced acceptance of sexuality, receiving Stephen's gaze 'without shame or wantonness'.

Stephen was content to commune with the wading girl on a spiritual level. The nearest he comes to physical contact is by looking into her eyes and this is emphasised by the way the syntax joins his and her eyes without any linguistic connection:

She was alone and still, gazing out to sea; and when she felt

his presence and the worship of his eyes her eyes turned to
him in quiet sufferance of his gaze . . .

Similarly, the woman of the Ballyhoura Hills 'had her eyes fixed
on [Davin's] face'. Later on, Stephen remembers Davin's story and
reflects that he had never been the object of wooing eyes.

Here, one suspects, the sombre note in Stephen's thoughts is
the result of his failure to achieve a satisfactory sexual relationship
with the only young woman in his life, Emma Cleary.

Emma remains a shadowy presence, but one gathers that –
against all the odds – she and Stephen are attracted to each other.
Emma seems too contentedly middle-class for Stephen: she is conventionally coy when it comes to physical relations, reserving her
ardour for the revival of the Irish language, her intimacy for a
favourite priest. In *Stephen Hero* Stephen is physically attracted to
Emma but he complains that 'even her warm ample body could
hardly compensate for her distressing pertness and middleclass
affectations' and seeks to resolve his contradictory impulses by asking her to spend one night in bed with him.[59] [175]. In *Portrait* he
is more circumspect in every way. He sees her on the steps of the
National Library as tediously demure and contrived but then
immediately pauses in uncharacteristic doubt:

> And if he had judged her harshly? If her life were a simple
> rosary of hours, her life simple and strange as a bird's life,
> gay in the morning, restless all day, tired at sundown? Her
> heart simple and wilful as a bird's heart? [216]

The imagery recalls the bird-girl on Dollymount Strand and it is
not altogether surprising that Emma's 'wilful heart' [217] excites
the dream-vision which inspires the villanelle of the temptress, the
one example we have in the book of the vocation to which the
bird-girl called Stephen.

This slight poem, which is incongruously at odds with
Stephen's ambitions, is fashionably nebulous but some things are
clear enough. The poet wants the beloved to turn away from
ardent ways and to cease displeasing him with her talk of *enchanted*

days. But to no effect; the final stanza reads:

And still you hold our longing gaze
With langorous look and lavish limb!
Are you not weary of ardent ways?
Tell no more of enchanted days.

Presumably, the poet wants her to turn her thoughts to him and physical love here and now. The inspiration of the poem is identified as Emma and described as a temptress. How is Emma a temptress? To what does she tempt Stephen? Something more than masturbatory verse? I think so. Though *ardent ways* might be associated with the hot passions of sexual attraction, it is more likely that Emma's ardour was reserved for her contributions to nationalist politics and the language revival. And if it is granted that the *enchanted days* she talks of so obsessively – and to the tedium of the lover – are not characterised by amorous dalliance – past or future – would it not be reasonable to associate them with the romantic days of the glorious Gaelic past which the revivalists hoped would return again in a free and Gaelic Ireland? In that case we may see the villanelle as an anti-*aisling* or at least the polar opposite of the traditional *aisling*: the poet, far from being converted by the lady's talk of suppression, liberation and consequent happiness, wants her to stop talking about such matters and to share her physical beauty with him. He sees that she does not represent the true soul of Ireland but that she has been led astray by her enthusiasms for false ideals.

And yet he felt that, however he might revile and mock her image, his anger was also a form of homage. He had left the classroom in disdain that was not wholly sincere, feeling that perhaps the secret of her race lay behind those dark eyes upon which her long lashes flung a quick shadow. He had told himself bitterly as he walked through the streets that she was a figure of the womanhood of her country, a batlike soul waking to the consciousness of itself in darkness and secrecy and loneliness, tarrying awhile, loveless and sinless, with her mild lover and leaving him to whisper of innocent transgressions in the latticed ear of a priest. [220f]

Though Stephen may find the corporeal Emma a frustrating combination of physical attraction and mental repulsion, he is fascinated by her as an image or a figure or a type of Irish womanhood. She is described in precisely those terms which Stephen used to describe the peasant woman who confronted Davin in the Ballyhoura Hills. In both cases there is the suggestion of women struggling in confusion because they have not yet achieved a confident awareness of themselves, as opposed to the roles in which Irish life has cast them. And in both cases there is the suggestion of Ireland as a country which has yet to achieve a true sense of national identity, an identity other than those offered by the British imperialists or by the dominant forces of Irish nationalists.

Towards the end of the book there is a passage which clarifies Joyce's use of the bat imagery in *Portrait*. In Kildare Street Stephen imagines 'the sleek lives of the patricians of Ireland':

> How could he hit their conscience or how cast his shadow over the imaginations of their daughters, before their squires begat upon them, that they might breed a race less ignoble than their own? And under the deepened dusk he felt the thoughts and desires of the race to which he belonged flitting like bats, across the dark country lanes, under trees by the edges of streams and near the poolmottled bogs. A woman had waited in the doorway as Davin had passed by at night and, offering him a cup of milk, had all but wooed him to her bed; for Davin had the mild eyes of one who could be secret. But him no woman's eyes had wooed.

The bats, blind creatures of the dark, represent the subconscious thoughts and desires which are repressed in Irish society and which will only be brought to life and light when the true national psyche or the consciousness of the people is revealed by a great national poet, who will thus have created the uncreated conscience of the race.

Davin and Emma and a growing majority believe that the Irish people will only be able to achieve their true identity when the country is freed from British misrule and the people are able to rechannel all their energies into the creation of a Free State. Stephen – spectacularly – disputes this. He sees all the forces behind the demand for independence from Britain as designed to enslave rather than liberate. If Emma and the woman of the Ballyhoura Hills are in bondage it is not primarily that of the English tyrant but that of the repression of language, nationality and religion.

Stephen will try to escape from these psychic chains, to fly by these nets, and eventually he will leave the country. The final pages of *Portrait* make it clear that Stephen's departure from Ireland is merely physical and possibly temporary. He implies that his destination is Tara – the soul of Ireland, the spiritual or symbolic capital of Ireland. He will, he is saying, be a writer in the service of Ireland – the true Ireland – and his writings express the true soul of Ireland.

In that, of course, he was adopting a position taken by many nineteenth century writers who had sought to use literature as a means of creating a sense of national identity and pride which would serve the needs of nineteenth century Ireland, where the Anglo-Irish class was on the wane and where the remainder of the population had not for more than two hundred dark years had any national or political apparatus.

Joyce was well aware of this and had paid special attention to the career of one such nineteenth century writer, James Clarence Mangan. Towards the end of a paper on Mangan which he read to his fellow-students, Joyce used terms that anticipate parts of *Portrait*:

Mangan is the type of his race. History encloses him so straitly that even his fiery moments do not set him free from it. He, too, cries out, in life and in his mournful verse, against the injustice of despoilers, but never laments a deeper loss

than the loss of plaids and ornaments. He inherits the latest
and worst part of a legend upon which the line has never
been drawn out and which divides against itself as it moves
down the cycles. And because this tradition is so much with
him he has accepted it with all its griefs and failures, and
has not known how to change it . . . In the final view the
figure which he worships is seen to be an abject queen
upon whom, because of the bloody crimes that she has
done and of those as bloody that were done to her, madness is come and death is coming, but who will not believe
that she is near to die and remembers only the rumour of
voices challenging her sacred gardens and her fair, tall
flowers that have become the food of boards . . .

We may imagine Mangan as the literary equivalent of the political Davin. Davin is said to have 'worshipped the sorrowful legend of
Ireland'; Mangan is seen to worship 'an abject queen upon whom . . .
madness is come and death is coming'. Davin's nurse had shaped and
limited his rude imagination by teaching him the Irish myth
'upon which no individual had ever drawn out a line of beauty and . . .
its unwieldy tales that divided themselves as they moved down the
cycles'; Mangan had inherited 'the latest and worst part of a legend
upon which the line has never been drawn out and which divides
against itself as it moves down the cycles'. Stephen saw Davin as
utterly trapped by the nets of language, nationality and religion;
Joyce presents Mangan in the strait-jacket of a history which he is
unable to alter. Perhaps the comparison with Mangan helps us to
understand the privileged place which Davin occupies in Stephen's
world. Stephen sees him – as he had seen Mangan – *as a type of his
race*. There was much that Stephen admired in Davin's commitment
to his country even though he felt it was utterly misdirected and
misconceived. Similarly, Joyce's analysis of Mangan's shortcomings is
tempered by a desire to explain if not to excuse those shortcomings:

Mangan, it must be remembered, wrote with no native
literary tradition to guide him, and for a public which cared
for matters of the day, and for poetry only so far as it might
illustrate these.

Which is to say that before Mangan there had been no great work of literature written in English in Ireland. Throughout the nineteenth century Irish writers had sought ways of producing a characteristically Irish literature in English, not the easiest of objectives when one considers that almost all living contact with the Gaelic literary tradition had been lost and that Irish writers were trying to achieve some independence within the overwhelming influence of the English language and its rich literary tradition. Mangan, for example, seems to have lacked confidence in his own voice and to have found dramatic relief in the ventriloquism of esoteric translations. Stephen Dedalus does not seem like one who would not accept such a compromise:

– This race and this country and this life produced me . . .
I shall express myself as I am. [203]

But little had changed since Mangan's time. No great writer – not even Yeats, whom Joyce admired though not unreservedly – had established an independent Irish tradition in English. The problem and the prize remained.

The race and the country and the life which produced Stephen did not produce the language of Shakespeare and Jonson and Shelley and Byron and Newman. The tradition of expressing Irish life in English had never been validated by a major writer. What if Stephen had inherited a dialect which would always mark his subservience, a dialect which would always be peripheral to the major intellectual currents of the world, a dialect which would confine him to a subculture which had not yet produced one major literary talent and might never? This was the horrible possiblity suggested by Stephen's encounter with the Dean of Studies; this is what caused Stephen's soul to fret.

There is great relief in Stephen's entry for April 13:

That tundish has been on my mind for a long time. I looked it up and find it English and good old blunt English too. Damn the dean of studies and his funnel! What did he

117

come here for to teach us his own language or to learn it from us. Damn him one way or the other! [251]

One detects something more than bravado here: there is the will to overcome the greatest difficulties and succeed. Stephen was well aware of the fate of his predecessor, Mangan, who had been restricted by the strait-jacket of history, who had been deluded by the myth of Ireland as an abject queen. Stephen had seen on Dollymount Strand his image of Ireland as young and joyful. He was content to know that his vision of the soul of Ireland was not shared by the conventional nationalists: he would bide his time, knowing that their cult was coming to an end. As he said in a lecture which he delivered in the Physics Theatre:

> With Mangan a narrow and hysterical nationality receives a last justification, for when this feeble-bodied figure departs dusk begins to veil the train of the gods and he who listens may hear their footsteps leaving the world.

They would be replaced in time by a new spiritual order which would delight in human life and be beautiful, alluring, mysterious.

The hero of *Portrait* looks into the eyes of women to see if the spirit of Ireland is looking out. The author of *Portrait* was drawing on his own experience at school and university but he was always influenced by his later discovery of the woman whom he identified as the soul of Ireland, his national muse, his inspiration. That is an entirely different chapter of the story but I would like to end by quoting from a letter which Joyce wrote to Nora in 1909. He was back in Dublin, being introduced to people as destined to be the great Irish writer of the future. Joyce commented to Nora:

> I thought I heard my country calling to me, or her eyes being turned towards me expectantly. But O, my love, there was something else I thought of. I thought of one who held me in her hand like a pebble, from whose love and in whose company I have still to learn the secrets of life. [E287]

THE ARTIST AND THE LABYRINTH

RETROSPECTIVE

Stephen in *Portrait*, like Joyce in the Mangan lecture, is looking ahead, convinced that it is he rather than the nationalists who sees – through the eyes of women – into the soul of Ireland, confident that it is he the writer, rather than the nationalist politicians, who will provide a national identity for the Irish people. Almost a century later, how do we react to such claims?

The fact that so many of us are fascinated by his work is a proof of sorts that Joyce succeeded in becoming a considerable writer; but what of his ambition to create in his writings the conscience or identity of modern Ireland?

This is the sort of vast intellectual space in which I feel very uncomfortable but there are some physical features which all can see. Joyce was born into a political tradition – Parnellite parliamentarianism – which had almost become extinct by the time he began to write. Despite some brief encounters with socialism and despite occasional outbursts of Anglophobia, Joyce never developed along any traditional political lines, and in fact many found his apolitical stance – at the very least – an embarrassment. Joyce seems to have had an instinctual antipathy to the political ideology which dominated Ireland in this century. The central act of this ideology was the military campaign waged between 1916 and 1922 by nationalists like Davin. (Davin was based on Joyce's college friend George Clancy who was murdered by British counter-terrorists). When they achieved the Irish Free State they sought to build it on those virtues – Irish nationality, Gaelic language and Roman Catholic religion – which Stephen Dedalus intended to avoid at all costs. To a great extent the Free State did inculcate these marks of identity on the succeeding generations. Those who showed less than total reverence for the Gaelic Catholic ethos of the State or who questioned the means by which it had achieved its limited independence from Britain were discouraged. Joyce was – despite the fact that his works were never actually banned – the least approved of Irish writers. While his works were read and admired by a tiny minority of people it could not be argued that his writing had any influence on anything to do with the creation of a national identity.

Things began to change in the sixties – fifty years after the Easter rising. Developments in telecommunications and travel made national isolationism impossible. Full televisual coverage of the bloodshed and destruction in Northern Ireland and the spill-over into the Republic led to a general reappraisal – if not always a denial – of the kind of nationalist violence out of which the Free State had emerged. At the same time, despite a large amount of good will, it was obvious that the millions of pounds and class-hours spent on the Gaelic language had been spectacularly unsuc-cessful. And at much the same time the once absolute power of the Roman Catholic Church in Ireland began to be seen to be limited. The sixties also saw the establishment of Anglo-Irish literature in universities and – thanks largely to Ellmann's 1959 biography – the emergence of Joyce as, literally, the best known Irish figure of all time. And so it may be that future generations of Irish children will study Joyce's life and work and will be more influenced by it than by any other Irish writer or by any other figure in history.

There is a sense in which Irish people of this century saw and continue to see the nationalist victory as a new beginning. Joyce seems to have taken the opposite view, dismissing the nationalism of his own time as the last deluded act of homage to a disappear-ing myth. It is too early to say who was right. All that one can say for certain is that the absolute faith in the nationalist victory – which characterised the first half-century of independence – has been shattered beyond restoration; meanwhile, the gentler spirit of Joyce's humour – epitomised by Bloom – seems a goal which all human beings, and not only the Irish, could aim at.

THE
POET
JOYCE

Eamon Grennan

"I am not a poet."
Joyce to Padraic Colum.

My generic title offers a variety of possible topics. It might be possible to argue, for example, that poetry was for Joyce a central imaginative zone in which he revealed with the least number of disguises and overlays of 'genius' the most intimate recesses of his own consciousness. The poems, as it were, emerge from a seminal area of self and identity. 'Can you not see the simplicity behind all my disguises?' he asks Nora, telling her at the same time that 'my true love for you' is identical with 'the love of my verses'.[1] Such a topic would take into account the youthful 'love poems' of *Chamber Music* (published in 1907), written, as he said, as 'a protest against myself', against the outer actions of his dissipated life and as a log book for the 'journey of the soul'.[2] Such a topic might confirm Ezra Pound's observation (made in 1920) 'that the real man is the author of *Chamber Music*, the sensitive. The rest is the genius; the registration of realities on the temperament, the delicate temperament of the early poems'.[3] Pursuit of such a topic might also see how, in his only other volume of poems (*Pomes Penyeach*, published in 1927), the 'real man . . . the sensitive'

121

resorted to what his brother called 'a few incidental songs of a very personal nature'[4] to utter his raw distress over the passing of youth, the onset of age, the vanishing possibility of passion (he is, by the way all of 40 plus years at the time), and to give expression to a melancholy but tender sense of himself as son and father, a familial self beyond the critical isolation of the self as artist. Such a topic might argue, in other words, that in verse Joyce probed – without the protective carapace of irony, humour, multiple perspectives – his own most deeply rooted, unmediated, and in a sense inarticulate identity.

I could also have chosen to deal in a more specifically stylistic way with the poems, asking along the way why the greatest and most revolutionary prose stylist of the century was so timid in verse; asking what in the nature of poetry (as he conceived of it) and in his own nature made him in verse the decidedly minor figure he is. What kept Joyce, in biographical, circumstantial, and aesthetic terms, so conservative and conventional as a poet (even if the metrical and rhythmic freedom of a couple of poems in *Chamber Music* might seem remarkable enough, while the manner of one or two of the pieces in *Pomes Penyeach* could suggest a liberation of consciousness into verse that might, just might, anticipate something in the later manner of Thomas Kinsella)?[4] Such an investigation of style might reveal some of Joyce's underlying assumptions about the relationship between language, imaginative expression, and actuality.

There was also the possibility of tracing the curiously recurring presence of *Chamber Music* through the biography. It appears in at least one of his clandestine and more or less unconsummated affairs. But its most interesting appearance is in 1909 as an element in the graphically sexual letters exchanged by Joyce and Nora. It is just at this time that Nora 'discovers' the book, giving the poems a fresh lease of life for Joyce himself.[5] In this new context he can clearly see how the poems relate to his love for Nora (although not written for her), for they hold 'the desire of my youth and you, darling, were the fulfilment of that desire'.[6] Through these letters, mixing the idealised lyricism of the poems with the graphic coarseness of active lust, Joyce discovered in rudimentary form a mode of expression that would, when developed, approximate, as he believed a literary style could and should, the complex fullness of reality. In his need to express his loving and lustful fervour for Nora he stumbles on a style that will animate in language the brimmingly various (and rootedly sexual) consciousness of Leopold and Molly Bloom. This rediscovery and validation of the poems leads to a new creative fluency, the rudimentary preparations for which can be seen in the remarkable transitions observable in the letters from the lyricism of 'My beautiful wild flower of the hedges! My dark-blue, rain-drenched flower!' to the pornographic urgency of 'Fuck me in your dressing gown (I hope you have that nice one) with nothing on under it, opening it suddenly and showing me your belly and thighs and back and pulling me on top of you on the kitchen table', to the mundane details of 'O, I am hungry now. The day I arrive get Eva to make one of the threepenny puddings and make some kind of vanilla sauce without wine. I would like roast beef, rice-soup, capuzzi garbi, mashed potatoes, pudding and black coffee. No, no I would like stracotto di maccheroni, a mixed salad, . . . ' and so forth.[7] By setting the poems in this startling epistolary context (he frequently quotes from them, and he is making during this time a fancy manuscript of the whole collection on parchment and covered in vellum as a gift for Nora, a book that was to be her particular treasure and which 'missal-like volume . . . lay throned . . . on a reading desk, ecclesiastical in style' in their flat in Trieste).[8] Joyce found a way to accommodate in language the whole self, an imaginative accommodation that would lead to the expansive wholeness and harmonies of *Ulysses* and even of *Finnegans Wake*.

These, then, were among the possibilities. With a mixture of modesty and desperation, however, I finally narrowed my focus to *Chamber Music* alone. (*Pomes Penyeach*, after all, in spite of some interesting features, is more a ploy than a book proper, a ploy to prove that Joyce, under fire for the lunacies of *Work in Progress*, could still be 'grammatically sane' if and when he wanted to be).[9] So my subject here is the verse in *Chamber Music*, those poems and what, simply, (or at least some of what) they can tell us about the writer Joyce.

JAMES JOYCE

Let us begin with a sample:

My love is in a light attire
   Among the apple trees,
Where the gay winds do most desire
   To run in companies.

There, where the gay winds stay to woo
   The young leaves as they pass,
My love goes slowly, bending to
   Her shadow on the grass;

And where the sky's a pale blue cup
   Over the laughing land,
My love goes lightly, holding up
   Her dress with dainty hand.

(VII)

Of all Joyce's works *Chamber Music* – complete by or in 1904 and published in 1907 – was the only one to get an almost unanimously positive critical reception. 'It is a slim book and on the frontispiece is an open pianner', is Joyce's own laconic description, but the collection was widely praised in Ireland and England. Arthur Symons, who had been instrumental in their publication, was not alone in being 'reminded of Elizabethan, more often of Jacobean lyrics' (as well as, no doubt, of his own symbolist poems and those of his friends of the nineties: 'No one who has not tried', he said, 'can realise how difficult it is to do such tiny evanescent things').[10] In Ireland, Tom Kettle praised 'these delicate verses which have, each of them, the bright beauty of a crystal'. Other reviewers were happy to inform their readers that 'Mr Joyce flows in a clear delicious stream that ripples', or that 'the casual reader will see nothing in his verses to object to, nothing incapable of an innocent explanation' in the 'old-fashioned sweetness and flavour' of the collection. They had much of music and quaintness', in spite of some 'bold liberties taken with rhyme and rhythm': they were 'sweet, reposeful and sublime': they formed 'a very promising little volume', and were a 'welcome contribution to contemporary poetry'.

One discordant, dissenting voice was raised in this chorus of approval and praise: 'I don't like the book' said young James Augustine Joyce himself when he saw it. 'Nearly all the poems seemed to me poor and trivial: some phrases and lines pleased me and no more'.[11] Posterity has not been as hard on this 'capful of light odes' as their own author has.[12] Nor, however, has posterity echoed the fulsome tributes of those early critics, being more inclined to offer a measured appreciation of the distinctly minor work of a major writer, his status unquestionably due to his work in prose. In spite of a certain liking for the poems, most readers now would be likely to find themselves in agreement with Richard Ellmann's judgement of 'the rather anemic style Joyce reserved for his verse',[13] or with another critic who describes the poems as 'a limited selection from Joyce's life and a simplification of it for the convenience of tenors'.[14] For this reason, the few critics who have written about the poems at length have resorted to various tactics of validation. William York Tindall's definitive edition, for example, resorts to a marvellously inventive over-reading in psycho-allegorical terms (stressing scatology rather than eschatology), and is in spite of its mischievous excesses the anatomy lesson to which we're all indebted.[15] Chester Anderson's tactic is a scrupulously exacting stylistic analysis and evaluative summary. And Robert Boyle's excellent essay on "The Woman Hidden in James Joyce's Chamber Music" revises the published order of the poems (back to Joyce's original order) with fascinating results.[16] Like these critics, I have taken an approach that is, I suppose, a species of validation, thereby hoping to cast a little more light on the meaning of this small plot of ground in the Joycean landscape.

One of the curious facts connected with *Chamber Music* concerns a dedication. On the copy of the poem XXI which Joyce gave to Constantine Curran in 1904 he had written 'Dedication. To Nora'. Since poem XXI, the last line of which is 'His love is his companion', was the opening poem of the sequence as Joyce himself arranged it (the 'Yale' Ms), Tindale presumes that 'in dedicating this poem to Nora he was dedicating the whole suite'.[17] Whatever the truth of this last point, and it has to remain in doubt, (along with the possibility of other poems being about Nora), the fact of the matter is that the published volume contains no dedication, neither particular nor general. The actual reason for this is not known. As I read the poems over, however, I wondered if it might not be connected with the sense, the book as a whole was giving me, of being in itself a sort of dedication of the poet himself to certain crucial elements in his art. At any rate, it was this sense of *Chamber Music* as the young Joyce's own act of self-dedication as a literary artist that caught and held my attention, and this is what I want to share in what follows. It is possible, I feel, that it was his own awareness of something like this that prompted him, not long after publication, and when he had become a somewhat more tolerant reader of his own book, to refer to 'the expression of myself which I now see I began in *Chamber Music*'.[18]

There are three forms of self-dedication I want to address. The first of these is to craft, the craft of language. Thirty years and more before Yeats' celebrated injunction, here is an Irish poet who has certainly learned his trade and, with a youthfully dandified air, flaunts it. In fact, in 1903, Yeats' first praise of the cocky young poet was couched in precisely such terms: 'Your technique in verse is very much better than the technique of any young Dublin man I have met during my time'.[19] Yeats' judgement was echoed by the critics and reviewers, who stressed Joyce's mastery over the technique of poetry, 'the poems' integrity of form', their 'accomplished execution'.[20] Even a casual ear will pick up the elegance with which the following quatrains are managed:

Strings in the earth and air
  Make music sweet;
Strings by the river where
  The willows meet.

There's music along the river
    For Love wanders there,
Pale flowers on his mantle
    Dark leaves on his hair.

All softly playing,
    With head to the music bent,
And fingers straying
    Upon an instrument.

(I)

Here craft coaxes language towards the condition of music. Its chief strategy is repetition, dominating sound, rhythm, structure. Language for this poet has an aural plasticity which he moulds into units of harmony which are, in light of the poem's subject, especially apt. They give the whole piece a rarefied, enclosed, self-reflecting air. Language, it would seem, is listening to itself, and that wandering 'Love' might be, among other things, a love of language for its own sake. Such innocent narcissism (and yet it is also the love of another, 'With head to the music bent', something beyond the self though an expression of the self) could conjure up JF Byrne's portrait of the young poet at work in 1900 in the National Library: 'he would write and rewrite and retouch, it might almost seem interminably, a bit of verse containing perhaps a dozen or a score of lines. When he had at last polished his gem to a satisfying degree of curvature and smoothness, he would write out the finished poem with slow and stylish penmanship and hand the copy to me'.[21] Plain, simple, conventional – the poem's diction has no surprises: it is a clear distillate of the imagined scene. The syntax is on the same model, being straightforward, unnoticeable, paratactic. Stanzas two and three form virtually (and, in an earlier draft, actually)[22] a single sentence, of which the last six line-units are all adjectival or adverbial qualifications of the main clause contained in the first two lines. What this careful dedication to language creates is a ritual simplicity – something at once refined and unsophisticated, a careful but casual gesture in words. This can be heard in the unassertive nature of the verbs (all except 'is', 'make' and 'wanders' being participles) and the way this is complemented by the clean line and firmness of presentation. It is also obvious in the way the colloquial relaxation of 'There's music along the river' is given a ritual turn by that Yeatsian 'For' and the adagio pace of the line that follows: 'For Love wanders there'. The vowel play of the whole thing is distinct and impressive, the poet sounding vowels and dipthongs [i, e, e, e, u, i, make a rich chord of the first two lines, for example: rich and pure] into elegant harmonic structures.

Here, then, is an example of a poem put together as Stephen Dedalus wanted, 'not word by word but letter by letter'.[23] And so, for all its conventional evanescence of content, there's a sense of the concrete in the poet's own awareness of and dedication to language. For him, as for the young Yeats, 'words alone are certain good'. While elements of the actual world have been erased, the language itself has body. Such a sacramental commitment to language is consummated in Joyce's prose. But it is proper that its beginnings should be in verse, in poetry. For poetry, to be honest, always begins, by being dedicated to, and in some sense about, language itself, whereas even great prose seems to begin not in this pure air but somehow committed to content, to some expository urge or need. So it is in his beginnings as a poet that Joyce aptly inaugurates the stylistic revolution that would import into the practise of prose, poetry's dedication to the word itself, its betrothal to language. The poems of *Chamber Music* are the artist's baptism in craft, his offering up of his artistic life to style.

The next dedication of self revealed by these poems is a dedication to tradition. This is seen in the writer's receptive openness to other voices. In fact, the poems of *Chamber Music* are compounded of 'other voices': the poet has no real individual voice. What we hear instead is the voice of tradition (the tradition of love song, love poetry) through which, as appropriate persona, this speaker expresses himself. Such a habit of composition reveals something of the natural structure of Joyce's imagination.

Evidence of such imaginative hospitality – which will achieve its perfected form in the catholicity of influence to be heard in the orchestral harmonies of *Finnegans Wake* – appears in the bits and pieces that remain to us of poems preceding *Chamber Music*. Among these is a translation from Horace (a literal taking-on of the voice of another poet), the Yeatsian title of a lost juvenile collection (*Moods*), and fragments from a collection called (after Whitman) *Shine and Dark*, composed in Joyce's last year at Belvedere.[24] Titles such as 'Wanhope', 'Tenebrae', 'Valkyrie' and 'The Final Peace' suggest a Romantic Gothic influence, and this may be detected in the fragments themselves (eg 'There are no lips to kiss this foul remains of thee,/O, dead Unchastity!'). This can also be crossed with Keatsian pathos, Yeatsian cadence, Tennysonian gesture: for example, the Lady of Shallott, la belle Dame sans Merci, and Wandering Aengus all converge on this harmless, exemplary quatrain: 'They covered her with linen white/And set white candles at her head/And loosened out her glorious hair/And laid her on a snow-white bed'.[25] Elsewhere as Richard Ellmann points out the verse-making can show traces of Byronic posturing or pseudo-Elizabethan simplicity ('For she was passing fair,/And I was passing mad').

Such imitative mood-making was Joyce's apprenticeship for *Chamber Music*, and he showed a proper degree of self-knowledge in preserving none of it except the 'Villanelle of the Temptress' for *Portrait*, and an elegant translation of Paul Verlaine (a poet who cast an influential shadow over *Chamber Music*, the poems of which were described by one critic as being 'of the same kindred with harps [Yeats?], with woodbirds [the Elizabethans?] and with Paul Verlaine'.[26] But in the main, the nature of this early imitation is a species of parrotting, merely miming a manner. As William Archer said after seeing some of the poems, 'You feel and imagine poetically [in the manner of poetry?], but I do not find that as yet you have very much to say'.[27] In *Chamber Music*, not only did he have something to say (about the nature of love and the 'journey of the soul'), but he has also a different relationship to his influences. Now they are digested, not just mimed. They do not give Joyce his own voice, necessarily, but a voice that is a genuine compound of traditional accents. His reading, that is, gives him ways and means of translating his own experience into an individual poetic mode. Turn anywhere in these poems and you'll hear echoes of other poets: Nashe, Shakespeare, Derrick, Dowland, Byrd, Shelley, Byron, Blake, the last Romantics of the nineties, Yeats of *The Wind Among the Reeds*, the harder, more 'modern' note of Meredith, and even a contemporary Irishman, Paul Gregan, 'in whose lyrics he found an affinity' and whose own obvious influences are Yeats and AE.[28] (Gregan's *Sunset Town* appeared around 1900). A major influence is Ben Jonson, whom Joyce read avidly and 'exhaustively' in Paris in 1902, whose distinct simplicity of diction and syntax, as well as his 'sinewy qualities and classical exactness' left a clear mark on lucid stanzas like the following: 'What counsel has the hooded moon/Put in thy heart, my shyly sweet,/O Love in ancient plenilune,/Glory and stars beneath his feet'. (XII)[29] Economy and steadiness of expression here suggest a deliberate chastening and limitation of style, factors which – along with the Elizabethan's irony and elegance – may have drawn Joyce to Jonson.[30]

Since these influences have been documented elsewhere, revealing what Anderson calls Joyce's technique of 'multiple theft', I won't rehearse them here.[31] I would like, however, to add to the list a possible influence I have not seen mentioned, namely that of the great Italian lyric poet, Leopardi. Joyce's mention of Leopardi in the essay on Mangan (who is 'weaker than Leopardi, for he has not the courage of his own despair')[32] betrays acquaintance and admiration, and although Joyce said 'I dislike Italian verse', his Italian studies must have included some of the *Canti*. With these facts in mind, it is not impossible to hear in the song, 'Lean out of the window,/Goldenhair',(V) a faint echo of Leopardi's 'To Silvia'.[33] In Leopardi's poem the poet also leaves his book and his room ('Leaving my books . . . I leaned out from the balcony towards the sound of your voice') to hear a girl's song, just as Joyce's lover-poet does: 'I have left my book,/I have left my room,/For I heard you singing/Through the gloom'. A second, equally faint Leopardian echo may be heard in the song (XXXIV) that 'brings the 1905 sequence [the one Joyce himself arranged: see below] to an inconclusive conclusion'.[34] Here the echo of Leopardi's 'To Himself' is joined to those of Yeats, *Macbeth*, and the Song of Solomon. Joyce's opening lines – 'Sleep now, O sleep now,/O you unquiet heart' – could be a memory of Leopardi's opening, 'Or poserai per sempre/Stanco mio cor' ('Now you will rest forever/My weary heart'), even if that 'unquiet heart' of Joyce's derives more directly from Yeats' poem, 'The Old Age of Queen Maeve'.[35] Joyce's concluding, 'Sleep on in peace now', with its conjunction of sleep and death might be an echo of Leopardi's 'T'acqueta omai' ('Be you at rest now'), since both of them invoke implicitly the Catholic funerary formulation, 'requiescat in pace'. Again the Leopardian presence is at best a faint possibility, no more. But with a magpie author like Joyce, such possibilities are in the grain of the work, and none should be too quickly dismissed.

Quotation of this short lyric may help to demonstrate how Joyce digests his influences:

Sleep now, O sleep now,
   O you unquiet heart!
A voice crying "Sleep now"
   Is heard in my heart.

The voice of the winter
   Is heard at the door
O sleep, for the winter
   Is crying "Sleep no more!"

My kiss will give peace now
   And quiet to your heart –
Sleep on in peace now,
   O you unquiet heart!

Macbeth, the Song of Solomon, Yeats, maybe Leopardi: the echoes are obvious enough. What is worth pointing to, however, is the smoothness with which these various voices have become the one voice of the poem. That this is a poem *about* voices seems particularly apt, its two voices being parts of the poet. In style and substance, that is, the poem enacts the drama of multiple voices becoming one voice, that voice being at once the voice of 'Love' and the literary tradition, which throughout this sequence is identifiable (so that, as poem XXXIII shows, 'the end of love is the end of poetry'). In such poems the voice of the lover has no actual identity: it is the voice of that kind of poetry. The poet is betrothed to the tradition, and the lover's persona, as well as the object of his love, is the tradition itself.

This dedication to the tradition also serves to explain the non-actuality of the woman of *Chamber Music*. 'How would I write the most perfect love songs of our time' Joyce rhetorically asked his friend Skeffington, 'if I were in love'.[36] And in *Stephen Hero*, when Maurice asks Stephen 'who the woman [of the poems] was, Stephen looked a little vaguely before him before answering, and in the end had to answer that he didn't know who she was'.[37] In 1909, when the poems had become an important part of the passionate exchange between Joyce and Nora, he tells her that the girl of *Chamber Music* was not her: 'She was perhaps (as I saw her in my imagination), a girl fashioned into a curious grave beauty by the culture of generations before her, the woman for whom I wrote poems like 'Gentle Lady' or 'Thou Leanest to the Shell of Night'.[38] Not an actual woman then, but the representative of this kind of poetry, and by extension of the literary tradition itself, to which the sequence as a whole is an elaborate act of homage and self-dedication on the part of the young poet. Perhaps this is the reason, in particular, why he removed the dedication to Nora, and, in general, why, when he saw the proofs of *Chamber Music* in 1907, he remarked, 'It is not a book of love-verses at all, I perceive'.[39] In this initial literary action of his career, an act of dedication to tradition itself, Joyce lays the ground of an imagination extraordinarily hospitable to the widest possible range of literary allusions, an imagination to which nothing will seem alien.

At this early stage, however, that 'nothing' must be qualified in an important way. For an important footnote to this whole issue concerns not the inclusive but the exclusive nature of the poet's influences. Those influences are, as can be seen at a glance, aggresively non-Irish. Yeats may be a heavy presence. But not the Celtic Yeats of *The Wind Among the Reeds*, the book which Joyce regarded with great admiration, saying that 'in aim and form' it was 'poetry of the highest order'[40] but rather the Yeats who gathered into himself as a poet of desire and love ('aim') elements of that tradition ('form') which Joyce contrived to let speak through him. And whatever tonal features he may have admired in Paul Gregan's *Sunset Town*, its explicitly Celtic features seem to have left him unmoved.[41] The poet of *Chamber Music* (even its title is unCeltic) stood aloof from the Celtic paraphernalia apparent in the collection of new poets edited by AE in 1904, *New Songs*. With his English, French and Italian influences on show (Dante's *Vita Nuova*, for instance, prompted Stephen Dedalus to arrange his poems into 'a wreath of songs in praise of love')[42] the critics were not going to confuse Joyce with the Celtic School to which Little Chandler in 'A Little Cloud' dreams of belonging 'by reason of the melancholy tone of his poems'.[43] To identify himself further as an Irish poet, Chandler intended to 'put in allusions', of the sort, no doubt that crowded the lines of poets like Gregan, Colum, and others among those whom Yeats called 'AE's canaries'. Joyce's 'allusions' are English and classical, both overt and (in the various echoes and borrowings) covert. (Coleridge and Shakespeare seem explicitly alluded to in XXVI). As to Irish allusions, I find only four: 'harps' in III, 'choirs of faery' in XV, ('choirs', mind you: perhaps a borrowing from Gregan, who refers to 'the faery choir')[44]; the not wildly Celtic suburb of Donnycarney in XXXI (perhaps his 'Sally Gardens' song), and the satirically barbed 'piping poets' of XXVII. Joyce's own eventually measured approval of the poems stresses this Celtic disconnection: 'Some of them are pretty enough to be put to music. I hope someone will do so, someone that knows old English music such as I like'.[45]

As an initiating gesture in self-portraiture, then, the poems are marked by their refusal to join any club except that of his own choosing (the one, as it turns out, in which most of the competition is dead). It was his encourager and critic, Symons, who noted that Joyce was 'not in the Celtic Movement', and 'free of schools', observations which had to please this inner emigré who had gone stylistically into exile before ever he left with Nora from the North Wall in 1904. The poems may be the first move in the game of antithesis which Joyce played with Ireland and Irish art for the rest of his life. But whereas this first move was exclusive and, in a sense, elitist, the later moves were increasingly inclusive and democratic. The poems manage to suggest at the same time a neutrality (an interest only in style) and a hostility: it is a mixture fertile with possibility, a sort of early summary of how Joyce's imagination actually works. This particular feature of *Chamber Music* shows that the impulse of dedication is also accompanied by an important impulse of divorce, which in itself, however, is an even more deliberate dedication to a literary context larger than that provided by the Irish Literary Revival. As well as being a species of self-excommunication, this dedication to tradition is, as it were, Joyce's First Communion with the totality of a literary past he wanted to emulate and eventually to incorporate.

The third form of self-dedication observable in *Chamber Music* is to narrative. There are two major arrangements of the poems: the published one is by Stanislaus Joyce, whom his brother allowed to organise the sequence, telling him 'to do what I liked with it'. This odd decision, surrendering that last act of will that would arrange the individual pieces into a pattern, suggests the degree of Joyce's own detachment from the poems by 1906, involved as he was in the prose of *Dubliners* and *Stephen Hero*. ('A page of A Little Cloud gives me more pleasure than all my verses', he says).[46] Stanislaus' pattern has a musical logic and bias: 'arranged them . . . in their present order – approximately allegretto, andante cantabile, mosso – to suggest a closed episode of youth and love'.[47] Arranged thus, the collection, as Tindall says, 'proceeds clearly according to moods'.[48] Joyce's own arrangement (preserved in the Yale manuscript) is more essentially and explicitly narrative, proceeding 'with greater fidelity to actual experience'.[49] It shows an active instinct to organise experience into story shapes, an instinct already alive in 1902 when he decided to divide the suite into two parts, 'the first being relatively simple and innocent, the second more complicated and experienced',[50] on the analogy both of Blake's Songs and, even more relevantly, I'd suggest, of the implicit narrative patterns in sonnet sequences such as those of Sidney and Shakespeare. In 1909, when Joyce briefly describes the collection, it is clear that in spite of the published arrangement he still has his own narrative design in mind, into which he has incorporated his brother's changes: 'the central song is XIV', he says 'after which the movement is all downwards until XXXIV which is vitally the end of the book. XXXV and XXXVI are tailpieces just as I and III are preludes'.[51] Since XIV is the seventeenth poem in his own ordering, exactly midpoint in the original sequence, it shows the architectural care for balanced and symmetrical narrative natural to his imagination.

After the dedications to language and tradition, the dedication to narrative may be seen as a bodying forth of his imagination, making it present in the world with its significant performance. Narrative, that is, is the more expansive syntax of imagination, shaping the individual elements of the sequence into larger meanings. Since these elements are in themselves essentially musical, Joyce's own arrangement of the sequence brings music and will together, marrying them to one another to produce a unit of richer possibility. *Chamber Music*, therefore, with its musical centre and its narrative circumference, is a miniature model of the imagination that would produce the greater works. It is possible that Joyce's perfunctory permission to Stanislaus to do as he liked with the poems for publication was in part a result of his feeling that this imaginative compound of music and narrative could achieve its full potential for him only in prose, recognising, that is, that the poems, even with his own narrative design in place, were still of necessity dominated by the musical and tonal elements.

Arranged according to his original intentions, however, the poems do tell a coherent story, providing a portrait of the artist as a young lover and, as Robert Boyle says, intending 'a projection of the woman he desired to meet in the world outside himself' as well as 'a large philosophy dealing with human love'.[52] The story is conventionally romantic: the lonely young poet singer with only his own love for a companion, yearns for a girl; he finds her; celebrates her lightly-clad springtime beauty; leaves friends and seeks a haven from the austerities of the world in her 'sweet bosom'. When 'Love is at his noon' he seeks a more fully sexual, fleshly union with her, and seems to find it, in the accents of the Song of Solomon ('My sister . . . my love . . . My breast shall be your bed'). After this climax the shadows increase: desire being satisfied, a sense of death, attended by the 'modern' ironic note, sets in: the love affair fluctuates, the woman is seen in a more ambiguous and sinister light, love itself is malicious and tender, is 'sweet imprisonment'. The end of the affair approaches in autumn, as the lover tries to persuade the beloved that 'love that passes is enough'. Something in the manner of Yeats' Ephemera', the love is reduced to memory, and the lover, 'for old friendship' sake' welcomes 'The ways that we shall go upon'. The end of love signifies the end of this kind of poetry; the poet (as we have seen) bids his 'unquiet heart' to be at peace. Then, in two 'tailpieces' (added by Stanislaus, but which Joyce must have seen would accentuate his own narrative design) the singer goes alone into exile (anticipating the end of *Portrait*), and has an apocalyptic dream that ends with an anguished recognition of his solitude: 'My love, my love, my love', he cries to his own heart, to his idea of love, to the lost girl, 'why have you left me alone?'

Yearning, discovery, disappointment: the narrative enacted by *Chamber Music* composes a lyrical abstract of Joyce's experience of love in Ireland up to mid-1904 and the meeting with Nora (who, as he told her in 1909, 'made me a man').[53] (Most critics assert as a probability that some of the poems concern and are addressed to her, but I remain unconvinced. At very most, it might have been a transformed, rarefied image of her, but no more). Frequenter of brothels and idealiser from a sanitary distance of a few of the girls of his acquaintance, the young Joyce is at the same time desperate for a conjunction of the erotic with the spiritual. In a sense, the narrative charts the failure of that ambition, that hope. Embodying Joyce's early sense of human love and the loss of that sense of it, it is a lyrical narrative about the image of love itself, and as such is the true lineal successor to that love of the Virgin Mary which dominated his boyhood, importing some of that religious fervour into this zone of secular passion. As such it stands between that religious love and his love for Nora. Most important, the sequence shows clearly enough the instinct of Joyce's imagination to fashion those scattered fragments of experience caught and distilled as poems into the larger coherence of narrative. This dedication to narrative represented by *Chamber Music* crowns the other two more primary forms of dedication – to language and to literary tradition – and confirms his imagination (as that to language baptised and that to tradition enabling it to make its First Communion). After these three sacramental attachments, his imagination is ready, for future enterprises.

It is in this final form of self-dedication – to narrative – that Joyce also discovers, I believe, the limitations for him of poetry as an art for the expression of reality. Part of the reason why he showed little interest in the poems in 1906 and 1907, as has been suggested or implied, is his awareness that the poems, in spite of their narrative arc, failed to embody and represent adequately the reality that was their subject matter. In the poems, the realities of self, sex, and spirit receive an abstract, distilled expression. He wants a much closer approximation to the actual, and this the poems alone cannot deliver. (He discovers, almost inadvertently, that closer approximation through the letters to Nora in 1909, and the way their coarseness and sexual immediacy joins with the language and sentiments of the poems to form a new, a novel, sense of wholeness. But that, as I said at the start, is another story). 'It is not a book of love-verses at all', he says. By this he means, I imagine, that the poems do not truly or adequately represent the nature of love, and he can only justify them by saying that 'at the top of each page I will put an address or a street so that when I open the book I can revisit the places where I wrote the different songs'.[54] These mundane addresses or street names (the very stuff of his prose) are for him more evocative of actuality than the poems themselves. For the poems etherealise his subject, distilling and vapourising the experience. And it was (certainly by 1907) the actual experience he was after, and a style that would get as close to that as the nature of language would allow. 'Absolute realism is impossible, of course', he conceded not long after the poems were published, but 'I would like to put on paper the thousand complexities' in the mind of a young drunken labourer he saw accompanying his mother into a trattoria.[55] True narrative, as far as he is concerned, demands that layered richness of texture, whereas his lyrical habits as displayed in *Chamber Music* are exactly antithetical – distillation, draining away, vapourising.

It is possible to get a closer look at this process, and so to understand a little better his abandonment of verse for prose, by comparing a poem with the experience that gave rise to it. Here is Ellmann's account of the incident that stands behind the poem. 'What Counsel Has the Hooded Moon' (CM XII): during an excursion into the Dublin Hills with Mary Sheehy, Francis Skeffington and other friends, 'Joyce, swaggering a little in his yachting cap and canvas shoes and sporting an ashplant, spent most of his time watching Mary. He admired her beauty, and interpreted her silence in company as a contempt like his for the people around her. He did not give himself away now or at any other time, but they exchanged a few words on the way back from the hills. Mary, gazing at the moon, thought it looked tearful, while Joyce, with mild daring, contended that it was 'like the chubby hooded face of some jolly fat Capuchin'. 'I think you are very wicked,' said Mary, and he replied, 'No, but I do my best'. After they separated he tore open a cigarette box [as Stephen Dedalus does for his vilanelle] and wrote, 'What counsel has the hooded moon'.[56] And, now, here is the poem:

What counsel has the hooded moon
    Put in thy heart, my shyly sweet,
Of love in ancient plenilune,
    Glory and stars beneath his feet –
A sage that is but kith and kin
With the comedian capuchin?

Believe me rather that am wise
    In disregard of the divine.
A glory kindles in those eyes
    Trembles to starlight. Mine, O Mine!
No more be tears in moon or mist
For thee, sweet sentimentalist.

As you can hear, all the hard sardonic facts have been distilled out of the poem. Even the anti-clerical joke has been given a graceful, enigmatic, stylising twist. Like the fingernails of the God of creation, the facts have been refined out of existence. As Joyce chooses to write poetry, it becomes an agent of, in every sense, sublimation. It is the process described later in *Portrait* when Stephen writes the poem 'To E – C –' (for whom Mary Sheehy is the main model): 'During this process all these elements which he deemed common and insignificant fell out of the scene. There remained no trace of the tram itself nor of the tram-men nor of the horses: nor did she appear vividly. The verses told only of the night and the balmy breeze and the maiden lustre of the moon'.[57] The narrator here exercises an implicit critical judgement on Stephen such as Joyce himself exercised on *Chamber Music*. For he saw that the poems themselves, in spite of their narrative pattern, could not represent the facts of life which he wanted to represent in narrative. His sense of what poetry is, in other words, his own practical aesthetics of verse, will not allow it. And for all Stephen Dedalus' notions of the Incarnation as a metaphor for artistic creation, what his and Joyce's verse does, in effect, is not make the word flesh, but rather make the flesh word. As in the 'Villanelle of the Temptress' in *Portrait*, in the poems of *Chamber Music* the facts are rendered down to a few imagistic details, the language is driven by a generalising energy, detaching the 'subtle soul of the image from its mesh of defining circumstances'.[58] Such an effect is enhanced in the poems by a boneless syntax that simply lets the elements of a poem float together, and by a speaker who is no more than a ghostly presence. Language, music, internal pattern, the playing of old notes – those first two dedications to language and tradition, in fact – are what in the final analysis remove the poems from the area of genuine narrative possibility. This may be exemplified in the first poem of the sequence proper (as Joyce himself would have arranged it):

The twilight turns from amethyst
    To deep and deeper blue,
The lamp fills with a pale green glow
    The trees of the avenue.

The old piano plays an air,
    Sedate and slow and gay;

She bends upon the yellow keys,
   Her head inclines this way.

Shy thoughts and grave wide eyes and hands
   That wander as they list –
The twilight turns to darker blue
   With lights of amethyst.

Here all is frozen gesture; language and syntax encase and make conventional the moment, giving it the generality of song. In his contemporary work in prose, however, the elements that verse distils out are left in, accentuated. And it is in his prose poems, in fact, in the epiphanies, that Joyce discovers a management of language that will allow him to pursue his own narrative urge. The epiphanies, indeed, may be seen as the bridge from the poems to the major work in prose. The following example offers a simple comparison with the poem just quoted:

She stands, her book held lightly at her breast, reading the lesson. Against the dark stuff of her dress her face, mild-featured with downcast eyes, rises softly outlined in light; and from a folded cap, set carelessly forward, a tassel falls along her brown ringletted hair . . .
   What is the lesson that she reads – of apes, of strange inventions, or the legends of martyrs?[59]

In this slight prose sketch the diction, for all its calculation, does not strain after effects of purity and remoteness, as it does in the verse. This language is more straightforward than the posed simplicity of the poem. The rhythm varies, as the motion of each sentence – turning to a different syntactical impulse – is different. And things are being included, enumerated, given physical body and presence, rather than being forced, under the pressure of poetic sublimation, to 'fall out of the scene'. The poem is a sort of secret, in code. The prose seems to wish that the reader share exactly what the writer has seen. Here facts are enacted, rather than souls evoked. The surfaces are in clear view ('her book held lightly at her breast', the dark stuff of her dress, the folded cap set carelessly forward, a falling tassel, 'her brown ringletted hair', rather than 'Shy thoughts and grave wide eyes and hands/That wander as they list'). In this dedication to surfaces and the known, as well as in the concluding questions, the sense of the 'I' conveyed is of a self mentally alert and sensually attached to facts. Such qualities, of course, could be part of a poem. But Joyce's own aesthetic presumptions about the nature of verse would not allow them. In prose he could invent his own aesthetics, and not be subject to an inherited set, those that in a sense defined Stephen Dedalus. In a certain sense, *Chamber Music* might be seen as charting the limits of Joyce's own identification with Stephen. In prose, the poet of essences becomes the painter of accidents, enabling his imagination – in a way verse as he conceived of it and practised it could not – to realise fully itself. (Verse enabled his imagination to realise, and to begin, its engagement with language, with tradition, with the idea of narrative – things other than itself).

So, in rich and various ways, *Chamber Music* is, as he says himself, the beginning of Joyce's 'expression of myself' that proceeds through the great works in prose. And valuable and informative (and in its own terms successful) as it is, the accent must always fall on its being a beginning. In it, 'the poet Joyce' dedicated himself and discovered his limits, and it brought him nearer to being that quite different creature, the writer. But it is in the triple dedication represented by *Chamber Music* – to language and craft, to tradition, to narrative – that the fundamental structure of Joyce's imagination is established, and it is by means of this structure that the 'writer' becomes truly, in the great works of his maturity, his own early image of 'the poet', whose life was intense, 'taking into its centre the life that surrounds it and flinging it abroad again amid planetary music'. From chamber music to planetary music: may not the whole career, that life in art, be seen as no more nor less than the ramifying redefinition of 'the poet Joyce'?

NOTES

1 James Joyce, *Letters*, ed. Richard Ellmann (New York: The Viking Press, 1966), II, 181.

2 Richard Ellmann, *James Joyce* (Oxford University Press, new and revised edition, 1982), p.127.

3 Quoted in Ellmann, p. 479.

4 I'm thinking especially of 'I Hear an Army' in *Chamber Music*, and 'A Memory of the Players in a Mirror at Midnight', in *Pomes Penyeach*.

5 James Joyce, *Selected Letters* (New York: Viking, 1975), pp. 160-61.

6 *Selected Letters*, p.161.

7 ibid., pp. 180, 190, 192.

8 Ellmann, p.381.

9 *Letters*, III, 6.

10 For these and subsequent quotations from revires, see *Letters*, II, 333.

11 ibid., pp. 219, 182.

12 Lynch in *Ulysses* (revised text, p. 408).

13 James Joyce, *Giacomo Joyce* (NY: Viking, 1968), p. xviii.

14 William York Tindall, in *Poetry*, 80, May 1952, p. 107.

15 *Chamber Music*, ed. with Introduction and Notes by William

York Tindall (New York: Columbia University Press), 1954.

16 Chester G. Anderson, 'Joyce's Verses', in *A Companion to Joyce Studies* (eds. Zack Bowen and James F. Carens, Westport Connecticut and London: Greenwood Press, 1984), pp. 129-55. Boyle's essay is in *Women in Joyce*, eds. Suzette Henke and Elaine Unkeless (Chicago: University of Illinois Press, 1982), pp. 3-30.

17 *Chamber Music*, p. 88.

18 *Letters*, II, 217.

19 ibid. p. 13.

20 ibid. p. 333.

21 J F Byrne, *The Silent Years* (New York: xxxxxxxxxx 1953), pp. 63-4.

22 *Chamber Music*, p. 108.

23 *Stephen Hero*, (New Directions, 1963), p. 32.

24 *Ellmann*, pp. 50-51, 80ff.

25 ibid., p. 81.

26 ibid., p. 76, and *Letters*, II, 333. The critic was Tom Kettle.

27 Stanislaus Joyce, *My Brother's Keeper*, (New York: Viking Press, 1958), p. 142.

28 See Ellmann, pp. 83, 121.

29 For Jonson, see Boyle, p. 23, and Herbert Gorman, *James Joyce* (N.Y.: Rinehart, 1948), p. 116.

30 See Tindall, *Chamber Music*, p. 31, Boyle, pp. 22-3, Anderson, p. 138.

31 See Ellmann, Tindall, Boyle and Anderson, *passim*.

32 James Joyce, *Critical Writings*, edited by Richard Ellmann and Ellsworth Mason, Faber and Faber, 1959), 80.

33 Along with echoes from Yeats, the Elizabethans, and 'The Lady of Shallott'. See *Chamber Music*, p. 187.

34 ibid., p. 221.

35 Anderson, p. 147.

36 *My Brother's Keeper*, p. 148.

37 *Stephen Hero*, p. 36.

38 *Letters*, II , 237.

39 *Chamber Music*, p. 102; *Letters*, II , 259.

40 *Chamber Music*, 25

41 Many of Gregan's poems are crammed with such features of landscape, mythology and mood.

42 *Stephen Hero*, p. 174.

43 *Dubliners*, (New York: Viking Press, 1961), p. 74.

44 In one of the poems of *Sunset Town* (p. 40).

45 *Letters*, II, 219.

46 ibid. 182.

47 *Chamber Music*, p. 44

48 ibid. p. 47.

49 ibid.

50 *Letters*, II, 27.

51 Ellmann, p. 262.

52 Boyle, p. 28.

53 *Selected Letters.*

54 *Letters*, II, 219.

55 Ellmann, p. 266.

56 ibid. p. 150.

57 *A Portrait of the Artist as a Young Man*, (New York: Viking Press, 1972), p. 70-1.

58 *Stephen Hero*, p. 78.

59 In *The Workshop of Daedalus*, Edited by Robert Scholes and Richard M. Kain (Evanston, Illinois: Northwestern University Press, 1965), p.49.

DIRECTING
EXILES

Vincent Dowling

In 1973, on my return from an extended visit to the US, I was appointed Director of the Peacock (the smaller stage of the Abbey Theatre). At the first meeting I attended, for a group of emerging or 'hopeful' playwrights, one of them, a taxi-driver, said to me, 'You should do Joyce's *Exiles*. It is the best play ever written!' He said it with such simple conviction that I decided there and then to read it again, and, at once! I remember I had read *Exiles* in the 1950s and had thought it a stiff, intellectual, non-theatrical piece! Well, in my flat, in the house where the Synge family spent their Summer holidays in Crosthwaite Park, Dun Laoghaire, (a most appropriate place to read *Exiles*, don't you think?) I put down the paperback book having finished Act I and said to my partner-in-life Olwen, 'if the rest of this is as good, I will produce it as part of my first season as Director of the Peacock'. At the end of the second act, I was so excited that I was afraid to read the third act in case I would find in it the cause why *Exiles* was dismissed by every theatre person who knew it except my taxi-driver friend. I need not have worried. The third act was just what I felt it should be and had to be.

I saw at once that what I had mistaken previously for 'stiff and intellectual and non-theatrical' was the accurately re-created dialogue and mode of speech of my own Dowling, middle-class Dublin relations. I felt, too, that while Richard's search for freedom for himself, Bertha and Robert, was a brilliantly intellectual one, the carrying through of its conclusions was powerfully emotional, given the depth of his passion, his need for Bertha and his reliance on her. Here was emotional conflict indeed.

Less importantly, I saw the need for minor cuts, though in the end I put most of the 'cuts' back! Perhaps Joyce did not fully trust actors or realise fully how they could communicate a sub-text!

In the production of any play, casting is the biggest, most important decision the director has to make. Second in importance is design – sets, costumes, properties, light and sound. It would seem to be obvious that these decisions should arise from the play itself and from the circumstances in which it is being produced. Sadly, many of today's productions are *impositions* of a director's political or moral philosophies on an author's work. This 'concept', as it is euphemistically referred to, is a distortion of an author's intent and a manipulation of an audience's trust, in my opinion. 'Style is the pressure of the raw material' Synge is alleged to have said. Well it is true for me and I approached the production of James Joyce's *Exiles* in that spirit. The pressures were for me:

> The text, the actors, the designers, the director (myself), the space we were working in (The Peacock stage of the Abbey Theatre) and the time we were doing it, 1973.

I will start with the space. The Peacock is flexible. You can play in the traditional procenium arch or 'in the round'. To be more exact, with the audience on three sides of a stage that is placed in the centre of the auditorium proper. The fourth side is a wall with an exit door in it. Opposite that exit door is 'The Loge' containing about 24 seats. Thus the main audience (150 people) is equally divided between the two 'long' sides of the auditorium, steeply raked down to the square of stage, in a kind of cockpit. I wanted the action to take place in the greatest possible intimacy with the audience, so I decided to use the theatre in this latter configuration. However, as the designer I chose an actor/designer named Gerry Sullivan, and myself agreed that the play needed a detailed setting reflecting the personalities and class of the main characters and the Sandymount Strand environment seen through a window (used by the child in the play), we used 'The Loge' as a practical curtained window with the strandscape outside it. The exit door we re-decorated in Georgian style. The wall became a book case. A fire and brass accoutrements plus a set of beautiful armchairs and a sofa, in an exquisite sepia coloured material, with a love seat and fine occasional tables and a whatnot, (mostly from an antique furniture shop – Cusacks – near Kelly's corner) combined to create Richard's and Bertha's carpeted drawing room.

The New York Players' Theatre on the Upper East Side of Manhattan is part of The Church of the Heavenly Rest. Its name and associations provided a delightfully ironic context for Joyce's irreverent genius. We were able to create or re-create a traverse configuration within the space to accommodate the special needs of the play's action.

An unexpected bonus came from the added focus given to the stage action by the intense concentration of the audience opposite, if one chanced to raise one's eyes above the actors. Who these actors were going to be presented no problem in Dublin. Alas, in the New York production one fine actor was so overawed at acting the character of the great James Joyce himself, (Richard), that he never relaxed into the role! However, Dublin was the first production of *Exiles* for me, and the actors, you might almost say, cast themselves.

Clearly, I felt, for Richard we needed a consummate actor, highly intelligent, with manners and class, private in personality capable of a cold exterior, righteous, indeed, savage indignation and a fierce inner passion. We needed Bosco Hogan and we got him. Looking at the tape of the television performance of this production today I am convinced that Bosco could not have been bettered, nor could Bertha. In Nuala Hayes we found everything the play demanded – beauty, strength, vulnerability, sensitivity, sensuality and a curious country woman's mixture of common sense and wisdom. She also had Bertha's hands. In Kevin McHugh, I knew we had all the obvious charms and complex contradictions of Robert and in Maire O'Neil the delicate beauty, the 'protestant' mask, the inner loneliness of Beatrice. May Clusky as the housekeeper, and the boy Archie played by Donald Reynolds with a touch of Italian in his Dublin voice, completed the most perfect cast for a play it has been my good fortune to assemble.

I have heard Joycean scholars complain that Richard – the Joyce figure in the play – and Robert, who also loves Bertha – the Nora figure – are ill-defined, ill-distinguished figures, almost the same personage split in two. Even the names, it is argued, are ominously similar, like those of female characters, Beatrice and Bertha!

Though I can't help seeing the general point, the complaint still amazes me. I could hardly agree less. Even now, sixteen years after the event, however I try, the four Irish actors I cast in my original production walk in my head through the vivid world of *Exiles*. In ordinary life could any two actors be so different – or any two actresses? On stage, in the performances, the differences are even more marked. Of course there are surface and inner similarities in Robert and Richard. But they are the subtle and brilliantly observed similarities that arise from long acquaintance, shared experience and background. The characters are aware of these similarities, as part of their human predicament. The investigation of these areas and responses was part of the joy in the rehearsal process.

Another unusual, almost unique, pressure was added to this production – a resident critic! My season with the Peacock was intended to be experimental in a number of ways. The experiment I proposed for *Exiles* was that each newspaper would send a critic to join the production team from day one; he would present his criticism each day as part of the process and continue to do this up to the opening, so that the critic would contribute to the production rather than judge it. I made it clear that these critics would not review the production; someone else from their publications would do that. They would be free, however, and encouraged to write, later on, of their experience.

One critic came to a rehearsal and wrote a good article. Almost all the other critics rejected the offer, fearing, I believe, an attempt to muzzle them. One critic, whom I had long recognised as one of the few critic/artists I had encountered anywhere, joined us – Sean Page. Sean's contribution to the success of this production of *Exiles* was equal to that of any actor, designer, technician or myself as director.

What can I say about the actual five week period of rehearsal? Very little, except that joyfully we teased out every fibre of our material. Perhaps this will be of interest. Normally I do an enormous amount of research on and about a play, its author and the time a play is written and set in. In the case of *Exiles* I knew something of James Joyce, but not that much. I had read *Portrait of an Artist* and *Dubliners*. I had failed to make much progress with *Ulysses*, less with *Finnegans Wake*. Of course, I had seen, and read for parts in, stage and screen adaptations of various Joyce works. I had turned down a major part in Joseph Strick's movie of *Ulysses* to play Fluther in *Plough and the Stars*, in the first production of a play in the new Abbey Theatre. You can't win them all!

Of course, I knew Dublin intimately and the Dowlings belonged to a middle-class, articulate, literate, Victorian milieu instantly recognisable to me in *Exiles*. So I decided to trust the players and my own experience and imagination, but, above all, to trust James Joyce's play, which my intuition and experience had told me was a powerful piece of drama. The production of the play was a success. It was even a success with the critics; more importantly it was a success with serious theatre practitioners, wherever they came from. Most importantly it was a success for all of us engaged in the production. We found James Joyce and his Nora and got to know them personally in *Exiles*. We got to understand him as an ordinary extraordinary *Dub*, Irishman and human being. We got to know ourselves better and our potential. I like to think we helped to rehabilitate a neglected masterpiece. We were not the first to do this. But we were one of the few.

I want to do this play again. World theatre is richer for *Exiles*, poorer that Joyce did not write more plays.

THE RHYTHM
OF ULYSSES

Clive Hart

– Rhythm, said Stephen, is the first formal esthetic relation of part to part in any esthetic whole or of an esthetic whole to its parts or of any part to the esthetic whole of which it is a part.[1]

Joyce was, above all, a shaping artist, a master of formal relationships. He had at least this much in common with Sir Philip Sidney that he scorned the notion of direct self-expression, of merely looking into one's heart and writing. Perhaps, after all, only fools do that. I want to explore some fairly simple propositions about the way the shape of Joycean narrative may be related to fundamental narrative structures, and to suggest how that relationship reveals something of the essential qualities of Joyce's approach to his art and of his sense of the world. I had originally intended to speak only about *Ulysses*, but although the rhythmic patterns of that meticulously organised book will be my final focus, I find that I need to preface my remarks with a few comments on the formal qualities of *Exiles*, of *Dubliners*, and of

Portrait. Like all of Gaul and *Ulysses* itself; my lecture is divided into three parts: first, a description of the shapes that concern me; second, the early works; third, *Ulysses*.

The shaping qualities that I shall be describing fall into two main categories: those that affect the sequence of relationships in the perceived events – in the story – and those that concern the distribution of textual elements – in other words, the words. That the link between these two has been weakened in modern writing almost to the point of total severance has long been a critical commonplace. While I want to take that severance into account, my main concerns will be, first, an examination of Joyce's response to the available shaping patterns, and, second, the relationship of the shapes to my sense of what I perceive as Joyce's quietist tendency, his disposition to avoid suggesting change. It has long been my view that in Joyce nothing ever happens except the attainment of self-awareness.

I

I beg your indulgence while I sketch in a couple of rather abstract patterns. Without such a preliminary summary I cannot readily establish my sense of Joyce's rhythmic procedures. I begin by suggesting that all western art is an opposition of two and three, of twoness and threeness. Put as baldly as that, this is, of course, a ridiculous, pompous statement; if uttered by, say, a character in a work by Samuel Beckett, it would receive a rude noise in response. As it happens it is, nevertheless, an opposition much explored by Beckett and I mention in passing that I turn to examine it in Joyce partly from hindsight after considering it in Beckett, where the patterns are presented with great clarity.[2] I have two different shapes in mind: put at their simplest they are; first, those that present a narrative consisting of one thing leading to another, one thing leading to a quite different thing, after which – full–stop; and, second, those that pursue that course without stopping, pursue it further by adding a third part in which there is a return to the starting point, or to something like the starting point.

Both structures are very ancient, but they enter western artistic consciousness by different routes. The two-part structure is coherent with linear, salvational religion – with a religion that promises an endpoint in eternity. By contrast, the three-part, reflexive structure is coherent with cyclic mythologies and religions which, instead of promising a happy endpoint, promise eternal recurrence, promise something like the metempsychosis that is an important thematic strand of *Ulysses* – Molly's met-him-pike-hoses, a happy malapropism relating eternal recurrence to sexuality in ways that I will briefly take up later. The first is consistent with the Christian religion, the second with much of the pagan thought that re-entered the west as a powerful counter-force during the Renaissance. It is, in particular, the structural basis of the Neoplatonism that so deeply influenced the arts after the end of the fifteenth century. I am going to suggest that Joyce is happier with a modified Neoplatonic reflexive structure because he cannot swallow the idea that change is either possible or desirable, and does not find a linear ameliorative process in any way true to human experience. In that important sense he is a man without faith.

The linear structure of the Christian story, and of hosts of salvational stories like it, is, familiarly enough, the basis of much western narrative. Boy meets girl, boy loses girl, boy gets girl, is, give or take some important qualifications, the story of the loss of Eden followed by redemption. And they all lived happily ever after. The story disappears off the end of the page, into Heaven. It is no longer our concern, so to speak; we enquire no further; life has stopped. We are given a very strong sense of an ending. This structure – explored by many narratologists – is not only linear, but also essentially bipartite. There is a before and an after, an Old Dispensation – an Old Testament – and a New. After having been the basis of many narrative works of art of the Middle Ages, it clashed interestingly with the pagan tripartite structure with which, after the Renaissance, it formed an unstable amalgam. And at some later periods, such as, in particular perhaps, the mid eighteenth century on the continent of Europe, it was largely supplanted by the symmetries of neo-classicism. The most obvious examples of these structural patterns in the arts are probably to be found in music: compare, on the one hand, the two-part structures that form the basis of much baroque music, with, on the other, the reflexive three-part patterns of musical neo-classicism and its successors: the slow-fast structure of a *sonata da chiesa*, the two halves of the *Goldberg Variations*, the two acts of Purcell's *Dido* – very different from the reflexive basis of classical sonata form. Consider it in other fields: the two main parts of the Mass; or the mediaeval church itself which, architecturally speaking, is essentially bipartite – the nave and the chancel, representing the world and Heaven respectively, life and the after-life. On the other hand the palace *style classique*: tripartite and symmetrical; and of course churches built in neoclassical times play energetically with the possibilities of incorporating classical cyclic form into Christian sequence.

The second of my basic structures, the tripartite and reflexive, the neoclassical and symmetrical, returns us, in its final phase, to life: a-b-a, an out-and-return journey. The focus, in other words, is human. Man's quotidian experience, to which we return at the end, provides the basis for judgement of the more remote experiences at the centre. The hero goes out into the world with the intention of returning with the boon. The prince finds and wakes the sleeping princess (a boon achieved by positive means), or he slays the dragon (a negative route to happiness). Sometimes one part of the cycle is subjected to closer scrutiny than another; or the various parts may be distributed between related works. Fielding's *Joseph Andrews* sketches in the first two parts very hastily in order to concentrate almost all of its attention on the last part, the process of return. He is concerned above all, as Joyce was to be, with the way the pattern of circularity feeds back into life.

Of course the idea of a journey of return can readily be adapted to Christian purposes. It is not wholly different from Christian linearity: the third stage may be a return with a decided difference indicating a transformation or glorification. Dante offers a brilliant amalgamation of the two structures in the *Divine Comedy*. He travels to the extreme of the universe, and, as we learn at various stages of the poem, he comes back bearing the boon of celestial knowledge which he passes on to the rest of mankind. The

structure of the narrative and that of the experience are nevertheless differentiated: at the end of the narrative he leaves his other
self and us, the readers, in the presence of God – that is to say at
point b, the end of the linear Christian journey.

The three-part structure, characteristically pagan, has affinities
with Renaissance humanism. I am thinking in particular of that
three-part, out-and-back metaphysical journey so fundamental to
the Neoplatonism which spread from Florence in the later decades
of the fifteenth century. The material and temporal structure of
the cosmos follows a symmetrical, pulsating movement out from
God and back to Him. God's unity develops itself into ever more
diverse forms, to become, finally, the multiplicity of the world we
live in. That multiplicity will later collapse back into the godhead:
a spiritual circuit sometimes referred to by such phrases as Emanation, Action and Reabsorption. This view of the pattern of the
cosmos is the most immediately crucial influence in creating a tendency for the earlier two-part structures to be superseded by
three-part, a-b-a forms.

The Neoplatonic three-part pattern was often mythologised,
and especially as the metaphor of the Three Graces. That
metaphor itself takes various forms. The most common and relevant goes something like this: Love meets Beauty and the result is
Delight; Delight then returns us to an understanding of the nature
of Love. In the case of human experience, God descends to
embrace His beautiful world, which delightedly reflects His love
back to Him. And, most important in the present context, the
human imagination may mirror the pattern in reverse, going out
to meet God and returning to mundane life with the boon of
Grace. The famous tripartite aesthetic theory that Stephen enun-
ciates to his friend Lynch (to the accompaniment from Lynch of
obscene puns of the word 'whole') follows the inverted out-and-
return Neoplatonic pattern: wholeness is Love; harmony is Beauty;
radiance is Delight. Needless to say, Joyce's handling of the
Neoplatonic pattern is usually ironic – as here with the jejune
aesthetic theory – and it is often painfully so.

II

Like Sir Thomas Browne, Joyce is an amphibian, living in at least two antithetical conceptual worlds. Although he is rightly celebrated as one of the most innovative of modernists, he works most happily when he is also closely involved with familiar forms. In an important sense all his books are teasingly open-ended, while at the same time they are carefully concluded. For Joyce, closure is not a dirty word. He loves it more than almost any other modern – with the possible exception, I suppose, of Eliot. Pound, you may recall, predicted that when he reached number 100 of his cantos (the same as the number of cantos in Dante's perfectly shaped *Divine Comedy*) all would become clear. When he not only reached 100 without attaining formal clarity, but carried on well beyond it, people reminded him of his prediction. He answered to the effect that he had long since ceased being serious about that promise of closure, that the work had to be allowed to continue to grow organically. Not for Joyce, that kind of response. While Joyce never began with a fully formed plan, to be developed without deviation until the end, he always worked towards the vision of a form – and it is important for my purposes that it is a closed form – which he attempted to perfect in the Dantean mode. But, as I suggest, the perfection is ambiguous; or perhaps I should say that the perfection applies to only a part of the whole concept of the work. It is a perfection, a closure, achieved mainly by the use of reflexive structures – parts mirroring or reflecting parts – but there can of course be a good deal of irony when one relates closed formal structure to linear narrative content.

Because the pattern is perhaps clearest in it, I shall glance first at *Exiles*. In the first place this is a three-part, a-b-a structure in a quite simple sense: it is a three act play. The shape of the play echoes that of the three-act *pièce bien faite* so firmly established by Ibsen. The fundamental structure of such plays is often a-b-a in the sense that the middle act contrasts with the first and third, which in some ways correspond to each other. The first establishes the issues in need of attention; the second explores possible resolutions; the third returns us to the issues, typically either to resolve them or to show the failure of resolution.

In *Exiles*, the middle act takes place in a different physical environment, and at a different time of day: night as opposed to the morning of the first two acts. In other respects the play obeys the classical unities; Joyce's break with them in respect of place is a pointer to his focus on the possibilities of the a-b-a journey. At the love-nest in the centre of the play – a parody of an Arcadian grotto – Robert, the principle of profane Love, meets Bertha, the principle of Beauty. But the result is not the Neoplatonic Delight of an ennobled sexuality. The two of them may or may not have a sexual encounter (despite their several protestations the play remains ambiguous on the point), but in any case the result is – well, very nearly nothing at all in terms of changes to people's active lives. There are, as you would expect, significant internal changes: they all learn something; but on the surface almost nothing happens. It is a pattern that Beckett was later to develop much more fully in his plays, and of course it had also been explored a good deal earlier – by Conrad, for example. But in Conrad the learning process tends to have profound effects on what people do: once they have seen the horror, which is what Conrad's truth often and notoriously amounts to, they can never be the same again. In Joyce, as even more so in Beckett, the changes, if any, are subtler. In respect of action, of how you go about living from day to day, the cyclic pattern returns the characters, and the readers, to a point very similar to that at which they found themselves in the beginning. It is not changing the world that matters, so much as learning about it.

The two ideas – a linear structure and a circular a-b-a structure are interestingly combined in *Dubliners*. The more closely one reads *Dubliners*, the less it seems like a collection of stories. It is much more, even, than the careful arrangement in the four celebrated stages – childhood, adolescence, maturity, and public life – that Joyce enunciated in a letter.[3] There is a linear sequence in it which establishes it is a kind of *Bildungsroman*, a novel of personal development in which the main character keeps changing name and sex as he grows up. But there is also a cyclic structure containing, so to speak, no *Bildung*, except for that achieved by the reader.

If we treat the last story, 'The Dead', as a coda, as a separate and special case, the remaining fourteen stories arrange themselves quite neatly into four symmetrically patterned groups: 3-4-4-3. It is in fact a chiastic symmetry, the first and last sets of three corresponding in inverse order, and likewise the inner sets of four. The first three might, on the analogy of the labels Joyce gave to the substance of the chapters of *Ulysses*, be called stories concerning religion, literature, and commerce, while the last three concern, reversing the order, politics, music, and religion – just the sort of patterning Joyce was soon to develop more fully and more expressly. At present I shall not try to explore in detail the patterns created by the inner chapters, but the relationships are, I think, fairly specific. Speaking in general, one can say that the inner stories are all about versions of seduction: male and female, old and young, homosexual and heterosexual. In the case of *Dubliners* these inner stories are crucial; they form the outermost point of the Neoplatonic journey. If one wanted to be more precise about the outermost point I think one might say that the exact middle is the moment of peripeteia from the seventh story, 'The Boarding House,' in which the first marriage of the book is arranged, to the eighth, 'A Little Cloud', where the first painfully inadequate married relationship is explored. In the first half there is an emphasis on celibacy, in the second on marriage. Early in the eighth story Joyce ironically describes the main character, aged thirty-two, as being 'just at the point of maturity'.

The circular structure of *Dubliners* works against its linear aspirations, creating a still more ironic version of the journey than is to be found in *Exiles*. There is no escape from the seductions, the temptations, no salvation to provide a modern, lay equivalent of the redemption of mankind after the seductions of Adam and Eve. We are returned, without a boon, to our present state, from which partial relief is offered only by the more humane tone of the coda, by 'The Dead', which stands outside the main cycle of experience.[4]

I hope that what I have said may be true of the collection as a whole. With some distortion of the symmetries I suggest that is also true of each story. Their individual structures, that is, their rhythms, are helpful for an understanding of *Ulysses*. They are variations on a-b-a, each exploring possibilities of movement out from captivity, only to sink back to the starting point with nothing achieved. First imagined by Joyce as a further story for the collection, *Ulysses* is broadly speaking a *Dubliners* story writ large, though with a crucial difference: the much stronger emphasis on the growth of awareness.[5]

Portrait includes a further interesting combination of linearity and a still more meticulously arranged circularity. Although it actually deals with only a tiny proportion of the life of the young man during the twenty years that it records, it follows a linear chronological course and seems at first close in spirit to the familiar nineteenth century novels of personal development. With regard to its artistic shaping, there are nevertheless two important qualifications to be made. First, the mission, as I read the book, ends in failure. I have not the space to argue this in detail, but I suggest that in an important sense *Portrait* comes full circle at the end. The novel begins – not with a view of an infant, as is sometimes misleadingly stated – but with a view of literature, with a representation of the literary world as it is perceived by an infant ('Once upon a time and a very good time it was . . . '); and it ends with a series of childish, clichéd orotundities:

> Welcome, O life! I go to encounter for the millionth time the reality of experience and to forge in the smithy of my soul the uncreated conscience of my race. (*AP* 252-53)

Did anyone – as Stephen himself tellingly asks of another of his utterances earlier in the book – did anyone ever hear such drivel? (*AP* 179). As we are frequently reminded, Stephen is a son, not a father, an adolescent not a master craftsman; he is an Icarus who will fall into the ocean and be reabsorbed into the matter from which he emerged. *Portrait* gets nowhere; an ironic account of artistic development, it ends where it began, in immaturity.

As in the case of *Dubliners*, then, its linearity gives way to circularity, a circular pattern of the a-b-a kind. A closer look shows that that structure is in fact the whole basis of the book's design.

There are five chapters, and hence, of course, there is an easily
identifable middle one. Furthermore, each chapter is itself built on
the a-b-a pattern, with a contrasting and climactic middle section:
those middles are not only climactic but each time explore what
for Stephen is an aspect unknown. At each stage of life, in each of
the five chapters, Stephen finds himself in a new world distant
from his previous experience, and each time he returns with what
seems to be a boon, with the dragon slain, the princess under his
arm. Each time – and right to the end – the boon proves to be an
illusion. The centre point of the central chapter is the famous
series of sermons on Hell. That, in the long run, should be seen as
the far point of Stephen's journey of personal development: a descent into Hades. Welcoming the learning experience, he chooses
life instead. But at the end he still has to begin to live. And as has
often been pointed out, at the end he is no more than a newborn
infant, an artist in potential, perhaps, but one who has only just
emerged from the womb, almost literally wet behind the ears.

III

In *Ulysses*, a boy-gets-girl story with a difference, Joyce plays com-
parable games with the two structures. The Christian narrative is
about arrival at one crucial event: salvation. The familiar parallel in
secular art is the pattern of a Jane Austen novel: salvation through
a combination of marriage and the attainment of self-knowledge.
Joyce deals obliquely with the idea of a climax in marriage, in
order to focus as fully as possible on self-knowledge. Instead of
evoking an arrival at salvation, he turns the story back on itself to
bite its own tail, to plunge back into the life that is already
known, repudiating the possibility of transcendence. It is, once
again, an out-and-return story that gets nowhere. (My invocation
of the myth of the Three Graces may suggest some similarity with
the Hegelian pattern of thesis, antithesis, and synthesis explored in
connexion with *Ulysses* by Richard Ellmann.[6] Despite the triads
common to both, I believe that the a-b-a structure I propose is in
fact the contrary of Ellmann's: the one is a pattern of return, the

other of progress). But the process of return is not, as it usually is in Beckett, a hopeless or helpless getting-nowhere. Nor am I suggesting that *Ulysses* is in any way didactic. It does not seem to me to convey a message, but rather to offer a demonstration of the idea that salvation is not necessary – and not only not necessary, but positively to be repudiated as a way of understanding the needs of life.

If I am to pursue this pattern effectively, I need to be able to discern the outermost point reached by the a-b-a structure of the storyline of *Ulysses*. Where the main character goes, in the most important senses of that term, will of course be crucial to my sense of the shape of the perceived events. That shaping is, of course, achieved by the independent structuring of the words. It may help if we recall Joyce's model, the *Odyssey*. In keeping with epic tradition, we are there plunged *in medias res*. If we take that concept literally – being carried into the middle of things – as for example Milton did when beginning *Paradise Lost*, the *exact* middle is to be found right there, at the start of the odyssey proper. The outermost point of Bloom's journey, as of that of Odysseus, is perhaps to be found in his beginning, in his meeting with Calypso, in his capitulation to that temptation towards emotional inactivity that she offers. The first 'a' of the verbal structure may thus be understood as relating events which correspond with the 'b' of life's experience. What follows for the next eleven chapters, Bloom's wanderings and encounters, may be construed as an ever deeper analysis of how he got to be where he found himself at the start, in the arms of the witch. Joyce introduces, of course, a significant twist: Molly is Bloom's Calypso as well as his Penelope. The boon that Bloom brings back to his own life, like a fairytale prince curing the ills of his kingdom, is, I suggest, his encounter with the fact that his relationship with Molly is satisfactory even in its Calypso form. It used to be fashionable to propose that Bloom followed a linear as well as a circular path, profiting from his day's experiences in some fashion (dependent on the critic's taste) that would enable him to amend his life with Molly. On the day after Bloomsday everything will be different in the Bloom household: health will return to the marriage. Many earlier Joyce critics – I shan't name them – strike me as having been obsessed with conventional norms of sexual and emotional health. Joyce was anything but conventional in these matters. Noting the importance for Joyce of the concept of return, I suggest that the only change proposed or needed is understanding followed by acceptance – acceptance of the identity of Penelope and Calypso, an identity making it possible for the circle to be fully and satisfyingly closed.

Ulysses, you might say, is about life conceived of as essentially satisfactory – warts and all – if only we could get to establish the right perspective on it. We don't need to be saved from it; we need, rather, to be saved into it. I would describe Joyce – certainly the Joyce of *Ulysses*, his greatest creation – as both profoundly unreligious and profoundly apolitical. But I would want to follow those negatives by a very positive if also trite consequence: he is profoundly human, profoundly life-affirming. Too much, perhaps, for some tastes: he affirms the value of life to a degree that makes many people feel uncomfortable. I see nothing in *Ulysses* to suggest that he feels any need to change the life people lead in the twentieth century. For many readers that is not a welcome view of the appropriate human response to the reality in which they find themselves. Welcome or not, it seems to me to have been Joyce's.

With Bloom as the central though not always explicit concern, *Ulysses* explores the out-and-return structure in a multitude of ways, which many microcosmic reflections of the main pattern. Some are direct, such as the chiastic arrangement of the eight paragraphs of Penelope, taking Molly's language and imagery as far as possible from her initial focus on home and Bloom, only to return there at the end. Or, in the same vein though with more edge, the tumescence–detumescence of Nausikaa: up like a rocket, down like a stick. Bloom is there seen tempted once again by a Calypso, travelling once again to a distance from his home centre, and again returning with awareness that his encounter with Nausikaa-Gerty-Calypso is to be accepted as good. Some are inverse and dismembered in cubist ways. In relation to the verbal structure, Wandering Rocks is at the centre. At *its* exact centre, the middle section of the nineteen that make it up, Bloom is again depicted at his furthest remove from home, painfully salivating over the pornographic *Sweets of Sin*. The two long outermost sections, those depicting the journeys of Conmee and the Viceroy, do not show a movement towards that remote centre followed by a return; both proceed instead away from the centre, to northern and southern extremes of the city. The movements of both Church and State are severed from the out-and-return journey lying at the centre of the book, the disjunction stressing once again their powerlessness to engage effectively with it. Wandering Rocks is an exploration in passing of how things may sometimes fall apart, the centre not holding, rather than of how, as the book in general explores, they may be made to cohere.

Out-and-return is deeply rooted in the psychology of *Ulysses*, in the psychology of Joyce himself, for whom memory was the most prized of human faculties. 'Here we are again' is a fundamentally important movement of the spirit for both writer and reader. Joyce's recreation of the spirit of Dublin life is mirrored in his reintroduction of characters and events from earlier books ('I know that man', one says comfortably to oneself when reencountering Bob Doran or Tom Kernan – to say nothing of Stephen Dedalus), and it is mirrored still more fundamentally in the interplay of repetitions and recalls. As he proceeds through the book, the reader goes out in imagination only to find that he is increasingly recalled to his earlier reading experiences, remembering, juxtaposing, comparing, to make sense of the relationship of end and beginning. One is repeatedly invited to leave remote regions and go home; after the return one will for the first time truly understand one's past.

In this, the out-and-return journey of language is at least as important as are the representations of reality. Words, phrases, images, return to create a sense of home, of security in the acceptance of familiarity which is at the root of *Ulysses*. Its language is of course intimately related to the physical and psychic journeys of the characters – intimately, but not on a one-for-one basis. In relation to the book's total structure, the out-and-return journey is expressly indicated by Joyce's shorthand descriptions of the aims and techniques of the chapters in the inversely correspondent opening and closing parts: we end with versions of the experiences with which we began. Language has not proceeded towards a series of climactic insights through a linear journey of discovery. The linguistic climax is found, once again, towards the centre of the journey, after which language folds back into itself. But the outermost point of the linguistic journey is not coincident with the outermost limit of Bloom's psychological journey. The journey through words is ours and the artist's, not his. Our exploration of the problem and it feels as if we encounter it expressed in all possible linguistic ways – is only loosely coupled to Bloom's. The most obvious evidence of the disjunction is the fact that in the end we return to the simplicity of the final monologue of which he knows nothing. Both Bloom and we come full circle, though our circle is wider. There is no hint in Joyce that he, or we, need to purify the language of the tribe. The artist goes out to remote linguistic regions to slay verbal dragons, but the boon he brings back is an awareness of the sufficiency of ordinary human discourse. In Neoplatonic terms, Love in the form of loving language – poetry – goes out to meet the Beauty of experience – Beauty which may inhere in things as mundane as Stephen's washing-basket, and the result is aesthetic Delight. Nothing whatever is pressed on us by this least didactic of writers, but we are invited to conduct our lives in the fluent, fluid, all-encompassing natural language explored in Molly's monologue, and we are invited, by implication, to remember our beginnings, to present the world to ourselves with the clarity of the book's brightly lit opening chapters, a clarity to which Joyce's wide-ranging linguistic journey returns us.

NOTES

1 James Joyce, *A Portrait of the Artist as a Young Man* (1916) (New York, 1964). (*AP*)

2 Clive Hart, *Language and Structure in Beckett's Plays*, (Gerrards Cross, 1986). (The Princess Grace Irish Library Lectures, 2).

3 *Letters of James Joyce* II, ed. Richard Ellmann (London 1966) 111.

4 For a fuller discussion, see My *Joyce, Huston, and the Making of 'The Dead'*, (Gerrards Cross, 1988). (The Princess Grace Irish Library Lectures, 5).

5 *Letters* II, 168.

6 Richard Ellmann, *Ulysses on the Liffey* (London, 1972).

JOYCE AND
HOMER:SEEING
DOUBLE

Barbara Hardy

If imitation is the sincerest form of flattery, it is also the most attentive form of reading. As Joyce read Homer he judged and analysed his art. *Ulysses* implicitly offers a commentary on its chief source and model. Joyce's critics have understandably subordinated Homer to Joyce, making the *Odyssey* an instrument for the understanding of *Ulysses*, but the process can be reversed. Joyce's creative revision, with its implicit analysis and judgements, can improve our reading of Homer, even if, like Joyce, we work wholly or mostly with translation. We can attempt a shift in instrumentality.

What we see in Joyce can help us to see similar or different things in Homer, and to pick up fresh sightings with which we return to *Ulysses*. To see double may be to see better. Not only do we read Joyce in the light of Homer, and *vice versa*, shuttling to and fro in a gradual intensification of scrutiny, but certain features become stressed or focused by turning up twice over. The mere habit of looking for correspondence sharpens sight. The modernist reflexiveness so prominent in Joyce can turn our attention to the less conspicuous modes of self-awareness and self-commentary in Homer. Knowing Joyce's delight in finding equivalents for Homer's objects can prompt us to search for indirect and obscure renderings. Moving from Homer's representation of women characters we can take a harder look at Molly Bloom. Sensing the prominence of Homer's gods can lead us to search for modern equivalents.

It seems likely that Joyce wanted certain parallels and equivalences to creep slyly and slowly into the reader's mind. Perhaps his change of mind about putting in the names of the Homeric episodes came in part from a desire to try readerly attentiveness, though the teasing isn't just a test. It demands energy, provokes thought, and provides pleasure. Joyce was of course intent on the Homeric connections, but must have responded subliminally to much in his models. Some of the responses leave only faint or implicit traces in his text, to be articulated, generalised, and taxonomised by the critic.

II

Narrative point-of-view

To begin with the title of *Ulysses*, to which its text is exquisitely responsive, as Coleridge said of another genre-conscious work, *The Winter's Tale*. Joyce's title reminds us of Homer's hero, but translates his name into another language, thus announcing model and variation. The title assumes the introductory function of Homer's traditional address to the Muse, which also begins with the hero: 'The hero of the tale which I beg the Muse to help me tell is that resourceful man . . . '[1]

This invocation is missing in the twentieth-century work, but Joyce's Latin title, like Homer's submissive request, begins dialogue. Homer's address is much more than an act of dedication; it is a request for help, and indeed for more than help, for heavenly dictation: 'This is the tale I pray the divine Muse to unfold to us. Begin it, goddess, at whatever point you will'.

Homer's text begins with a pronounced awareness of the work of art as art, of its beginning, and of everything represented by the Muse – history, earlier stories, and the unconscious mind. This insistence on an external source and inspiration is made even more clearly in the *Iliad*, where the narrator explains that some points of view are inaccesible to him, so that he has to delegate to the omniscient Muse the telling of certain events. The Muse-eye-view is clearly convenient for epic sweep and breadth, as well as deriving from superior wisdom and knowledge. Perhaps the oral traditions made the request for dictation by the Muse not only a rhetorically effective filler or bridge, but a genuine acknowledgement of traditions and sources. The so-called omniscient author's voice familiar from Chaucer and eighteenth–and nineteenth–century novels, is often accompanied by such admissions of limit and restriction, and reminders of uniscience and ignorance. We don't need the stimulus of Joyce to recognise the self-consciousness and multiplicity of narrative mode in Homer.

Homer's address to the Muse is as sophisticated as the narrative voices analytically and complexly present in *Ulysses*. It is this multiplication and splitting of narrative point-of-view which has so fascinated modern critics that they have used it to describe and judge the authoritarian and egocentric nature of Victorian novelists, especially George Eliot. Some artists have a greater imaginative range than others, as Coleridge and Keats recognised when they contrasted the egotistical sublime of Milton or Wordsworth with the protean powers of Shakespeare. But I do not believe a rhetorical multiplication of narrative voice implies a greater ability to slough off subjectivity: Joyce's proliferated voices are many, and created in an astonishing range of idiolect, but in some ways they are more restricted than Homer's, whose representation of women characters, for instance, has more variety than Joyce's.

Colin MacCabe[2] believes that Molly Bloom is a Penelope who attacks and subverts phallic fetishism, but though her man-made voice subverts conventional punctuation, syntax, and lexis, it does so in order to utter views of women congenial to many conventional men, including Joyce. It also draws on an old tradition of subversive female garrulousness which goes back to post-Homeric Greek poetry and drama, medieval and renaissance texts, Shakespeare and Dickens; it is probably Dickens' talkative women, free, wild, and irrational, who were present to Joyce's imagination when he wrote Molly's internal monologue. It is possible to see a certain feminist, even separatist, streak in Molly, but her last word is an acquiescence, and a speaking performance of love-in-memory; very different from the fidelity of Penelope. Molly's fidelity is largely – not wholly – retrospective and nostalgic. It is in grave danger of sentimentality, especially when we apply Joyce's own rigorous definition of the sentimentalist from *Ulysses*, as 'one who would enjoy without incurring the immense debtorship for a thing done'.[4] Molly's appreciation of Bloom is in the present, but love and sexual union are in the past, valorised by nostalgia. Her dissolving of ambiguous masculine pronouns in the final unambiguous 'he', for Bloom, is a *nostos* deeply gratifying to a husband's and a monogamist's ego. Penelope's fidelity has to be fought in the public world, is nearly lost, and she has every appearance, unlike Molly, of being willing to incur the debtorship for love.

Modern Greek scholarship has suggested[5] that the *Odyssey*, a product of shame culture, not guilt culture, was free from the association of the female with the instinctual and the irrational. Homer's women characters, I suggest, contrast most strongly with Joyce's in their rationality. Molly is earth-goddess, allowed some licence and licentiousness, but kept domestic, unlettered, unpolitical. Penelope's imagination is forced to be political: as her son grows beyond her governance, she recognises the maturing with rueful intelligence, sometimes submits, but never stops thinking and acting. She deals with her suitors, procrastinating, manipulating, preparing for compromise, acquiring goods. Homer creates a character most congenial to feminist readers. She does not transcend history, of course, and her submissions to Telemachus – however diplomatic – modify the assertion of her power. She has also – like Beatrice and Cleopatra – been sentimentalised by male critics: JW Mackail,[6] for instance, calls hers the portrait of 'a perfect wife', but this is the critic's patriarchal diminution, not Homer's representation of woman's knowledge and initiative.

Penelope is the most prominent among several powerful and rational women characters, who act energetically, diplomatically, and creatively in the public world. Unlike Joyce, Homer crosses easily from one sex to another. Bloom changes sex in a masochistic fantasy, and puts on the woman the better to be humiliated. But Homer's similes compare Odysseus to a woman and Penelope to a man without any sense of transgressing fixed bounds.[7] Homer's men and women characters are created equal. Arete is as powerful as Alcinous. Helen stage-manages the great scene of Trojan reminiscence when Telemachus visits Agamemnon's court. Athene rebukes Odysseus for pointless, habitual, and mechanised narrative when he goes on inventing fictitious autobiography after landing in Ithaca. And of course she guides, presides, instructs – and represents reason.

Molly's strength is her irrationality, which is attractive and spirited, though conventional in stereotype. But she is no Penelope. It is as if Joyce were least attentive to Homer's most impressive woman character, the person whose inner and outer life show most clearly Homer's distance from any association of woman with intuition and instinct. Penelope has both, but she has judgement and cunning too. She is the best dreamer of dreams in Homer, but also an analyst of dreams, and one whose imagery of the horn and ivory gates is invented as a warning – not unneeded by Odysseus – against glib interpretations of dreams. She has more inwardness than Odysseus, but shares his diplomatic skill. She too can compromise, wait, and deceive. She too is creative: if Odysseus makes a booby-trap in the shape of a wooden horse, she weaves a web which pretends to be a shroud but is a defensive weapon against male trespass and aggression. She is pained by isolation, but manages alone until Telemachus grows up and Odysseus comes home. She devises the archery test which Odysseus wins by the strength and skill of his archery. He builds the olive-rooted great bed, but she thinks of using it as an identity test. In the intimate feeling of her great nightingale lyric, and the subtle conversation with Odysseus on the eve of victory, she is presented not only as a character, but as a mind. Women characters are not stereotyped in Homer, and they are many and various. Joyce makes Molly incorporate Helen, Calypso, Circe and Penelope, in their most conventionally domestic and 'feminine' roles and aspects. Unlike Molly, Penelope is developed, changed, exposed. She is also perfectly matched with Odysseus: both are creative, clever, rationally acquisitive, and called by the same approving epithet, '*echephron*', which WB Stanford tells us means something like 'mind-restraining' or 'thought-controlling'.[8] She is strengthened, like Clarissa Harlowe, by being bonded with brilliant sisters. Her character is as opaque as Hamlet's. Does she recognise, intuitively guess, or not know that the slave is Odysseus? The lack of an answer testifies to Homer's vitality as a creator of women characters. Joyce uses more narrators than Homer, and Molly's narration is structurally more prominent than Penelope's; the one plays the third part in a triad, the other is one of many internal tellers of memories, dreams, lies, and truths. But narrative equality is a matter of quality not quantity.

After an appreciation of the two great love-scenes in the *Odyssey*, – one on the eve of victory where spouses speak like strangers, in conversation familiar, strange, and erotic; the other after the recognition and bed-test, where they pass the night in lovemaking and telling stories of a twenty-year parting – we may return to *Ulysses* with a heightened perception of its lyrical and erotic beauty. But its last episode of love and memory is in part warmed by old flames, unlike the fresh reunion in the *Odyssey*. Richard Ellmann lyrically wrote of Molly and Bloom 'In their dark bed at dead of night the summer sunlight shines'.[9] But they are separated in the present, and the woman wakes while the man sleeps. Penelope and Odysseus have a reunion of one night, and contemplate briefly their past losses, and those that lies ahead. Both Joyce and Homer join tenderness with toughness, but Homer's is the marriage of true minds.

Colin MacCabe says that the last action in the *Odyssey* is the drawing of the bow, the phallic assertion, but Penelope and Odysseus have some way to go after that act, both in the story and its projected future. In this respect the epic and the novel are alike. Both end in a form of closure, in homecoming, love, and sleep, but both look ahead, in Molly's fantasies, Bloom's fresh demands and breaks with routine, and Tiresias' prophecies of Odysseus' gentle death, and the second journey to Hades. Molly is a modern version of Penelope, a technically unfaithful wife, faithful in her fashion to a new unheroic Odysseus heroic in his fashion. But the sympathies of a modern reader are likely to find the Homeric woman the more politically congenial. Joyce seems to have been better able to match and rewrite Homer's eccentric, inventive, pacific hero, than his rational, politic, and creative heroine.

A more prominent narrator – in terms of narrative space and time – is Demodocus, the blind bard. He is an interesting anticipation of the nineteenth-century narrator, anonymous in his subdued identity. He is the professional teller within the tale, the court bard in Alcinous' kingdom. He is given a few particularising details. He has been gifted with blindness by the Muse, the better to see with the inward eye. (Another wounded artist, like Philoctetes). Odysseus observes him closely, and through that observation we see him being helped, we see his lyre hung up and brought to him, we see him sent a special piece of meat by Odysseus, and we hear his sung story of Troy. Demodocus moves Odysseus to tears, as he feels himself and his past relived in story. (Anticipating *Aeneas* and *Hamlet*). Demodocus also provides the professional standard for narration, to be invoked when Odysseus performs his share and shifts from listener to teller. It is to be supposed that he had a special interest for the chief, or last, author of the *Odyssey*, if he was indeed blind Homer. The blind bard is perhaps a replica of the poet and is in any case a portrait of an artist. He also carries a large share of the narrative burden of the epic, joined by the chief subdued anonymous narrator, the bard at Menelaus' court, and Odysseus. Where does he appear in *Ulysses*?

We might be tempted at first to say that he is Stephen Dedalus, the professional poet and story-teller within Joyce's novel. But apart from the arts of poetry, music, and narration, the two characters have nothing in common. Demodocus is one of the covert presences or ghosts in the novel. In Episode 8, 'The Lestrygonians', Leopold Bloom helps a blind man across the road. He is barely characterised, the emphasis being almost entirely placed on Bloom's sympathetic imagination, as he characteristically speculates about the man whose hand he touches, and then about blind men in general, remarking their compensatory musical gifts and then Bloomianly fantasising about a blind man's sexual life:

> Look at all the things they can learn to do. Read with their fingers. Tune pianos. Or we are surprised they have any brains. Why we think a deformed person or a hunchback clever if he says something we might say. Of course the other senses are more. Embroider. Plait baskets. People ought to help. Work basket I could buy Molly's birthday. Hates sewing. Might take an objection. Dark men they call them.

> Sense of smell must be stronger too. Smells on all sides bunched together. Each street different smell. Each person too. Then the spring, the summer: smells. Tastes. They say you can't taste wines with your eyes shut or a cold in the head. Also smoke in the dark they say get no pleasure.

> And with a woman, for instance. More shameless not seeing. That girl passing the Stewart institution, head in the air. Look at me. I have them all on. Must be strange not to see her. Kind of a form in his mind's eye. The voice temperature when he touches her with fingers must almost see the lines, the curves.

The structure and content of Bloom's storytelling is in direct opposition to that of his Homeric prototype, shy, reticent and private, but also outgoing, protean rather than personal. Odysseus was not impersonal; he had to invent fictitious identities, but his stories are truthtelling lies, all containing something of himself and his history, sometimes even including himself as a character in the fiction, as in the last story he tells Penelope, in his beggar's disguise. Bloom's story about the blind man, fuelled by curiosity and scraps of information from his wonderful rag-bag mind, characteristically ends with a retreat from empathy, 'somehow you can't cotton on to them someway', as the anonymous blind man disappears into the Dublin streets. He seems at first sight to be one of the many nonce characters that people those streets and this novel, like the carpet-whacking skivvy and the chemist, about whom Bloom's fancies curl, but the blind man is not quite a nonce character, though he never appears again, except in report. Bloom wonders if he is going to 'Levenson's dancing academy piano', as he sees him turn into Frederick Street, but the blind 'stripling' is actually going to the Ormond Hotel, and is mentioned by Miss Douce (in Episode 11, 'The Sirens') as having been in to tune their piano for the smoking concert: 'I never heard such an exquisite player' and 'The real classical, you know', 'And blind too, poor fellow. Not twenty I'm sure he was'. Simon Dedalus, who has brought up the subject by noticing that the piano has been moved, goes into the saloon, lifts the piano lid, tries the soft pedal, and strikes the tuning-fork left behind, to hear its pure soft buzzing throb and dying call. The identification of the piano-tuner with Demodocus is implicit, not explicit, and for some Joyce critics the identification, even if agreed, may seem trivial. (Charles Peake, for instance, regards even the Pluto/O'Connell parallel as insignificant).[10]

What I think important is Joyce's desire to record, however mutedly, significant details in Homer's text. Our reading of *Ulysses* may not be radically affected by observing such details but our sense of Joyce's respect for Homer certainly is. Here he reduces one of Homer's prime narrators to a minor character, but in an honouring and tender way. The echo of that forgotten tuning-fork is the distant echo of Demodocus' lyre. The blindness is something Joyce makes Bloom most thoroughly imagine, in that loving compassionate spirit which is especially concentrated in the anticannibalistic Episode 8, 'The Lestrygonians'. Odysseus is attentive and sympathetic to Demodocus. And if Homer was a blind bard especially responsive to blind bards, Joyce's own troubled eyesight brought him close to that sympathy. Demodocus is not metempsychosed into a narrator. He narrates nothing except the name of South Frederick Street, and is the passive object of narration. Demodocus was culturally too remote – and perhaps pathologically too close – to find an equivalent in Joyce's twentieth-century Dublin. Stephen's was the professional art matched by Bloom's Odyssean narrative proficiency. But Demodocus was not forgotten. The blind stripling, whose blind dreams Bloom significantly tries to imagine, shows Joyce's appreciation of an important character in 'the real classical' text, the inward-seeing visionary teller who is contrasted with the great extrovert keen-sighted archer. It would be surprising if Joyce did not respond to the subject of blindness in Homer, since this goes beyond the presentation of the bard. When Odysseus throws the discus further than his rivals, it is observed that his discus lay so far ahead that a blind man using touch alone would be able to indentify it. And there is the cruel and grotesque episode of the blinding of Polyphemus. Joyce transformed the heated stick with which Odysseus put out the Cyclops' eye into a cigar, as he told Stuart Gilbert, but blindness he dealt with most compassionately. And of course blind bards are part of Irish, as of Greek tradition.

Such details may not seem important in the structure of *Ulysses*, if we think of it as an isolated and hierarchically ordered novel. But if we hear its dialogue with the *Odyssey* then all transformations and revisions count. Joyce's novel contains a reading of Homer, as well as using certain Homeric episodes for structure and thematic permutation.

Demodocus is also interesting when we compare the narrators in the novels, shuttling from one to the other and back again. Joyce borrowed Penelope's web to designate art and growth. He also promoted his Penelope to be a primary narrator, perhaps inspired by the original Penelope's dreams, prayer, and narrations to Odysseus, though failing, as I think, to recapitulate her initiative, power, and controlling reason or *echephron*. When Joyce's critics admire the multiplicity of narration in *Ulysses* they tend to think of the primary sustained voice, but if we count not only the three primary narrators in the *Odyssey* – four if we count the Muse – and also the many internal narratives, like those of Helen, Menelaus, and Penelope, then Homer's variegation of voice must be admired also, as it probably was by the responsive Joyce, who repeated it, consciously or not.

III

Reflexive Forms

Joyce and Homer blend professional and non-professional narrative. Many of Homer's narrators are unprofessional, within the over-arching professional narrative of the epic narrator aided by the Muse: Nestor, Telemachus, Menelaus, Helen, Penelope, and of course Odysseus, expand, vary, and deepen narrative by truthful and fictitious reminiscence, autobiography and pseudo-autobiography, fantasy, dream, and hopeful projection. (These narratives are not pure but mixed with lyrical outburst and reflective commentary). In *Ulysses* there is no narrative continuity, voices being fragmented, dispersed, and varied, though some stability is given by the dominant and recurring narratives of Stephen, Bloom, and the conclusion of Molly. The professional voice is that of Stephen, who continues the portraiture of the artist, still a young man, but whose reverie is that of the creative mind off-duty. Stephen is not responsible for shaping the novel like Dickens' David Copperfield or Proust's Marcel, both narrating personally and professionally. The mix of professional and unprofessional narrative makes for pronounced generic self-consciousness. When the professionals, like Demodocus, speak, it is always in a context which draws attention to art and entertainment, but the amateurs too are often praised for telling a good tale – Helen by Menelaus, Odysseus by Eurycleia, for example – and sometimes expressly compared to the divine singers and tellers. But narrative is also seen as natural. The formulaic comment, introductory or conclusive, which so often announces, marks off, and professionalises, everyday narrative discourse, is never merely formulaic. When Menelaus congratulates Helen on her tactful story of the wooden horse, in which she played a Trojan part, his response is readable as irony and forgiveness. This Lacedaemonian drama of telling is softened and sweetened by the anodyne Helen politically puts in the wine, so that the past can be recalled without pain, but Homer subtly allows Menelaus a dignified rather than a dulled response. In Ithaca, when Eurycleia says that the disguised beggar is a spellbinding storyteller, as good as a divine minstrel, Penelope's eagerness to listen is provoked. And the listening loosens her tongue: she tells intimately as never before, breaking isolation and silence, relating her history, her emotional conflict, (she is torn like the nightingale spring) and her dreaming. Helen's anodyne is not only needed in Menelaus' hall, but reminds us of the pangs of telling and listening. These are experienced by Penelope, Telemachus, and Odysseus, whose anguished responses to story echo across the epic narrative to form a rhythm both regular and varied. Telemachus and Odysseus reveal their identity in the pain of finding personal life becoming public story, and Odysseus begins a long line of distressed tellers, including Aeneas, the Ghost in *Hamlet*, Egeon in *The Comedy of Errors*, and Othello. He recalls his past in the hall of King Alcinous, changing from agonised listener to agonised teller. Unlike the reluctant Aeneas, whose story is wrung from him by Dido, Odysseus brings the burden of narrative on himself. He thanks Demodocus for his narrative, with a gift of boar-chine, a compliment to the Muse-instructed and Muse-loved profession of bards, and the praise of Demodocus' tale of the Achaeans, told as if he 'had been with them' or had 'heard the story from one who was'. Then he asks for the story of his wooden horse, and this most personal episode, cunningly compressed and summarised at the end of Episode IX, 'The Phaeacian Games', makes him break down and weep like a woman weeping for her dead husband. (The brief narrative simile itself, though generalised, lays fresh emphasis on the theme of Troy). The name-evader is then asked for his name, and makes the famous complaint about having troubles probed, and grief intensified, by remembrance of time past, which introduces the narrative core of this epic, his fabulous adventures. He gives his name and tells the truth instead of the wonderful half-truths in which he has become expert. His telling occupies Books IX to XIII (during which time Telemachus is still in Lacedaemon) and ends by declining to repeat the story of his time with Calypso, which he has already told because it could be told without revealing his identity. There is a satisfying rounding-off, and a reminder of the narrative's own blend of truths and fictions. In oral narration such reflexive

emphasis must have had its own charm and irony, just as the variation of speaker and the stress on affective response would draw
attention to dramatic elocution and impersonation, and release
opportunity for virtuoso performance.

What seems a much greater variation of narrative idiolect in
the novel is partly a result of its undramatic genre, that of the
read text, which needs such variety. This granted, Joyce's shifts of
voice are not much more varied than Homer's. Stephen's linguistic
self-consciousness alerts the reader to the narrative and linguistic
creativity of his fellows, not only in Bloom and Molly, the other
primary narrators, but also in the many locally coloured voices of
diurnal and nocturnal telling, memory and dream, and the literary
modes of Gerty's girlie magazine style, or the quick grand tour of
literary history in Episode 14, 'The Oxen of the Sun'. These
variations also remind us that Homer's composite or conglomerate
text – whatever the constructive or deconstructive theory of
authorship – draw on a great variety of sources, and mix the
modes and materials of history, realistic story, folklore and legend.
Joyce is engaging in a dialogue with Homer, but Homer's own
intertexuality – which Greek scholars have long been analysing and
debating – is as impressive. The mixing of modes, and the traces
of earlier texts, also increase the artistic self-consciousness of the
text.

Assuming the conclusions of recent Greek scholars about
chronology, we can compare the relationship of the *Odyssey* and
Ulysses to their author's earlier works. Self-reference is one of the
most interesting and moving forms of intertextuality and reflexiveness. When Shakespeare's most defenceless and naive fool, in
King Lear, echoes the song of his most rational and sophisticated
fool, in *Twelfth Night*, with 'He who has and a little tiny wit', it is
not only a fine theatrical in-joke but pierces the tragic storm to
another genre, another mood, another fiction, and another performance. We feel the pressure of genial presence and confidence, as
well as a discord or interruption. Something like this must have
struck listeners to the *Odyssey* as they heard echoes, recalls, and
revisions of the *Iliad*. We may be alerted to such effects by Joyce's
habitual self-echo, or become more aware of self-echo in Joyce if

we have responded to it in Homer.

In Homer the pressure of the *Iliad* is made self-conscious within the characters' memories, which join the two epics. Odysseus, Helen, and Menelaus recall their past and recall Troy to recall the earlier story. (If the *Iliad* were written last, the echoes would have been planted, in retrospect, as they are in Shakespeare's English history plays, where chronological order of event does not correspond with chronological order of composition). Ghosts from the *Iliad* haunt the memories of characters and audience (or readers). And the ghosts of Dubliners haunt *Ulysses*. Emily Sinico's death is remembered, and the mystery man in the mackintosh may be Mr Duffy. Ignatius Gallaher and Lenehan, Hynes and Gabriel Conroy turn up again, individualising the Dublin crowd in streets and bars, giving faces a special visibility, shifting the reader's memory back to the earlier text, and confidently asserting text and author. Joyce's *Iliad* is *Dubliners*, which has no epic hero, and *A Portrait of the Artist as a Young Man*. Because no one in *Ulysses* has an interiorised and passionate memory of *Dubliners*, as Stephen has of *A Portrait of the Artist as a Young Man*, the reader's memory must work more excitedly on its own. Just as it may not greatly alter a sense of the novel 'as a whole' to spot the King of Hades or the blind bard in their Dublin dress, so it may make little difference to some readers whether they spot Lenehan or not. But when a Dubliner's presence is suddenly evoked it erodes the firmness and solidity of the novel's world. Doors open out of the text into other texts. We may start wondering how much of their earlier history, if any, these revived characters bring with them. When Thackeray resurrects characters from earlier novels, as he loves to do, it is always with some sense of their movement in time, their ageing, growth, and degeneration. With Joyce the characters are produced less conspicuously and resonantly, but the self-consciousness of text, for author and reader, is similar. We might argue that the history of Dublin, like Thackeray's English history, is being advanced, so that readers may feel the sense of reality enhanced as these once major characters move into mere minor characterhood. And I suppose as with so much self-reference – Homeric, Shakespearean,

Joycean or Beckettean – the effect is to sharpen our sense of the reality of fiction and the fiction of reality. Life-continuities are here, but they are textual references too. They tease and test the reader's knowledge, goad and persuade the reader into re-reading, in comic self-promotion. If we see this serious and amusing self-advertisement we may recognise that Joyce is acting as public relations person for Homer too.

IIII

Surfaces and Objects

Joyce loved to find equivalent objects for the things in Homer, like the cigar, the lemon soap, and the kidney. He is the kind of artist who liked to set himself superfluous tasks, or tasks which may seem superfluous or arbitrary to organicist critics unable to admit the fun of playing games and asking riddles within a visionary fiction. Joyce used fiction as a means of exploring moral, physical, and historical consciousness, but along with such grand aims come lots of little ones too. Writing to or against a Homeric pattern is rather like writing a poem to a strict form. It introduces an external or arbitrary element, which may turn out to be less arbitrary than it seemed. Who knows at what stage Shakespeare consciously decided to write Sonnet 20, the sonnet most concerned with gender and the physiology of sex, entirely in feminine rhymes? Thousands of readers must have read the poem without noticing the relation of theme to rhyme-scheme, but for the poet, and the reader who spots this, it makes a difference. Joyce may have scattered sacred and profane objects through his fiction as many novelists have done, though it seems to me that the object-world of *Ulysses* is more solidly specified, more expressive and more animated than in the previous stories and novels. It may be Homeric influence, as well as a desire to make his readers hunt the slipper, which shaped his sense of things. He knew that Stuart Gilbert needed to be told that the heated olive-branch was transformed into a cigar. When we notice things for ourselves, or

even with the help of critics, there is an amused sense of – what?
– completing a bit of jigsaw, recognising adroitness and humour,
savouring incongruity and difference, or enjoying a perfected
match. Joyce might have given Molly her chamber-pot and other
items of bedroom furniture with having read in Episode IV,
'Menelaus and Helen', about Helen's marvellous accessory furnish-
ing, described in elaborate detail when she arrives on the scene, a
famous beauty in a rich setting. She comes from her perfumed
room, looking 'like Artemis with her golden distaff' (another
usefully repetitive simile), and she has carried in for her a comfortable chair, a soft wool rug, and the silver work-box 'a gift from
Alcandre, wife of Polybius, who lived in Egyptian Thebes, where
the houses are furnished in the most sumptuous fashion'. There
follows a brief inventory of other gifts given by Polybius to
Menelaus, and by his wife to Helen, bringing us back to the scene
with one of these, a basket on castors, silver with a rim of gold. It
is full of yarn and Helen's spindle with deep blue wool is laid on
it. The things are of course expressive (as Madame Merle says to
Isabel Archer in *The Portrait of a Lady*), socially and psychically,
they are also characteristic of the Homeric interest in objects,
which has in its turn created a scholarly archaeological and historical interest in epic things. This solidity of specification may be
something Joyce learnt or caught from Homer, a sense of the history of things. Things are resonant as well as dramatically vivid
props and properties: the dress Helen gives to Telemachus, the
rich gifts the prudent Penelope solicits from the suitors, as cover,
precaution, and gain, the treasures accumulated in war or on visits,
the furniture and food, all play a complex part in the story. They
also respond to each other, like the trees so important in
Odysseus' story, the weaving of Helen, Circe, and Penelope, the
musical instruments, the weapons of war. Joyce, like Homer,
creates a world full of solid phenomena and shadowy noumena.
Both heroes inhabit inner worlds and underworlds, both heroines
dream, prophesy, and qualify their fantasies with common or
uncommon sense. Both texts are fantastic and realistic. The surface
of objects, substantial, characteristic, expressive, and historicised, is
assertive. It is not just a realistic feature: Bloom's nightmare and

comic erotic fantasy, Circe's house, Penelope's dream and Molly's projects, Bloom's visions of his son, Odysseus' invocation of the dead, are all made unnervingly solid by their accessory details.

Joyce is also having fun, transubstantiating Homer's things in his modern Dublin. Bloom's appetite for the inner organs pleasantly revives meals and rituals from the *Odyssey*, and the parallel is clinched when the breakfast kidney is burnt but deliciously palatable. Helen's knowledge of drugs finds its parallel in a real Dublin chemist's shop, placed in the novel with the archaeological loving care with which writers of epics used swords, shields, bows, staffs, and ships with a legendary or historical existence outside the text. The researches of Joycean scholarship into people and places offers a parallel to Greek scholarship in archaeological and topographical zeal, like no other act of literary and historical investigation, deriving from Joyce's Homeric scholarship, conscious and intuitive.

An object in Homer which had fascinated me in itself and because of its apparent absence from *Ulysses* is the Phaeacian ship which takes Ulysses back to Ithaca after his rescue by Nausicaa and his entertainment by Alcinous and Arete. There are several features of this ship which makes it play a significant part in the story. It is a marvellous piece of technology: Alcinous tells Odysseus that the Phaeacian ships need no steersmen or oars, like other craft, but know by instinct what the crew wants, and also know all cities and lands, so that they can travel over expanses of ocean, and through mists, without danger, ('Episode III, The Phaeacian Games'). Its voyage, when it takes place, is amazing and dreamlike: Odysseus is lulled to sleep as soon as 'the blades' touch the water, and in spite of the inconsistency of these blades, and a latter reference to rowing, the ship, proceeds as Alcinous had described, and speeds to Ithaca where the crew land the still sleeping Odysseus and his treasure. It is the strangest of the many strange sea-voyages in the *Odyssey*. Its magic is not only magic, but a scientific prophecy. But the swift ship which takes Odysseus home never returns to its home. It is turned to rock by the wrath of Odysseus' enemy, Poseidon, and when the Phaeacians see the petrified ship, Alcinous remembers an old prophecy and they decide to give up their habits of hospitable convoy. Magic, technology, a hero's homecoming, stony metamorphosis. It seemed strange that Joyce had not launched the ship in his Greek-Irish island story. There was a candidate, but the ship which keeps on recurring, the Rosevean in no way corresponded. (Charles Peake observes its combination of good and bad, and says it suggests homing).[11]

In the Joyce school held in Dublin in 1988 my attention was drawn by John Ryan[12] to the original Rosevean, a wooden ship which used to sail from Bristol to Dublin with a cargo of bricks. As so often, Joyce was prompted by coincidence to find an object which exactly matched his source and was part of Dublin (and English) history and geography. The brick-bearing ship was there in the text – distractingly and slyly? – tucked away at the close of Episode 16, 'The Wandering Rocks', to be noticed by Stuart Gilbert as 'a miniature Argo'. But its cargo is not only of Argonauts, or of wandering rocks, but also of Poseidon's petrifaction, though like many of Joyce's objects it does heavy duty:

> Elijah, skiff, crumpled throwaway, sailed eastward by flanks of ships and trawlers, amid an archipelago of corks, beyond new Wapping Street past Benson's ferry, and by the threemasted schooner *Rosevean* from Bridgwater with bricks.

Another correspondence which must have been the product of imaginative meditation, not accident, is that of the two marriage beds. Amongst the influential and recurring objects in both novels is a bed endowed with power, presence, and history.

The correspondence of the beds has a remarkable equality about it. Joyce wanted to revive and revise Homer's great deep-rooted bed, but his own recreation is entirely orginal. Adding his bed to Homer's rehistoricises and re-mythologises the object. And there is a special comedy about the differences, as with the moly-soap and the burnt-kidney offering. No bed is as strongly and per-manently made as the marriage-bed which Odysseus built. It is one of his great machines, like the wooden horse. It is more than a piece of furniture, its fertility drawing on the natural depth and vitality of the olive tree. Odysseus uses an olive-branch to kill the Cyclops, but from his point of view it is of course a restoring and life-giving thing. The bed is also a symbol of mutuality, as a marriage-bed, as a shared secret, as a sign and emblem of fruitful love and fidelity, and as a created object, inventive and wonderfully functional. Penelope participates in its creativity, not just passively but by using it for a test of identity. Just as she invents the devices of the web and the archery-test, so she transforms this image of their privacy and creativity, in another assertion of man's and woman's equal art and intelligence. And humour. The disguised beggar Odysseus made great play about liking to sleep rough – of course he often does, though with at least three soft beds – and when Penelope suggests that he should sleep in their bed, brought outside the room, it is a provoking comic signal for the right man. The bed-test is recalled when Odysseus goes to see his father, Laertes, and proves his identity, after the customary retarding yarn-spinning, by identifying the vine and olive trees he was given in his youth. Trees are important for him; the branch which helped him escape from Scylla and Charybdis was also an olive.[13]

No such creative carpentry has gone into the making of Molly Bloom's soft and jingly bed, but it has its magic too. It compounds the beds of Calypso and Circe as well as the stable marriage bed. Its metallic music jigs through the novel, even sounding 'jig-a-jig' in nighttown. The sound of its loose brass quoits is there as Molly first appears, turning over with a warm heavy sigh, and making Bloom recall the bed's history: her father bought it at an auction – 'Hard as nails at a bargain, old Tweedy' and it has come all the way from Gibraltar to Dublin, as travelled as Odysseus. In her soliloquy, Molly extends the bed's history, remembering that it may have been bought from Lord Nolan, and bringing in the new details of Boylan's spunk and Bloom at the bottom of the bed. (Bloom's position is both kinky and Homeric). For a moment she longs for a bed to herself, but when she gets out and then returns to the old lumpy jingly bed, she says 'I love my bed'. Her details are domestic particulars, but the bed has been the grand theatre of action in the previous section: 'Going to dark bed there was a square round Sinbad the sailor's roc auk's egg in the night of the bed of all the auks . . . ? Bloom's entry is ritualised in a precise description of how he 'removed a pillow from the head to the foot of the bed, prepared the bedlinen accordingly and entered the bed'. The answer to the catechism's question 'How'? mythologises the bed:

> With circumspection, as invariably when entering an abode (his own or not his own): with solicitude, the snakespiral springs of the mattress being old, the brass quoits and pendent viper radii loose and tremulous under stress and strain: prudently, as entering a lair or ambush of lust or adder: lightly, the less to disturb: reverently, the bed of conception and of birth, of consummation of marriage and of breach of marriage, of sleep and of death.

The slowed account makes an appropriate register for the imitation of Homer. In the *Odyssey* a careful description presents the making of the bed, related by Odysseus in a form of slow-motion and circumstantial description which is apt for the insistence of maker and husband. Joyce is writing a cold catechism, but it bears the traces of his acquaintance with Homer's animated narration:

> Who, if you please, has moved my bed elsewhere? Short of a miracle, it would be hard even for a skilled workman to shift it somewhere else, and the strongest young fellow alive would have a job to budge it. For a great secret went into the making of that complicated bed; and it was my work and mine alone. Inside the court there was a long-leaved olive-tree, which had grown to full height with a stem as thick as a pillar. Round this I built my room of close-set stone-work, and when that was finished, I roofed it over thoroughly, and put in solid, neat fitted, double door. Next I lopped all the twigs off the olive, trimmed the stem from the root up, rounded it smoothly and carefully with my adze and trued it to the line, to make my bedpost. This I drilled through where necessary, and used as a basis for the bed itself, which I worked away at till that too was done, when I finished it off with an inlay of gold, silver, and ivory, and fixed a set of purple straps

across the frame. (Episode XXIII, 'Odysseus and Penelope').

The rebuilding of this sacred object is one of the most elaborate feats in Joyce's reading and rewriting of Homer.

V

The subject can be illustrated, not exhausted. The sun that rises, moves and sets in Homer, proceeds in less regulated description through Bloom's one day. Comparing the suns, we realise the audacity with which Joyce compressed epic time-span into less than twenty-four hours. But as so often, to contrast is to compare. Homer's art is a feat of compression too, eschewing linearity, depending on the natural-seeming impetus of memory, in the epic art of Demodocus and the natural art of Odysseus. And *Ulysses* is a long novel. The ending of the *Odyssey* is open – to a renewal of action after the momentary terminus of the bed, with night prolonged to Athene for love-making and telling, and to the future ordeals and death of Odysseus in the future prophesied by Tiresias. Richard Ellmann has called *Ulysses* 'the most concluded book ever written',[14] and this is so, but there are future projections in the reported conversation of husband and wife, and in the monologue of Molly. The classical poem – perhaps because its last section,[15] the Second Nekyie, was an addition – is less rounded-off and closed than the modernist novel, but both share an inclination to prolong events beyond an ending and to imagine a future as they have depended on imagining a past.

NOTES

1 The text used for quotations from *The Odyssey* is the translation by EV Rieu (Harmondsworth: Penguin Books, 1972).

2 Colin MacCabe, *James Joyce and the Revolution of the Word* (London: MacMillan, 1978).

3 See my essay, 'The Talkative Woman in Shakespeare, Dickens and George Eliot', to be published in *Problems with Feminist Criticism*, ed. Sally Minogue (London: Routledge and Kegan Paul).

4 The text used for quotations from *Ulysses* is the Penguin edition (Harmondsworth, Penguin Books in association with The Bodley Head: London, 1969).

5 See ER Dodds, *The Greeks and the Irrational* (California: UC Press, 1951) and Charles H Taylor Jr, 'Odysseus, The Inner Man', in *Homer's Odyssey; A Critical Handbook*, ed. Conny Nelson (California: Wadsworth Publishing, 1969).

6 John Murray, 'Penelope in the *Odyssey*, in *Classical Studies*, (London 1925).

7 See Book VIII, 'The Phaeacian Games', and Book XIX, 'Eurycleia Recognises Odysseus'.

8 'Athene's Odysseus; The Man of Action', in *Homer's Odyssey, A Critical Handbook*, ed. cit.

9 *Ulysses on the Liffey*, (London: Faber and Faber, 1972).

10 *James Joyce: The Citizen and the Artist*, (London: Edward Arnold, 1977).

11 Op. cit.

12 Unpublished lecture.

13 See George E Dimock Jr, 'The Name of Odysseus', in *The Hudson Review* (Vol IX, No 1, Spring 1965).

14 See especially Stuart Gilbert, *James Joyce's Ulysses* (Harmondsworth: Penguin Books, 1963) and Richard Ellmann, *The Consciousness of Joyce* (London: Faber and Faber, 1977).

15 Preface to *Ulysses: The Student Edition* (Harmondsworth: Penguin Books, 1986).

THE GHOSTS
OF ULYSSES

Maud Ellman
The Richard Ellmann Memorial Address.

The Sheeted Mirror

In the recent film *Ghost Dance*, directed by Ken MacMullen, Jacques Derrida is interviewed by an ethereal young woman who asks him if he believes in ghosts. 'That's a hard question', he smiles, 'because, you see, I *am* a ghost'.[1] Eerily, this reply turned out to be prophetic, not for Derrida, who is no deader than the rest of us, but for the questioner herself, who died before the movie was released and her image was set loose to haunt the screen. In the film, however, the living man is just as insubstantial as his dead inquisitor, for both have been dispatched into the afterlife, translated into bodiless projections. Through the photographic image we survive the grave but also die before our death, disenfleshed before our hearts have ceased to beat. To be or not to be is no longer the question.

What could be blinder than refusing to believe in ghosts? Our ghost-free civilisation depends upon the myth that presence is superior to absence, and that absence is a lack of presence rather than an independent power. Although most of us have grown embarrassed by racism, sexism, homophobia, and all the other violent exclusions which reveal the sacrificial logic of the modern state, we persevere in *vivocentrism*, the fiercest and perhaps the founding bigotry of all: the illusion that the living may eradicate the dead through burial, cremation, and forgetfulness. It is to protect the living from the dead that our culture insists upon their opposition, policing those extravagant and erring spirits who refuse to be confined to either realm.

Shakespeare, however, knew better than to underestimate the vigour of the dead, or the irrepressible activities of emptiness. The very task of poetry, he said, was to give to airy nothing a local habitation and a name; thus curtailing its insidious meanderings. In Shakespeare's drama, it is usually women who are obliged to speak and represent the truth of nothing: just as Molly Bloom becomes the prophet of 'omission' in Penelope.[2] Gertrude, for example, sees nothing and hears nothing when Hamlet thinks he sees his father's ghost, who being cuckolded, dethroned and dead is three times nothing.[3] Ophelia, on the other hand, professes to think nothing: 'a fair thought to lie between maids' legs', Hamlet bawdily retorts, in an unconvincing effort to relegate the nothing that patrols the night to its local habitation as castration (III ii 116-17). And of course there is Cordelia, who knows that she can only meet her father's absolute demand for love by yielding him the nothing of desire: 'Nothing, my lord'.[4] However, Lear is not content with *having* nothing unless he can *be* nothing, too: and his daughter's answer guides him through his odyssey of destitution towards a vision of the rapture of unbeing.

This 'nothing', therefore, cannot be confined to women, although it circumambulates between the injured daughter and the guilty queen, because it always seems to come to rest in the ghostly figure of the father. 'The King is a thing . . . Of nothing', Hamlet says (IV iii 27-9). It is significant that he could be referring either to the king that's dead or to the king of shreds and patches who has seized his throne, because he knows that both are nothing, spectre and impostor (I i 44; III iv 103). The king is a thing of nothing. How can you murder nothing? This is the question that paralyses Hamlet, who fears moreover that by killing nothing he would be obliged to take its place, to be *and* not to be, by playing father. The true father, in Stephen Dedalus' words, is necessarily a 'ghost by absence' or a 'ghost by death', and those who take his role are always player kings. This is why Hamlet exults in the success of the play-within-a-play, as if he had already murdered Claudius by staging it: for he can only conquer theatre with more theatre, compelled to reenact the uncorroborable death which institutes the order of paternity.[5]

Nora Joyce once hinted that Shakespeare was the last poetic father that Joyce had still to murder: 'Ah, there's only one man he's got to get the better of now, and that's that Shakespeare!'[6] But because Joyce knew that language is a graveyard of quotations, he never tried to silence Shakespeare's ghost: instead he drew his 'lean unlovely English' into the echo-chamber of his prose, where all the ghosts of the tradition converse bone to bone (*U* 162: 471-2). This prose, Derrida complains, is 'of such plot and scope that henceforth you have only one way out: *being in memory of him* . . . Can one pardon this hypermnesia which *a priori* indebts you, and in advance inscribes you in the book you are reading?'[7] While Harold Bloom, argues that 'strong poets' struggle to destroy their antecedents, Joyce makes ghosts of his descendents too; and whereas the Romantics came too late, Joyce comes too soon.[8] 'He's read us all, and pillaged us, that guy', Derrida continues in his essay, 'Two Words for Joyce'. When I was reading this essay, however, I suddenly discovered my own name inscribed in Derrida's ghostridden text, and realised with another start that it was not addressed to me but to my father. 'Ellmann', he writes, has quoted many other writers who confess to the malaise of being written in advance by Joyce's texts.[9]

On this occasion I am conscious of a double malaise, for not only must I speak as Joyce's ghost but also as the phantom of my father, disappearing into two preemptive memories. Of course, I find my name lying in ambush in almost every critical account of Joyce, and yet that name is always destined elsewhere, to my father: and now that he is dead it only seems to come into its own, since it was always fated to become his sepulchre, and mine.

Here, speaking in his place and in his name, I taste the sublime fraudulence of Stephen Dedalus' dream of being author and begetter of his father. What holds him back, however, is the intuition that the father's name entails his death. The name survives its owner and for this reason it foreshadows his extinction in the very moment that it calls him into being. In *Ulysses*, Corny Kelleher identifies Bloom's father's name, Virag, as 'the father's name that poisoned himself': and the ambiguity of this locution unwittingly implies that the father was poisoned by his name.[10] In *Hamlet*, Rosencrantz and Guildenstern meet their death by means of the letters that Hamlet seals with his 'father's signet', suggesting that the father's name entails the death of anyone who bears its baneful signature. Indeed, the name could be regarded as the poison gift which is poured into the porches of the ear at birth, conferring ghostdom on the subject it identifies. To sign one's name, moreover, is to manufacture one's own ghost, one's own extravagant and erring spirit: for writing may be iterated anywhere, by anyone, independent of the life of its creator.[11] Thus when Stephen asks, 'What is a ghost', he could be wiser to inquire if anyone, or anything, is not a ghost, because the living are already mostly dead, dispersed among the names and images they leave behind to haunt succeeding generations (*U* 154: 147).

For Stephen, as for Hamlet, to ask 'what is a ghost?' is also to demand 'What is a father?' These unanswerable questions have beset the stage ever since Oedipus assumed the onus of the Theban regicide. To understand what Joyce means by ghosts, therefore, it is necessary to explore the echoes of the word itself and the adventures of the ghosts of Oedipus and Hamlet.

The Theatre of the Dead

What is a ghost? Stephen's own answer to his question is curiously undefinitive. A ghost, he says, is 'One who has faded into impalpability through death, through asbsence, through change of manners' (*U* 154: 147-9). Stephen is well aware that one can be transformed into a ghost without the bother of an actual demise, for every absence is a dress rehearsal of one's death, and even a change of manners may precipitate one's obsolescence. Odysseus, for instance, visited the Phaiakians in disguise and heard his own adventures from the mouths of strangers; thus learning that his legends had already usurped his life and reduced him to the phantom of his name. As Tennyson's Ulysses says, 'I am become a name', as if he had become a ghost before his time. Indeed, the name is the ghost bequeathed to each of us at birth, insofar as it prolongs our subjectivity beyond our death. Accordingly, Stephen's task in *Ulysses* is to reduce his father to a ghost in order to unleash the symbolic power of his name.

In *Totem and Taboo*, Freud argues that ghosts are compromise-formations which embody both reverence and horror towards the dead. He says that primitive societies first acknowledged death when they invented ghosts, yet this is also when they first denied it by asserting that the dead return.[12] The ghost, then, could be seen as the first pure symbol in that it bespeaks the absence rather than the presence of its referent; just as language recreates its objects in their absence, both affirming and denying their propensity to disappear. In this sense, words are the ghosts of things, their chattering afterlife. The very word 'ghost' seems to be marked by the disavowal of mortality, since it can either mean the spark of life or the disembodied image of the dead. To 'give up the ghost', for instance, is to lose one's life but also to release one's deadly emanation. Ghosts are almost always hungry, and they are usually angry too, for 'ghost', as the *OED* informs us, derives from the Teutonic word for 'fury'. A 'ghost' in optics is a bright spot, like a livid mole, produced by the reflection of a lens. It is, in other words, a mark of mediation, and to disbelieve in ghosts is to be duped by the illusion of transparency. Thus people who see ghosts, like Hamlet or Macbeth, know better than to overlook the fictive infrastructure of the visible.

In theatrical slang, 'the ghost walks' means that the treasury is full and that the wages will be paid. That this spirit, unappeased and peregrine, should represent the actors' very livelihood suggests a bond between the theatre and the resurrection of the dead, a bond affirmed in the dramatic chapters of *Ulysses*. For *Ulysses* is a book about mourning: about the death of love and its return as fury: about the ghosts who vampirise the ego like the famished spectres of the underworld. In 'Mourning and Melancholia', Freud describes how the ego incorporates the objects that it mourns in order to preserve them from oblivion, and populates itself with phantoms. But the object, once instated, feeds upon the ego until the latter is 'totally impoverished'. Mourning, therefore, is the struggle to release the ego from the very objects it is trying to embalm.[13] Whenever this struggle comes to a climax in *Ulysses*, the stage invades the narrative, and words give way to figures, thought to reenactment. In Scylla and Charybdis, for example, *Hamlet* provides the stage where Stephen hallucinates his parricide, for he disposes of his living father through the figure of the murdered king. If his living father is dead, however, his dead mother is very much alive, demonically vital. It is in Circe, the theatre of the dream, that he banishes her ghoulish spectre. Two theatres, then, the first for parricide, the last for matricide. Yet in the enclosed world of the stage there is no room for the true death: as the Greeks acknowledged by restricting murder to the wings and purging the theatre of event. In the theatres of *Ulysses*, similarly, love no longer touches and death no longer stings, for nothing real *takes place*, and every actor is the dummy of blind ventriloquism. But in another sense death *is* theatre, for it is always represented, never *lived*: and the drama in its turn could be regarded as the art of vicarious unbeing.[14]

What *is* the theatre, that ghosts should find it so enticing? In particular, why should the theatre conjure up *parental* ghosts? André Green suggests that in the family the child witnesses the daily drama of his parents' romance, and it is in the theatre that he rediscovers the fascination of spectatorship. The stillness of the audience recalls the speechless passivity of infancy, while the darkness recreates the state of sleep, where the unheeded wishes of the day return in the dramatics of the mind.[15] For the dream is the theatre of desire.[16] Freud argues that in dreams desires are performed rather than thought: words become deeds, fears become monsters. This is what happens in Circe, the dream theatre of *Ulysses*, which stages the apocalypse of Bloom's unconscious: for his desires are replaced by their embodiments, and his ego is dispersed among the ghosts of its libidinal positions. When he becomes a woman, for example, we know that he has longed for subjugation; when he creates Bloomusalem, we know that he has also lusted after power; and when he is accused of a dizzying spectrum of perversions, we know that his desires speak in his accusers' tongues, together with the added frisson of chastisement. According to Yeats, such dreams arise because 'the passions, when . . . they cannot find fulfilment, become vision'.[17] In the visionary stage of Circe, unconscious impulses are acted out, theatralised; and the unspeakable erupts in a whirlwind of phantasmagoria.

So ghosts have an affinity to theatre, as theatre has to dream, for each in different ways embodies words as visions. Hegel argues that drama consists of picture-thoughts which take the place of verbal narrative, just as pictures take the place of wishes in a dream.[18] Similarly, ghosts are the visions which arise when words have failed to purge the agony of loss. Moreover, a theatrical performance is a text incarnate which embodies written words in living voices. As Artaud has suggested, the word is made flesh and the dead letter is restored to life, resurrected from the mortuary of the alphabet.[19] To perform a play is therefore to revive the dead, since every actor is the phantom of a script, as each performance is the afterlife of writing.

Drama originates in ritual, and for this reason it preserves the magical power to *present* rather than *explain*. In the immediacy of the theatre, representation masquerades as presence, afterwards as now. As Hegel says, 'the language ceases to be narrative because it enters into the content', and the 'hero is himself the speaker', rather than the object of the speech.[20] Lévi-Strauss, however, criticises ritual as a regression, contrasting it to the creative alterity of myth. In the final volume of *Mythologiques*, he argues that myth is superior to ritual because it is 'essentially transformative', a narrative modified by each retelling. Ritual, by contrast, denies difference, surrendering the metamorphic power of the myth to the stupefying incandescence of the spectacle. According to Lévi-Strauss, ritual is a futile attempt 'to re-establish the unbrokenness of a reality dismantled by the schematism which mythic speculation has substituted for it'.[21] Rituals *act out* what myths *remember*: and

Lévi-Strauss agrees with Freud that psychic maturity depends upon converting reenactment into memory.[22] Artaud, on the contrary, celebrates the specious immediacy of the theatre as revolutionary rather than regressive. 'If theatre is as bloody and inhuman as dreams', he writes, 'it is . . . to demonstrate and to confirm in us beyond all forgetting the idea of a perpetual conflict, and of a spasm where life is cut through at every moment; where the whole of creation rises up against our state as finished beings'.[23] This is the kind of theatre that Joyce creates in Circe, where he exploits the regressive elements of ritual but only to undo the perilous coherence of the daytime self by unleashing the nightmare of its history. Here the barrier of the unrepeatable is broken and the past erupts into the present in the form of ghosts, dismantling discourse in a carnival of secular and sacred rites.[24]

In Scylla and Charybdis, however, Stephen seems to be defending Lévi-Strauss, becaue he uses 'dialectic', the technique of the chapter, to hold the world of ritual at bay.[25] But the style of the prose constantly breaks out of his control, making *scenes* as fast as he makes *sense*, as if the theatre were subverting the linear progression of the narrative, transfixing it with spectacle and incantation. Lacan, moreover, argues that it is dangerous to deny the realm of ritual because it irritates the dead out of their graves. Ghosts, he says, arise out of 'the gap left by the omission of a significant rite'.[26] The ghost of Hamlet's father, for example, rises from the grave 'unhousel'd, disappointed, unanel'd', because he died without receiving the last rites (I v 77). Stephen, on the other hand, refused to perform the ritual that would have kept his mother quiet in her tomb. As Mulligan mocks, ' – You could have knelt down, damn it, Kinch, when your dying mother asked you . . . to think of your mother begging you with her last breath to kneel down and pray for her. And you refused. There is something sinister in you . . . ' (*U* 5: 91-4). In the place of this omitted rite, this unsaid prayer, the ghost of Stephen's mother rises to demand her obsequies in Circe; and she brings with her the world of ritual, the denigrated principle of reenactment which Stephen has attempted to subdue with dialectic.

We shall return to Circe later: but because it is the father's ghost, rather than the mother's, who traditionally haunts the Western stage, it is important to examine the motif of parricide in *Oedipus* and Freud.

The Art of Parricide

Freud chose Oedipus as the archetype of the unconscious because he murdered his father and married his mother, but it is also his theatricality that implicates him in the realm of dreams. Moreover, Freud likened the action of the play to the process of a psychoanalysis, arguing that both consist of 'nothing other than the process of revealing'. For it is not the crimes themselves that *Oedipus* enacts but the tragic consequences of interpretation (SE IV 262). Freud first remarked upon the riveting power of the *play* in 1897, some thirteen years before he named the *complex* after Oedipus. But is is in *The Interpretation of Dreams* (1900 [1899]) that he first declared the universal application of the tragedy.

Here, as elsewhere in his writings, Freud yokes Oedipus with Hamlet, claiming that the difference between the plays marks 'the secular advance of repression in the emotional life of mankind' (SE IV 264). 'In the *Oedipus*', he argues, 'the child's wishful phantasy . . . is brought into the open and realized as it would be in a dream' (264). This means that Oedipus is the only man in history without an Oedipus complex, as Cynthia Chase has pointed out, because he fulfills his murderous incestuous desires rather than repressing them.[27] By contrast, Hamlet's wishes have gone underground, and we discern them only in the things he cannot do, rather than the things he does. Hamlet, Freud argues, is an 'hysteric' unable to take vengeance on Claudius who having killed his father and seduced his mother has acted out his own repressed desires.[28] Each of us was once a 'budding Oedipus', but having blinded ourselves to our unconscious fantasies we have grown up into hesitating Hamlets instead.

Freud points out that *Hamlet* was written soon after the death of Shakespeare's father: and it is curious that he composed his own interpretation of the play shortly after suffering the same bereavement. He described *The Interpretation of Dreams* as 'a portion of my own self-analysis, my reaction to my father's death', whose 'significance I only grasped after I had completed it' (SE IV xxvi). Thus Shakespeare's dreamer and Freud's analysis of dreams were both created out of mourning for paternity. And just as Oedipus tore out his eyes when he discovered he had killed his father, so Freud suggests that he was blinded by the parricidal act of writing. Remembering *The Interpretation of Dreams* he later wrote that 'Insight such as this falls to one's lot but once in a lifetime'. It is as if he saw so much that he could never see again, blinded like Oedipus by gazing back into the violence of infancy.

In his later work *Moses and Monotheism* (1939), Freud describes the text of Exodus as the mausoleum where the murdered body of Moses, the father of the Jews, was laid to rest (SE 23:62). He also hints, however, that fathers are not only buried but actually murdered by the writings of their sons. The distortions of a text resemble a murder, he says, because 'the difficulty is not in perpetrating the deed, but in getting rid of its traces' (SE 23:43). Indeed, what is uncanny about *Moses* is that Freud does not just read the myth of Exodus but reenacts it and bestows it with a second life, according to the principle that Shoshana Felman has elsewhere called a 'ghost effect'.[29] He tells us, for example, that he found himself 'unable to wipe out the traces of the work's origin': like a murderer who cannot obliterate the traces of his crime (SE 23:103). Among these traces was his exodus from Austria, which like Moses's exodus from Egypt has left a lesion in the centre of the text where it was interrupted and resumed.[30] Moreover, he confesses that the theme of Moses tormented him 'like an unlaid ghost' until he had completed its analysis. So Freud too seems to be besieged by ghosts, and like the Israelites he too has failed to cover up the traces of his essay's murderous nativity.

According to Freud, however, the guilty secret underlying the history of religion is not so much that the father has been killed as that he is never dead enough. The death of Moses and later the judicial sacrifice of Christ reactivate the 'ineradicable traces' of the parricide that instituted human history.[31] But the fact that the father is so constantly remurdered hints that he has never really been destroyed. Gertrude Stein once remarked that the detective novel was the only truly modern form of fiction because the hero is dead and the event is over before the story has begun.[32] However, Freud's argument suggests that the hero and the event were ousted at the very origin of human culture, and that history consists of the repetition of the traces of a murder which could never have occurred.[33] These repetitions could be seen as the equivalents in *history* to the 'traces' in his *text* which Freud was never able to obliterate: those 'unlaid ghosts' exacting reenactment.

In *Hamlet*, too, the father's murder has occurred before the play begins, unwitnessed and unverifiable. Yet this death, which never literally *takes place*, is *represented* time and again, by the dumb show and the mousetrap, by the testimony of the ghost, and by the carnage which completes the tragedy: 'Nine lives are taken off for his father's one', as Stephen says (*U* 154: 132). Moreover, the tragedy of *Hamlet* is haunted by the 'ineradicable traces' of *Oedipus the King*, and therefore it is necessary to return to Sophocles' treatment of the theme of parricide.

Greek tragedy arose at a particular historical turning point, because it was born, flourished, and passed away from Athens within the brief span of a hundred years. It was a social institution which the city set up beside its political and legal institutions, and the tragic competitions took place in the same urban space as the public assemblies and courts. (In fact, the legal system of today still retains the vestiges of tragedy, because the forces of crime and justice are personified by judge and jury and the sacrificial victim in the docks. The media's insatiable appetite for courtroom drama also testifies to the theatrical dimension of the law). However, Jean-Pierre Vernant and Pierre Vidal-Naquet have pointed out that Athenian tragedy arose out of a crisis in the legal system, when civil law began to encroach upon the jurisdiction of religious law and to override its immemorial injunctions. Much of the action in the *Oedipus* trilogy hinges on the ambiguity of certain words which implicate the sacred in the secular domain. Antigone, for instance, uses the word *nomos* to mean 'religious rule', whereas Creon uses it to mean 'an edict promulgated by the head of state'. Similarly, the hero's 'ignorance' condemns him in the sacred order of *Oedipus the*

King, whereas it condones him in the civil order of *Colonus*.[34]

Tragedy, then, resembles law in that they both exploit the sorcery of spectacle. But the theatre also brings to light the hidden conflicts of the legal code, just as hysteric symptoms stage the conflicts of repression. A symptom, like a tragedy, is a *display*: and both reveal a crisis in the law, whether in the psyche or the city. Freud himself hints at these analogies when he makes the extraordinary argument that the business of the dramatist is to induce hysteria in the spectator. A transference occurs in which the audience becomes possessed by the madness of the hero just as the hero is possessed – like an hysteric – by the vindictive secrets of his past. In *Hamlet*, for example, Shakespeare subjects the spectators to the same dilemma as the hero: for they are just as mystified as he is by his inability to act, yet at a deeper level they recognise his double-bind because they have repressed the same conflictual desires. It is this contradiction between 'knowing and not knowing', in Hegel's words, which deranges the defenses of the audience.[35]

Oedipus, however, may be even more hysterical than Hamlet, although his symptoms are somatic rather than obsessive. Freud argues in a famous formulation that 'hysterics suffer mainly from reminiscences'. What he means is that their memories have surfaced in the form of symptoms because they cannot be expressed in speech. Their afflictions are the ghosts of buried words. Similarly, Oedipus' memories have been carved into his body ever since he was exposed at birth, in his swollen ankles and his broken gait. In the play, however, his mutilation is inscribed into his name. For Oedipus means 'swell-foot', and thus his name assumes the function of a verbal scar whose significance has been forgotten and deferred. It returns upon him like an unlaid ghost, reopening the wound that marks the censored chapter of his history.[36]

Embedded in the name, moreover, is a pun which encapsulates the hero's tragedy, *Oîda*, the first part, means 'I know', whereas *poús*, the second part, means 'foot'. If Oedipus begins the play as *Oîda*, the know-it-all who solved the riddle of the sphinx, he concludes it as the sacrificial victim of his swollen foot, blind to the destiny enciphered in his symptom. Indeed, Vernant and Vidal-

Naquet contend that 'The whole of the tragedy of Oedipus seems to be contained in . . . the riddle of his name'.[37] As 'Know-foot', for example, Oedipus' name predestines him to solve the sphinx's riddle about feet: he alone is wise enough to know that it is *man* who walks with four feet in the morning, two feet at noon, and three feet at the close of day. However, this answer only resolves the question temporarily, for the Theban miasma descends again and Oedipus is forced to recognise that he himself is the solution of its riddle. Being brother to his children, child to his wife, and lover to his mother, Oedipus is infant, man and grandfather in one: dusk, noon and dawn.

However, Oedipus' name, like his lameness, speaks a language which is always destined elsewhere, to the other, since they both remain illegible to Oedipus himself. This is also true of the prophecies encrypted in his punning speech, which only the other can decipher. In effect, Oedipus is *haunted by himself*, because his words are constantly implying the opposite of what he means. At the beginning of the play, for instance, he boasts that 'it is I who will bring the criminal to light'. Since it is ironic that he should boast about his prescience, because there is a sense in which the culprit is indeed the only man who truly knows the crime.[38] Thus it is in the unheard meaning of his words that he conspires in his own catastrophe. Just as he had acted without seeing the implications of his deeds, so now he speaks without hearing the implications of his words. In the end he blinds himself to open up his ears, capitulating to the darkness of his own divided speech and the systematic ambiguity of signs.

Hegel argues that tragedy depends upon the contradiction between the 'power that knows and reveals itself to consciousness, and the power that conceals itself and lies in ambush.[39] In Oedipus' speech these powers meet in mutual interdestruction. Like the puns in *Finnegans Wake*, the puns in *Oedipus* could be seen as the linguistic equivalents of incest, because the 'monstrous commingling' of the members of the family is reenacted in the monstrous commingling of meanings.[40] The Theban miasma seems to symptomatise both the semantic contagion in the language and the incestuous confusion of the dynasty.[41]

It is in these ambiguities of speech that Oedipus unveils the ghostly meanings that he cannot bear to contemplate: confession oozes from his every pore, as Freud might say.[42] Whereas Odysseus manipulated double meanings to escape from one-eyed single-minded monsters like the Cyclops, Oedipus becomes the sacrificial victim of his puns, and the polytropic man is superseded by the parapractic. The subject who knows has now become the subject who *shows*.

Like Oedipus' name, however, Odysseus' scar serves as the repository of the hero's history in that it harbours the secrets of his origins. In both works the past emerges *après coup*, caught in the ghostly logic of deferral. It is only when Oedipus' destruction is complete that he can understand the meaning of his name. And it is only when Odysseus returns to Ithaca that his scar resurfaces with all its onomastic violence. When he is bathed by his old nurse Eurykleia, he tries to hide his scar 'lest all his story should come out': and indeed the narrative itself breaks open like a wound to tell the history of his name and mutilation.[43] Similarly, when Oedipus entreats the chorus at Colonus not to reawaken his old wound, he means that they must spare him the reiteration of his history:

Oedipus:

For kindness' sake, do not open
My old wound, and my shame.

Chorus:

It is told everywhere, and never dies:
I only want to hear it truly told (11. 515-18).[44]

Here the Chorus suggests that Oedipus' wound can never close upon itself because his legend has gone into diaspora; and indeed, the crime itself does not belong to Oedipus alone but to the conscience of his whole corrupted lineage. As he declares.

... I

Suffered those deeds more than I acted them
As I might show if it were fitting here
To tell my father's and my mother's story . . .
For which you fear me, as I know too well (II. 266-69).

Here Oedipus hints that his crimes were visited on him to pay for the offenses of his ancestors. Marie Balmary supports his theory, pointing out that Laius, Oedipus' father, took refuge in the court of Pelops, but later sinned against his host by eloping with his son. This boy, whose name was Chrysippus, subsequently killed himself in shame. The name Chrysippus means 'golden horse': and Balmary argues that Laius' crime rebounds on Oedipus in the images of horses which pursue him through the trilogy until he dies before the horsemen of Colonus. However, these equine revenants do not imply a return of the repressed, because they never belonged to Oedipus' consciousness. They are not the 'familiar strangers' of repression but the kind of phantoms that Nicolas Abraham describes as 'bizarre foreign [bodies]' transmitted from the parents into the unconscious of his child. 'What haunts', he says, 'are the gaps left within us by the secrets of others'. In the case of Oedipus the ghostly horses could be seen as the 'verbal stirrings of a secret buried alive in the father's unconscious': that is, the sins of Laius which are visited on his unknowing son.[45]

Oedipus' name is also an ancestral trace in that it aligns him with his grandfather, Labdacus, whose name means 'he who limps'.[46] Through the symbolic power of his name and limp, Oedipus becomes the ghost of his own grandfather, anticipating Stephen Dedalus' dream of begetting a begetter in his own image: 'Himself his own father', as Buck Mulligan expresses it (*U* 171:875). But the name is not the only way that Oedipus has overturned the generations. His incest has deranged the lexicon of kinship, too, and this is why he is evicted from the city like a beast. René Girard has argued that the charge of incest signifies the 'collective character of the disaster' and the interpsychic nature of the guilt.[47] After all, the only evidence of Oedipus' crime is circumstantial, and there are curious elisions in its reconstruction: as Sandor Goodhart has pointed out, the parricide is never proved.[48] The play suggests that it is not the acts themselves that constitute the crime but their contagion, since each retelling is a reenactment which exposes the incestuous and parricidal wishes of the teller. Indeed, Freud's theory of the play suggests that we are all the ghosts of Oedipus in that we reenact his tragedy in infancy. By the same token, the dread that Oedipus inspires does not depend on his offense alone but on its power to implicate the whole community; just as the force of *Hamlet* lies in the contamination of the viewers by the madness of the stage. Thus the secret that escapes from Oedipus' wound is nothing less than the terror of intersubjectivity.

The Mole and the Molecule

In Scylla and Charybdis it is Stephen's mole that assumes the function of Oedipus' scar. In this chapter Stephen is debating whether to excuse himself from paying back the pound he owes to AE (the mystic initials of George Russell) by claiming that his molecules have all been overhauled: 'Wait. Five months. Molecules all change. I am other I now. Other I got pound'. However, alarmed by this vision of his own unravelling, he bethinks himself that 'I . . . I by memory . . .' If the body changes every moment, weaving and unweaving its own substance, memory alone ensures that the I who borrows is the I who owes. History, Stephen finds, is rather an expensive luxury: 'A.E.I.O.U.' he admits at last (*U* 156: 205-6, 208, 213). But because he would rather be indebted than unselved he opts for memory and stakes the mole against the molecules.

– As we, or mother Dana, weave and unweave our bodies, Stephen said, from day to day, their molecules shuttled to and fro, so does the artist weave and unweave his image. And as the mole on my right breast is where it was when I was born, though all my body has been woven of new

stuff time after time, so through the ghost of the unquiet
father the image of the unliving son looks forth (*U* 159-60:
378-81).

Stephen is saying that despite the deconstruction of the flesh the
mole reprints itself afresh and thus affirms the continuity of
memory.[49] However, the image of the mole also alludes to the
ghost of Hamlet's father, whose son addresses him as 'old mole' (I
v 170). Stephen is punning on this epithet when he associates the
mole on his right breast with the ghost of the unquiet father. The
'ghost of the unliving son' is Hamnet, Shakespeare's son who died
in childhood (like Bloom's son Rudy whose spectre rises at the
end of Circe [*U* 496: 4956-67]). With the death of Hamnet, the
'son of his body', Shakespeare's name can only survive him in his
words, and Stephen sees his drama as the mausoleum of the pat-
ronym (*U* 155: 172). Indeed, a malaise about the father's name
pervades the tragedy of *Hamlet* from the start, when the ghost
arises instead of a name and as the symbol of the namelessness of
Shakespeare's lineage. The tragedy opens with the words 'Who's
there?': and everyone who witnesses the father's ghost is struck
with an aphasia about his name, resorting to such euphemisms like
'this thing', 'this dreaded sight', 'this apparition'; or Hamlet's antic
epithets, 'truepenny' and 'old mole'.[50] At the end, moreover,
Hamlet *fils* is sacrificed for Hamlet *père*, thus erasing both the
name and its descendence (see *U* 175: 1034). Shakespeare, who
played the spectre at the Globe, employed the tragedy to fantasise
the murder of his father and his son, and to taste his own death,
too, in a symbolic murder of himself. As Stephen says:

> The play begins. A player comes on under the shadow,
> made up with the castoff mail of a court buck, a well-set
> man with a bass voice. It is the ghost, the king, a king and
> no king, and the player is Shakespeare who has studied all
> the years of his life which were not vanity in order to play
> the part of the spectre (*U* 155: 165).

If the mole, then, stands for both the undead father and the unliving son, it marks the spot where death irrupts in life, where the ghosts of the future and the past look forth from the molecular decomposition of the present. It corresponds to the function of the *name* of Hamlet, in which Shakespeare's life converges with his art. For the molecules of Ham*n*et, 'the son of his body', were transfigured into the artefact of Ham*l*et, 'the son of his soul' (*U* 155: 171). As Stephen puts it, Hamnet Shakespeare died at Stratford so that 'his *namesake* may live for ever' (155: 173: my emphasis). In the play, the name survives the dissolution of the father's molecules, and indeed it only comes into its full symbolic force when he is dead, for the ghost ('old mole') is nothing but an ectoplasmic version of the name. 'That mole', as Stephen laughs, is always 'the last to go' (*U* 160: 391). Here, although the mole can mean the blemish on the breast, the burrowing beast, or the 'vicious mole of nature' in the soul, it also represents the father's *ghost* ('old mole'), which is the visionary emanation of his *name*.[51]

If the mole is associated with the name of the father, it appears to represent the triumph of paternity. But Joyce subjects the mole to the paranomasia that undercuts all of the master signifiers of his text. Acoustically the mole is related to the 'moly', which preserves Odysseus' manhood when he walks among the swine in Circe's den.[52] However, in Joyce's version of the Circe episode, Bloom surrenders his potato - the Irish equivalent of moly – and thereby forfeits his virility to Bella Cohen. 'I should not have parted with my talisman', he laments (*U* 431: 2794). Bella becomes Bello and Bloom becomes a woman until he has retrieved his potato from the prostitutes. Greedy for emasculation, Bloom has also forfeited another form of moly, *Molly*, to the gallantries of Blazes Boylan. Thus Bloom's virility depends upon possessing moly, or possessing Molly: but since both these charms show an alarming tendency to circulate, his potency is constantly in threat.[53]

Similarly, Stephen alludes to the mole of Imogen in *Cymbeline*, which also signifies the threat of cuckoldry. Imogen's husband Posthumus mistakenly believes she has betrayed him because his rival reports that he has seen the mole beneath her breast: 'Imogen's breast, bare, with its mole cinquespotted', as Stephen says (*U* 162: 474).[54] Though Imogen's honour is salvaged in the end, the play suggests that Posthumus can never fully certify his wife's fidelity. Similarly, Joyce implies that the father is necessarily a 'posthumous man', in Nietzsche's phrase: a ghost by absence from the process of gestation who can never guarantee his own paternity.[55] In *Cymbeline*, Shakespeare implies that the mole can make a ghost of both the father and the son because it marks the ineradicable possibility of bastardy. The mole in *Ulysses* also represents the fictional and ghostly nature of paternity, encapsulating both the name of the unfaithful wife ('Molly') and the nickname of the cuckolded and murdered father ('old mole') (*U* 170: 844).

Always the binarist, however, Stephen ignores the emasculating implications of the mole to relegate the mother to the molecules. As Penelope wove her web, so 'Mother Dana' weaves the flesh, unravelling its molecules incessantly. The mole is where the father's name transcends the mother's metamorphic flesh; just as the 'mole of boulders' in Proteus provides a point of fixity in Stephen's decomposing universe of sand and sea (*U* 39: 356). His equation of the mother with the dying body and the father with the deathless word (the name) scarcely constitutes original theology, but Stephen insists upon it doggedly. In his famous disquisition on paternity, he argues that the mother's role in parturition is self-evident, whereas the father's role is hypothetical, since he can never guarantee his offspring as his own. 'Fatherhood, in the sense of conscious begetting, is unknown to man'. A ghost by absence from the act of birth, he is potentially a ghost by death as well (*U* 170: 837-8; 155: 174-5). It is only through the 'legal fiction' of the name that he reclaims his dubious paternity (*U* 170: 844).

It is at this point of Stephen's argument that the parricidal motives of literary criticisms are unmasked. Yet if the father is as dead as Stephen says he is, it is strange that he discusses it so imperturbably. He elaborates his theory in the library, amidst his cozy if competitive fraternity, and neither Stephen nor his audience seems to be ruffled by his dreams of murder, incest, and adultery. What has happened to the agony of mourning, the rage, the guilt, and the garrulity: 'Words, words, words', as Hamlet says (II ii 192), which hollow themselves out with their own petulance? Even Stephen admits that he does not believe in his own theory

211

(*U* 175: 1065-7). For his abjuration of the father is a decoy, a displacement of his more insidious negation of the mother; and the whole theory serves as 'the creation he has piled up to hide him from himself', and in particular to blind him to his matricide (*U* 162: 475). Indeed, he only denies the father's actuality in order to affirm the 'mystery' of paternity. For it is on 'that mystery and not on the madonna which the cunning Italian intellect flung to the mob of Europe [that] the church is founded and founded irremovably because founded, like the world, macro and microcosm, upon the void. Upon incertitude, upon unlikelihood' (*U* 170: 839-42). This theory implies that what the father loses in the real he regains in the symbolic, in which the fiction of paternity obliterates the fact of motherhood. 'Loss is his gain', as Stephen says (*U* 170: 844; *U* 162: 476).

Ernest Jones argues that another phantom, the Holy Ghost, arose out of the same desire to erase the mother in the guise of a denial of the father.[56] According to Jones, the Christian trinity is the only holy family in mythology in which the mother has been ousted by a masculine progenitor; that is, by 'the mysterious figure of the Holy Ghost'. The myth of virgin birth expresses a desire to repudiate the father's role in reproduction, but also to atone for this emasculating wish by granting him stupendous potency. For God impregnates Mary with a word, a breath, a thought, and he does not even have to move an inch. The Holy Ghost takes care of everything. This spirit, Jones thinks, derives from infantile fantasies about the fecundating power of another kind of breath or *spiritus*: the gaseous exhalations of the anus. In other words, behind the myth of virgin birth lurks the belief that Mary was inseminated by a cosmic fart. This theory of flatulent conception disavows the father's sexual possession of the mother and thereby frees her for the child's incestuous imaginings. However, Jones goes on to argue that the story of religion represents the never ending struggle to overcome desire for the mother and to achieve atonement with the father. This is why Christianity has concocted an all-male family for the saviour, demoting the mother-goddess to a mortal woman who merely incubates the father's procreative breath. While the Holy Ghost usurps the position of the mother in the Trinity, the priests appropriate the mother's role within the Church, since it is they who feed the congregation with the blood and body of the Saviour, a masculine substitute for mother's milk. Indeed, they even dress like women, and by assuming the emblems of castration – the robes, the shaved heads, and the celibacy – they assert that women are no longer needed even to represent men's lack. In this way religion which began as a denial of the father has ended up with the obliteration of maternity.

'Himself his own father', Stephen also tries to disavow the mother and to rebeget himself in the eared womb of his own brain.[57] But he has not yet murdered his mother sufficiently to rid his mind of the tormenting image of her wasting flesh. It is in Circe that the mother he has tried to murder, first with silence, then with words rises up to teach him *amor matris* and remind him of love's bitter mystery (*U* 170: 843; 474: 4190). To borrow Molly's malapropism, it is his 'omission' of the mother in his analysis of *Hamlet* that causes her 'emission' in the dream (*U* 634: 1170). For this reason it is significant that Ernest Jones interprets *Hamlet* as a *matricidal* rather than a merely parricidal tragedy.[58] Moreover, Margaret Ferguson has pointed out that *Hamlet* is obsessed with the signifiers of maternity: for Shakespeare uses the word 'matter' twenty-six times, more than in any of his other plays, typically twinning it with 'mother' to suggest a pun on the Latin *mater*. Hamlet's opening gambit in the closet scene is a good example: 'Now, mother, what's the matter?'[59] In Circe, matter and maternity are also inter-implicated in that Stephen's denial of the mother bespeaks a denial of the matter of the body and also a denial of the written or acoustic *matter* of the word. It is this matter that returns to haunt him in Circe, the substance rather than the sense of words. A swarm of half-remembered words assails him, wrenched out of the daytime chapters of the books and deformed by the compulsions of the dream. It is the contrast between the logic of the day and the madness of the night which gives the second coming of these traces their uncanniness. If the father's ghost assumes the form of a disembodied spirit in *Ulysses*, the mother's ghost returns as the body of the word evacuated by the spirit of its meaning.

In fact, the matter and the meaning of the word have parted company before, and taken off on separate odysseys: like the *HELY'S* sandwichmen who wander off in Lestrygonians, each 'scarlet letter' wending its own way; or the literary flotsam that meanders down the Liffey into the alphabet soup of the sea (*U* 127: 126-8). In Circe, however, matter takes command, and surface takes the place of depth in word and flesh. Everything is *on show* in this chapter: the veil is rent which hides the inner workings of the mind or the inner significance of words. Indeed, this whole theology of meaning explodes into theatrics. Here as in *Oedipus*, the subject who knows becomes the subject who shows.

At the beginning of the chapter Stephen speaks of a language of 'gesture' which would render visible 'not the lay sense but . . . the structural rhythm' (*U* 353: 105-7). Circe itself is written in the language of gesture, for discourse is embodied as performance, and it is the rude and epileptic rhythm of the words that matters, rather than their 'lay sense', their vulgar meaning. That rhythm is diagnosed by the prostitutes as 'locomotor ataxy': a disease which involves the inability to coordinate the voluntary movements, or constitutional unsteadiness in the use of limbs (*U* 425: 2592). Indeed, the very body of the text is wracked with cramps, and the bodies of the people are ataxic too. 'The stiff walk', as Bloom declares, punning on the convulsive movements of the characters and the ghostly resurrection of the 'stiffs' or corpses of the dead. Bloom himself is attacked by spasms, stitches, tics, and palpitations; the ghost of Shakespeare is afflicted with a facial palsy; and even Stephen, who scarcely bears a body, jerks and gabbles, whirls and totters, drops his cigarette and stammers parapraxes.[60] Here, symptoms speak instead of words, and even the ratiocinative Stephen is reduced to the theatrics of hysteria.

Lurking behind Circe is the legend that hysteria originates in a wandering womb. For Bloom admits to menstrual cramps at the very outset of his nightmare: 'Bit light in the head. Monthly or effect of the other' (*U* 356: 210). Indeed, the heroes cannot keep their femininity at bay: Bloom forfeits his potato-talisman and turns into a woman, while Stephen is beleaguered by the mother who wombed him in sin-darkness. Like Lear, he must subdue the mother in order to be cured of his hysteria, so that he may speak in language rather than convulsions: 'O! how this mother swells up towards my heart; / *Hysterica passio!* down, thou climbing sorrow!' (*Lear* II iv 54-5). It is by crying '*Nothung*' and by brandishing his ashplant sword that Stephen overcomes the wandering womb, dispatching the castrating figure of his mother to the darkness (*U* 475: 4241-5). And it is not until he sends his mother back to hell that he is freed from the delirium of matter. At this point, the beasts become men again, having mastered and externalised the feminine, and to certify their triumph the police return. The ghosts disperse, and the flood of that-which-was retreats from the bedrock of the present.

If Stephen is a ghost-buster, however, Bloom the advertising canvasser facilitates the transmigration of commodities and souls. The reason that he relishes the inner organs of beasts and fowls, or envisages the human body as a bunch of pumps, is that he functions as intestine to the world of commerce, transforming and dispersing its consumer goods. Less interested in ineluctable modalities than in the metempsychoses of the large intestine, he flushes words and flesh into their afterlife. Joyce complained that Stephen had a shape that couldn't be changed; but Bloom, by contrast, represents the shape-changing wizardry of commerce.[61] While Odysseus meandered through enchanted seas, Bloom circulates 'on the waters of civic finance' (*U* 571: 983-4). This connection between ghosts and commerce may derive from *Faust*, where Goethe puns on the word for banknote (*Geldschein*) and the word for ghost (*Gespenst*).[62] Money is a ghost because it has no body of its own but is constantly reincarnated in the bodies of commodities. Moreover, money *wanders*, and for this reason it resembles both the 'extravagant and erring spirit' of the father and the odyssean wanderlust of Bloom. In Ithaca, for instance, we are told that Bloom once launched a florin on a mercantile odyssey. Having 'marked a florin (2/-) with three notches on the milled edge', he gave it to the grocer 'for possible, circuitous or direct, return'. The text demands, 'Had Bloom's coin returned?' and the implacable riposte is 'Never' (*U* 981-88). Like the florin, Bloom himself is sent into diaspora, destined for dissemination rather than return.

Though Bloom does return to the Ithaca of 7 Eccles Street it is only to discover that Molly's bed is thronged with ghosts of other men. He surrenders to these spectral lovers, much as Gabriel Conroy surrenders to the ghost of Michael Fury in 'The Dead' ('ghost' being derived from the Teutonic word for 'fury'). But it is precisely by renouncing carnal love that Bloom defeats the suitors in Penelope: because he leaves his body on a distant shore in search of a symbolic consummation in the seas of Molly's reverie. In this chapter it is his name which wins the day. For Molly concludes her monologue with the wild dissemination of her husband's name in a torrent of *blooms*, an ocean of flowers:[63]

> I love flowers Id love to have the whole place swimming in roses . . . flowers all sorts of shapes and smells and colours springing up even out of the ditches primroses and violets . . . and O that awful deepdown torrent O and the sea the sea crimson sometimes like fire . . . and the rosegardens and the jessamine and geraniums . . . (*U* 642-3: 1557-8, 1562-3; 1597-1601).

In Lotus-Eaters episode, Bloom assumes the name of Henry Flower, and he concludes the chapter gazing at the 'languid floating flower' of his penis in the bath: 'limp father of thousands' (*U* 71: 571-2). Like the mole, however, the flower cannot be reduced into a phallic symbol. For instance, the Earl of Rochester uses 'flowers' as slang for menstruation, the *female* blood which Molly consecrates in her apocalyptic image of the crimson sea. It is also important that *flowers* mean figures of rhetoric. Since Bloom associates the 'flow' of water with the 'flow' of poetry in Lestrygonians, the flow of flowers which concludes the novel seems to represent the infinite fecundity of figuration.[64] Molly's rhapsody plunges deep down into the matrix of the language, in which the myths of gender and identity dissolve into the 'flowers' of the rhetoric where they originate. It is in her ecstatic surge of floral imagery that Molly finally relinquishes Bloom's presence for his name, and thus bequeathes him with his ghostdom and his passport to eternity.[65]

Agenbite of Inwit

In the *Ghost Hunters' Guide*, the president of the British Ghost Club enumerates a dozen different kinds of ghost, including cyclic ghosts, poltergeists, ghosts of animals, haunted objects, and ghosts of the living; and for those who plan to take up ghost-watching, he also provides a handy guide to gear.[66] However, *Oedipus* and *Hamlet* show that the theatre is the place to look for the vindictive phantoms of paternity. Like a dream, the theatre embodies the unspeakable, replacing words with deeds, wishes with apparitions. Indeed, the theatre is a dream turned inside out, the outer image of the oneiric stagecraft of the mind. If Western drama has been dominated by the father's spirit, however, the theatre of *Ulysses* is besieged by the mother's unpropitiated flesh. In Circe, as in the unconscious, the corpse of language reasserts its obstinate materiality: like the white corpuscles in Buck Mulligan's mock Eucharist which stubbornly resist the transubstantiation of his shaving lather (*U* 3: 1-29). Milan Kundera once remarked that 'Death has two faces. One is nonbeing; the other is the terrifying material being of the corpse'.[67] It is the second face of death which is invoked in the unstageable delirium of Circe. By denying the matter associated with the mother the father establishes his ghostly kingdom: thus the flesh is made word. In Circe, however, word becomes flesh in the savage hieroglyphics of hysteria and the revenge of the cadaver of the word.

The ghost of my own father, Richard Ellmann, has been visiting me regularly in my dreams, and it is he who shall be given the last word. In the first dream I was gazing at his biography of Wilde that he finished on the day before he died, when the face of Wilde on the cover began to crinkle up into my father's own inimitable smile. And suddenly it was my father, not his book, who was before me, sitting in the yoga position he was always comically proud of being able to accomplish, I cried, 'Why did you die?' He explained, most gently 'Because I was tired'.

In the second dream, I was standing outside the intensive care ward where my father died. My sister Lucy came out of the ward, and placing her hands on my shoulders said, 'Daddy has gone into diaspora'. This word seemed to mean 'remission' in the dream, and I was seized with a crazy joy: he wasn't dead after all. Yet on awakening I wondered if diaspora was really a more accurate description of my father's state than death, because he has not been erased but circumfused among our dreams and his incomparable books.

The last time my father visited was the ghostliest day of the calendar, the 29th of February. In the dream, however, it was Bloomsday, and I was at an Irish shebeen revelling with two companions. Exhilarated by the music we shouted in unison. 'I want to dance!' We seized the piano. One of my friends began to play elaborate arpeggios, his fingers dancing over the keys. The other man, who I now saw was my father, said 'I want to sing a tenor aria but I need Maudie to help me reach some of the high notes'. I agreed, although I was nervous about singing in public, and I also thought it odd that my father should be so eager to perform, since he was virtually tone-deaf and had lost the power of speech before he died. He began tunelessly enough, but slowly, stealthily, his voice rose into a tenor of such unearthly sweetness that every listener was wonderstruck. I began to weep. 'Why are you crying?', my father asked. I said, 'I miss you'. 'How can you miss me when I'm right here?' 'But you're *dead*!', I exclaimed. 'Well, I guess there is *that* to consider!', he laughed, as if it were the least of inconveniences. Now that our song was finished I went to take my place among the audience again: but as I passed each person I demanded, 'Was that not my father?' And no one could deny it. The vision faded: I woke up to remember I was fatherless. But now, as I resume my place amongst the living, my dream begins again, and I leave you with my ghost-inspired question.

Was that not my father?

NOTES

1 My translation is condensed and approximate.

2 Molly uses 'omission' for 'emission' throughout Penelope, and the malapropism suggests that the role of woman in the text is to emit omissions or breed absences: 'how much is that doctor one guinea please and asking me had I frequent omissions where do those old fellows get all the words they have omissions with his shortsighted eyes on me cocked sideways' (p. 634: 1169-71). All references to *Ulysses* are to the Student Edition of the corrected text, ed. Walter Gabler *et al* (New York: Garland, 1984), abbreviated here as *U*, followed by the page number and the line numbers.

3 *Hamlet*, Arden Edition, ed. Harold Jenkins (London: Methuen, 1982), III iv 132, 144.

4 *King Lear*, Arden Edition, ed. Kenneth Muir (London: Methuen, 1972), I i 86.

5 For Freud's theory of the murder of the primal father by his sons, see *Totem and Taboo*, in the Standard Edition of *The Complete Psychological Works of Sigmund Freud*, tr. James Strachey (London: Hogarth, 1953-74)), Vol. XIII, pp. 141-60. Further references to the Standard Edition will be cited as SE followed by the volume number in Roman numerals and the page number in Arabic numerals. In *Hamlet and Oedipus* (1949; New York: Norton, 1971), p. 89, Ernest Jones cites Otto Rank's argument that the play-within-the-play, in which a nephew kills his uncle and in which there is no talk of adultery or incest, is in Hamlet's imagination the equivalent for fulfilling his task.

6 Cited in Clive Hart, *Structure and Motif in Finnegans Wake* (Evanston: Northwestern University Press, 1962), p. 163.

7 Jacques Derrida, 'The Words for Joyce', in *Post-Structuralist Joyce:*

Essays from the French, ed. Derek Attridge and Daniel Ferrer (Cambridge: Cambridge University Press, 1984), pp. 147.

8 See Harold Bloom, *The Anxiety of Influence: A Theory of Poetry* (New York: Oxford University Press, 1973), *passim*.

9 'Two Words for Joyce', pp. 151, 148.

10 Jean-Michel Rabaté points out this ambiguity in 'A Clown's Inquest into Paternity: Fathers, Dead or Alive, in *Ulysses* and *Finnegans Wake*', in *The Fictional Father: Lacanian Readings of the Text* (Amherst: University of Massachusetts Press, 1981), p. 87.

11 This is one of Derrida's principles: see, *inter alia*, 'The Violence of the Letter: From Lévi-Strauss to Rousseau', in *Of Grammatology*, tr. Gayatri Chakravorty Spivak (Baltimore: Johns Hopkins University Press, 1974), pp. 101-40.

12 Freud, *Totem and Taboo*, SE XIII 25, 61.

13 Freud, 'Mourning and Melancholia', SE XIV 243-58. See also Leo Bersani's discussion of the 'moribund nature of the ego . . . its status as a kind of cemetery of decathected object-choices', in *The Freudian Body: Psychoanalysis and Art* (New York: Columbia, 1986), pp. 93-100.

14 Bataille argues that death necessitates the *spectacle* 'without the repetition of which we would remain foreign to and ignorant of . . . the fiction, more or less removed from reality, of death'. Cited by Derrida in 'From Restricted to General Economy: A Hegelianism without Reserve', in *Writing and Difference* (Chicago: University of Chicago Press, 1978), p. 258.

15 André Green, *The Tragic Effects: The Oedipus Complex in Tragedy*, tr. Alan Sheridan (Cambridge University Press, 1979), pp. 2-8.

16 Antonin Artaud compares the theatre with the dream in 'The

Theatre of Cruelty: First Manifesto', in *The Theatre and its Double*, tr. Mary Caroline Richards (New York: Grove Press, 1958), p. 93. For suggestive analogies between the theatre and the structure of the psyche, see Philippe Lacoue-Labarthe, 'Theatrum Analyticum', in *Glyph 2*; *Johns Hopkins Textual Studies* (Baltimore: Johns Hopkins University Press, 1977), pp. 122-43; and Salomon Resnik, *The Theatre of the Dream*, tr. Alan Sheridan, New Library of Psychoanalysis, Vol. 6 (London: Tavistock, 1987), esp. Ch. 1, pp. 4-25.

17 WB Yeats, *'Per Amica Silentia Lunae'*, in *Mythologies* (New York: Macmillan, 1959), p. 341.

18 Hegel, *The Phenomenology of Spirit*, tr. AV Miller (New York: Oxford, 1977), p. 443.

19 Artaud complains about 'ossified' language in his letter to Jean Paulhan of 28 May 1933; and in the first manifesto for 'The Theatre of Cruelty' he announces that 'it is essential to put an end to the subjugation of the theatre to the text' (*The Theatre and its Double*, pp. 117, 89).

20 *Phenomenology of Spirit*, pp. 443-4.

21 Cited from *L'homme nu* in David Trotter, *The Making of the Reader: Language and Subjectivity in Modern American, English and Irish Poetry* (London: Macmillan, 1984), p. 37.

22 See Freud, SE XII 150: 'the patient does not *remember* anything of what he has forgotten or repressed, but *acts* it out. . . He *repeats* it, without . . . knowing that he is repeating it'.

23 Cited by Green, *The Tragic Effect*, p. 10; a less elegant translation may be found in *The Theatre and its Double*, p. 93.

24 See Adorno's discussion of the return of the past in the Sirens episode of *The Odyssey*, in *Dialectic of Enlightenment*, tr. John Cumming (London: Verso, 1979), p. 32.

25 See Joyce's schemata for *Ulysses* in Richard Ellmann, *Ulysses on the Liffey* (New York: Oxford University Press, 1972), Appendix (no page numbers). 'Dialectic' is the *technic* in the Linati scheme; the Gilbert/Gorman scheme designates 'whirlpools' as the technic and 'two-edged dilemma' as the sense.

26 Jacques Lacan, 'Desire and the Interpretation of Desire in *Hamlet*', in Shoshana Felman, ed., *Literature and Psychoanalysis: The Question of Reading: Otherwise* (Baltimore: Johns Hopkins University Press, 1982), p. 39.

27 Chase's point is specifically that Oedipus 'murdered his father and married his mother in an appreciation of expediency rather than in satisfaction of a desire'. See Cynthia Chase, 'Oedipal Textuality: Reading Freud's Reading of *Oedipus*', in *Decomposing Figures: Rhetorical Readings in the Romantic Tradition* (Baltimore: Johns Hopkins University Press, 1986), p. 180.

28 Freud, *The Origins of Psychoanalysis: Letters to Wilhelm Fliess, Drafts and Notes, 1887 - 1902*, ed. Marie Bonaparte, Anna Freud and Ernst Kris (London: Hogarth, 1954), p. 224.

29 See Shoshana Felman, 'Turning the Screw of Interpretation', in *Literature and Psychoanalysis*, pp. 94-207.

30 Furthermore, it is a cruel peripeteia that the lintels which the Israelites in Egypt marked with blood in order to be spared by the avenging god of Exodus should later be marked with swastikas, like Freud's own doorway in Bergasse Street, to single them out for the Holocaust. For photograph see *Bergasse 19: Sigmund Freud's Home and Offices, Vienna 1938: The Photographs of Edmund Engelman*, intro. Peter Gay (New York: Basic books, 1976), Plate 3.

31 Freud contends that an 'event such as the elimination of the primal father by the company of his sons must inevitably have left *ineradicable traces* in the history of humanity . . .' (*Totem and Taboo*, SE XIII 155).

32 See Gertrude Stein, 'What are Master-Pieces and Why are there so few of them', in *Look at me now and Here I am: Writings and Lectures 1909-45*, ed. Patricia Meyerowitz (Harmondsworth: Penguin, 1971), p. 151: 'the detective story which is you might say the only really modern novel form that has come into existence gets rid of human nature by having the man dead to begin with the hero is dead to begin with and so you have so to speak got rid of the event before the book begins'.

33 Freud himself always insisted that the murder of the primal father was a literal event: 'in the beginning was the Deed', he concludes in *Totem and Taboo*, quoting his own forefather Goethe (SE XIII 161).

34 See Vernant and Vidal-Naquet, *Tragedy and Myth in Ancient Greece* (Brighton: Harvester, 1981), pp. 1-9, 87, 39-44, 58.

35 *Phenomenology of Spirit*, p. 446.

36 Lacan says that 'The unconscious is that chapter of my history which is marked by a blank . . . : it is the censored chapter'. Quoted by Shoshana Felman in 'Beyond Oedipus: The Specimen Story of Psychoanalysis', in *Lacan and Narration: The Psychoanalytic Difference in Narrative Theory*, ed. Robert Con Davis (Baltimore: Johns Hopkins University Press, 1983), p. 1033.

37 Vernant and Vidal-Naquet, pp. 96-7. See also Cynthia Chase's brilliant elaboration of the name in 'Oedipal Textuality', p. 185 much of which I paraphrase below.

38 See Vernant and Vidal-Naquet, Ch. V. esp. pp. 90, 95.

39 *Phenomology of Spirit*, p. 446.

40 Girard's translation in *Violence and the Sacred*, tr. Patrick Gregory (Baltimore: Johns Hopkins, 1979), p. 75.

41 This plague could be compared to the fog in Dicken's *Bleak House*, which represents both the sexual confusions of the tale and the semantic vagaries of Chancery. See Christine van Boheemen, 'Bleak House and the Family Romance', in *The Novel as Family Romance: Language, Gender, and Authority from Fielding to Joyce* (Ithaca: Cornell University Press, 1987), pp. 101-31.

42 See Freud, *Fragment of an Analysis of a Case of Hysteria*, SE VII 78.

43 See Erich Auerbach, 'Odysseus' Scar', in *Mimesis*, tr. William R Trask (Princeton: Princeton University Press, 1953), pp. 3-23. I discuss this passage at greater length in 'Polytropic Man: Paternity, Identity and Naming in *The Odyssey* and *A Portrait of the Artist as a Young Man*', in *James Joyce: New Perspectives*, ed. Colin MacCabe (Brighton: Harvester; Bloomington: Indiana University Press, 1982), esp. pp. 81-4.

44 *Oedipus at Colonus*, tr. Robert Fitzgerald, in David Grene and Richard Lattimore, eds., *Sophocles I, The Complete Greek Tragedies* (Chicago: University of Chicago Press, 1954), p. 102. All further references to Sophocles are to this edition.

45 See Nicholas Abraham, 'Notes on the Phantom', in *The Trial(s) of Psychoanalysis*, ed. Francoise Meltzer (Chicago: University of Chicago Press, 1988), pp. 75-80.

46 This limp, like the name, reemerges every other generation in the dynasty, like the alternating names in Bloom's paternal line (Leopold – Rudolph – Leopold – Rudy). See Marie Balmary, *Psychoanalyzing Psychoanalysis: Freud and the Hidden Fault of the Father*, tr. Ned Lukacher (Baltimore: Johns Hopkins University Press, 1982), Ch. 1, esp. pp. 7-14, 19.

47 *Violence and the Sacred*, p. 77.

48 Sandor Goodhart, 'Oedipus and Laius's Many Murderers', *Diac-*

critics 8 (1978), *passim*.

49 Coincidentally, Fredric Jameson, following Gilles Deleuze and Felix Guattari, has used the terms 'molar' and 'molecular' to describe the same kind of divisions in our modes of thought. He defines molecular apprehension as 'the here-and-now of immediate perception or of local desire'; whereas molar thinking consists of 'large, abstract, mediate, and perhaps even empty and imaginary forms by which we seek to recontain the molecular. . .' An example of a molar concept, Jameson says is the 'mirage of the continuity of personal identity'. See Jameson, *Fables of Aggression: Wyndham Lewis, The Modernist as Fascist* (Berkeley: University of California Press, 1979), pp. 8-9.

50 I owe this observation to my former student Courtney Pellegrino: see *Hamlet* I i 24, 28, 31; I v 158, 170.

51 Hamlet's speech about the 'vicious mole of nature' which can undermine the goodness of the soul occurs in I iv 24.

52 Joyce told Frank Budgen that 'Moly is the gift of Hermes, god of public ways, and is the invisible influence (prayer, chance, agility, *presence of mind*, power of recuperation) which saves in case of accident . . . In this special case his plant may be said to have many leaves, indifference due to masturbation, pessimism congenital, a sense of the ridiculous, sudden fastidiousness in some detail, experience'. See Budgen, *James Joyce and the Making of Ulysses* (Oxford: Oxford University Press, 1972), p. 237.

53 The role of moly in this episode compares to the function of the 'phallus' in Lacan, which he defines as the penis that the infant attributes to its mother. See Lacan, 'The Meaning of the Phallus', in *Feminine Sexuality*, ed. Juliet Mitchell and Jacqueline Rose (London: Macmillan, 1982), pp. 74-85.

54 Posthumus uses the ring that Imogen has given him to bet that she could never be unfaithful. But by pressing her gift into his

rival's hands he symbolically exchanges Imogen as well, suggesting an unconscious desire for betrayal. It is curious, moreover, that Posthumus should give a love-token to the very man who means to cuckold him, because it hints that Imogen is being used to establish an erotic bond between the men. The mole, like the ring, becomes the currency of this unconscious intercourse.

55 Friedrich Nietzsche, 'Maxims and Arrows', no. 15, *Twilight of the Idols* (Harmondsworth: Penguin, 1968), p. 24.

56 Ernest Jones, 'A Psycho-Analytic Study of the Holy Ghost Concept', *Essays in Applied Psycho-Analysis*, Vol. II, p. 358-73.

57 Stephen speaks of 'uneared wombs' in Scylla and Charybdis (*U* 166: 664).

58 See Ernest Jones, *Hamlet and Oedipus*, Ch. 5, pp. 92-100.

59 *Hamlet* III iv 7; see Margaret W Ferguson, '*Hamlet*: Letters and Spirits', in *Shakespeare and the Question of Theory*, ed. Patricia Parker and Geoffrey Hartman (New York: Methuen, 1985), esp. pp. 284-7.

60 *U* 354: 163; 355: 183; 463: 3822; 465: 3881; 473: 4151-2; 457: 3641; 411: 2091-2. Joyce indicated in the Gilbert/Gorman scheme for *Ulysses* that Stephen (Telemachus) does not yet bear a body in the first three chapters of the novel. See Richard Ellmann, *Ulysses on the Liffey*, Appendix (no page numbers).

61 See Richard Ellmann, *Ulysses on the Liffey*, p. 4.

62 Marc Shell discusses this pun in *Money, Language, and Thought* (Berkeley: University of California Press, 1982), pp. 6n., 84-130.

63 I am indebted here to Jean-Michel's Rabaté's brilliant analysis of the flower motif in *James Joyce: Portrait de l'auteur en autre auteur* (Petit-Roueulx, Belgique: Cistre, 1984), pp. 86-7.

64 In Lestrygonians Bloom locates the power of Shakespeare's verse in 'flow of the language', and then a little later wonders how you can 'own water', since it is 'always flowing in a stream' (*U* 125: 165; 126: 94). The two flows are connected in that Joyce is also challenging the notion of private ownership in language. Molly's rhapsody overrides the myth of property because her ghostly lovers indicate that she does not belong to Bloom or any man. But she also moves beyond the boundaries of her selfhood, for even personal identity depends upon the notion of belonging to oneself, self-ownership.

65 Joyce said that Molly's monologue provides 'the indispensable countersign to Bloom's passport to eternity'. See Budgen, p. 270.

66 Peter Underwood, President and Chief Investigator of the Ghost Club (founded 1862), *The Ghost Hunter's Guide* (London: Javeline Books, 1986), Ch. 1, pp. 14-37.

67 Milan Kundera, *The Art of the Novel*, tr. Linda Asher (New York: Harper, 1986), p. 123.

F I N N E G A N S
W A K E
- NIGHT JOYCE
OF A THOUSAND TIERS

Petr Skrabanek

'There is no work more intellectual, more disengaged from worry about contemporary matters, more estranged from time and space, more foreign to politics, war, the torment of wretched Europe, none more preoccupied with the great interests of life, love, desire, death, childhood, fatherhood, the mystery of eternal return'. This is how the French Academician, Louis Gillet, described *Finnegans Wake*.

James Stephens said: 'it is unreadable . . . it is wonderful;.

On the other hand, St John Gogarty, in a fit of blinding envy suggested that *Finnegans Wake* was a gigantic hoax written by an idiot on the backside of beauty. Or, to quote from the *Wake* itself, 'the recital of the rigmarole' (174.04), 'a stinksome inkenstink' (183.06), 'a . . . riot of blots and blurs and bars and balls and hoops and wriggles and juxtaposed jottings linked by spurts of speed' (118.29).

After 'his usylessly unreadable Blue Book of Eccles' (179.26),

Joyce wrote the 'bluest book in baile's annals' (13.21). As a young artist Joyce started with Ibsen, and ended obscene. *Finnegans Wake* with its 'sexophonologistic Schizophrenesis' (123.18) however, in distinction to *Ulysses*, was never banned, despite its 'seedy ejaculations' (183.23) and the 'fluefoul smut' (183.15), as all the four-letter words have been 'variously inflected, differently pronounced, otherwise spelled' (118.26). The scatological eschatology also seems to have escaped the attention of vigilant censors.

The verbal diarrhoea, the riverrun, of the floozie in the jacuzzi, is punctuated by ten thunderous farts, totalling 1001 letters. Thousand and One Nights of tails within tales, of tumescence and detumescence, of drinking and pissing, of eating and defecation, 'turning breakfarts into lost soupirs' (453.11). In the upside down universe of the *Wake*, God's creative breath becomes Devil's fart, and *paternoster*, 'farternoiser' (530.36). The sound of *Finnegans Wake* is that of chamberpot music.

If *Ulysses* was a day book, a stream of consciousness of one man, Everyman Bloom, *Finnegans Wake* is a night book, a nightmare stream from the unconscious of all men, of Nomen. Bloom's day is followed by Noman's night. The action takes place 'nowhere', now and here, in Noman's land. 'This nonday diary, this allnights newseryreel', (489.35). The time is 'nowtime' (290.17), 'noughttime' (349.06).

Just like the proverbial Heraclitean river, you can never step into the same stream of *Finnegans Wake* twice. 'Every word [is] bound over to carry three score and ten toptypsical readings throughout the book of Doublends Jined' (20.14). The reader, like Theseus, is lost in the labyrinth of theses and antitheses fusing into new syntheses. Each pair of Heraclitean opposites form both a unity and plurality, but if Heraclitus was known as 'the weeping philosopher', Joyce, 'the tragic jester' (171.15) is 'agush with tears of joy' (178.12), as there is 'lots of fun at Finnegan's wake'. (*Fun* in Japanese means 'excrement'). It's 'hugglebeddy fann' (616.01).

The readers of *Finnegans Wake* are of two types; those who pretend to read it and those who read it to pretend. But each time the reader turns the revolving drum of the *Finnegans Wake* prayerwheel, it sends up new revolting blasphemies.

It took Joyce seventeen years to write seventeen chapters of *Finnegans Wake* – a labour of love, a love letter, and his artistic testament – the portrait of the artist as an old man. It contains more than 50,000 different words, three times as much as in the whole of Shakespeare, and in more than seventy seven languages. That makes it easier for foreigners. 'He would wipe alley english spooker, multaphoniaksikally spuking, off the face of the erse' (178.06).

Talking to the Polish writer Jan Parandowski, Joyce complained:

> the few fragments which I have published have been enough to convince many critics that I have finally lost my mind, which, by the way, they have been predicting faithfully for many years. And perhaps it is madness to grind up words in order to extract their substance, to create crossbreeds and unknown variants, to open up unsuspected possibilities for these words, to marry sounds which were not usually joined before although they were meant for one another, to allow water to speak like water, birds to chirp in the words of birds, to liberate all sounds from their servile, contemptible role and to attach them to the feelers of expressions which grope for definitions of the undefined . . . With this hash of sounds I am building the great myth of everyday life.

'With a meticulosity bordering on the insane' (173.34). There is a method in his madness.

Samuel Beckett was one of the first to appreciate the mastery of the achievement. I quote: 'There form *is* the content, content *is* the form. You complain that the stuff is not written in English. It is not written at all. It is not to be read, or, rather, it is not only to be read. It is to be looked at and listened to. His writing is not *about* something: it is that something itself'. One could add that, like any great work of art, the *Wake* has no goal or meaning. Like God himself, to paraphrase the God of the Jews, it is because it is.

Finnegans Wake defies the second law of thermodynamics by being in perpetual motion, while its source of energy, the writer, is dead.

By giving four sides to the *Wake* circle, Joyce achieved another impossibility: the squaring of the circle. *'Finnegans Wake* is a wheel and it's all square'. 'She bit his tailibout' [tail, butt] and 'all hat tiffin for thea' (229.25).

And each time the wheel of *Finnegans Wake* turns, the Humpty-Dumpty is put together again: the egg is unscrambled.

The riverrun, the last and the first words of the river-rain cycle, is the antithesis of the raven's 'nevermore'. Here the dove of baptism descends with its promise of eternal life.

Finnegans Wake is about beginnings and ends, but without an end or a beginning. Tim Finnegan of the ballad, stoned by too much whiskey, and appearing stone-dead, is revived by more of the same, *uisce beatha*, whiskey, the water of life, splashed on him during a lively wake. His baptism is by fire and water of the firewater. Like the Phoenix, he rises from his ashes. A *sine qua non* of resurrection is death. His dead penis rises too – a terrible beauty is born. The mortal HCE rises and falls. The immortal ALP remains horizontal. A mountain and a river. A bobbing pile of shit on the surface of urine. A storm in a tea-pot.

The water of life in the *Wake* is also the river Liffey, described by Joyce as having the colour of tea without milk, 'Tea' in slang means both 'whiskey' and 'urine'. *Le thé* in French is 'tea'. But the Lethe is also the water of forgetting, the river of death.

The last word joins the first, the Lethe and the Liffey, the river of oblivion and the river of life, merge in an 'obliffious' stream (317.32). Just for a moment. 'Lethelulled between explosion and reexplosion' (78.04). The short lull between the last and the first word is like the 'holy hour', the pub closure between 2.30 and 3.30 (now abolished). This bizarre by-law was described by Stephen Pile as an attempt to assist the Irishmen in their struggle to come out of the pub at some point between dawn and bedtime.

The pissed Finnegan discharges the dead water from his bladder and is revived with a fresh supply of whiskey. Pissing rain swells Liffey again, and makes Ireland, the Urinal of the Planets, green again. This is a great country, as we say here, but they should put a roof on it.

In Italian, 'riverrun' reads *riverranno*, they will come again, the

Finnegans wake up again, they will revive (*rivivranno*), the river-run ends and the circular dream begins again (*rêve-rond*).

Joyce said to his friend Budgen: 'the Holy Roman Catholic Apostolic Church was built upon a pun. It ought to be good enough for me': *Tu es Petrus et super hanc petram aedificabo ecclesiam meam* (Thou are Peter, and upon this rock I will build my church, Mt. 16, 18).

Joyce's foundation of *Finnegans Wake* is a parallel pun: You are Patrick and upon this sham-rock I will build my sham-work. 'Peatrick' suggests the rick of peat, the mountain, the Reek (Croagh Patrick), and 'peat reek' (whiskey distilled over the smoke of peat), but also the reek of the pot, as Patrick, like Jesus, is baptized with waters of the Jordan. ('Jordan' is an obsolete term for a chamber-pot). 'Tauftauf thuartpeatrick' (3.10) means 'I baptize you Patrick'. It's all in German, as Patrick was a disciple of St. Germanicus (*taufe*, I baptize, *Taube*, dove, *Teufel*, the Devil). Holy Joe, St. Bridgit and St. Patrick! 'Scentbreeched and somepotreek' (12.22) – shitty breeches and chamber-pot stink.

The pea-trick was a rigging game of itinerant sharpers, using a pea and three thimbles. A sleight-of-hand, similar to St. Patrick's demonstration of the unity of the Holy Trinity, using the three-leaved shamrock.

Finnegans Wake being written from Paris to the Liffey, is a French letter, Joyce's last 'wetbed confession' (188.01). Joyce thought of it as 'a French letter which does not succeed in coming off, never quite' (VI.B.12.126). It's a riverrun with a 'rubberend' (144.30). 'The letter that never begins to go find the latter that ever comes to end, written in smoke and blurred by mist and signed of solitude, sealed at night' (337.12). The letter is found by a hen in a heap of litter, 'literatured with burst loveletters' (183.10) in the 'sound seemetery which iz leebez luv' (17.35), the symmetry of uniting opposites buried in the graveyard of sounds.

An early version of the *Wake* started with 'Reverend', the addressee of the letter written by ALP. In its final form, the addressee is 'riverrun', i.e. the Liffey, and the letter is written by Shem. It echoes a line from Yeats' poem 'A Poet to His Beloved':

'I bring you with reverent hands the books of my numberless dreams'.

In Irish, 'riverrun' reads *ribhéar a rúin*, my darling river, a love-letter of Joyce to the Liffey. *Rún* also means 'a riddle', or 'mystery'.

The letter ends in the middle of a sentence with the 'affectionate largelooking tache of tch' (111.19), a stain of tea, the sperm drop of renewal. 'Life. . . is a wake, livit or krikit, and on the bunk of our breadwinning lies the cropse of our seedfather' (55.05). The sperm drop from a victim of hanging, as discussed in *Ulysses*. After all, the *Wake* is a 'Suspended Sentence' (106.13).

The last sentence evaporates into nothingness, dissolves, melts into the final 'thaw', the Irish sound of the affirmative *tá*, 'yes', the 'final breath, a nothing', as Joyce said to Gillet. The male and female opposites meet in the orgasmic little death, *la petite mort*, as the French call it. ALP, falling into oblivion, breathes *ma mort*, 'mememormee' (628.14), remember me in my death. Isolde dying with the initial of Tristan on her lips – T, the. The Liebestod – the love to death.

ALP is passing out, and her daughter is taking her place, 'A daughterwife from the hills . . . and she is coming. Swimming in my hindmoist. Diveltaking on me tail' (627.02).

The last page is Joyce's swan song, the last leaf, the last of the Liffey, the last tea leaf. 'Where there's leaf, there's hope' (227.18). 'Only a leaf, just a leaf and then leaves' (619.22). 'They lived und laughed ant loved end left' (18.20). And Joyce's advice to the reader is: 'tare it or leaf if' (118.34) – take it or leave it.

The first and the last page of *Finnegans Wake* recalls lines from Tennyson's *Dying Swan*:

> with an inner voice the river ran,
> adown it floated a dying swan

The 'great sweet mother' at the begining of *Ulysses* appears again at the end of the *Wake*. This comes from Swinburne's *Triumph of Time*:

I will go back to the great sweet mother,
mother and lover of men, the sea,
I will go down to her, I and none other,
Close with her, kiss her, and mix her with me,

My lips will feast on the foams of thy lips,
I shall rise with thy rising, with thee subside . . .

Swinburne's 'fair white mother' is substituted by 'cold mad father' (628.02), alluding to Finn MacCool, King Lear and Mananaan MacLir. The Liffey embracing the cold sea is like Molly dreaming about Leopold in his youth, 'that awful deepdown torrent O and the sea . . . and his heart was going like mad and yes I said yes I will Yes'.

In the poem *A Prayer*, there are proleptic seeds of the end of *Finnegans Wake*.

Cease, silent love! My doom!
Blind me with your dark nearness, O have mercy,
    beloved enemy of my will!
I dare not withstand the cold touch that I dread.
Draw from me still
My slow life! Bend deeper on me, threatening head . . .
Take me, save me, soothe me, O spare me!

The 'whitespread wings like he'd come from Arkangels' (628.10) on the last page represent both Zeus descending on Leda and the Archangel Gabriel of the Annunciation, who, like Zeus, made the maid pregnant. The virgin birth will lead to death and resurrection, and Leda will lay the Humpty-Dumpty egg, from which the twins, Shem and Shaun, jump out. 'See what happens when your somatophage merman takes his fancy to our virgitarian swan?' (171.02).

The swan seems to like it. 'As he was rising my lather' (writing me a letter) . . . 'I was plucking his goosybone' (424.36). 'I have been lost, angel. Cuddle, ye divil ye' (147.02). 'Bite my laughters, drink my tears. Pore into me, volumes, spell me stark and spill me swooning' (145.18). 'When he'd prop me atlas against his goose' (626.13), he 'shootst throbbst into me mouth like a bogue and arrohs' (626.05).

The Archangel Gabriel brings to mind the end of the last story in *Dubliners*: 'Generous tears filled Gabriel's eyes . . . the snow falling faintly throught the universe and faintly falling, like the descent of their last end, upon all the living and the dead'. The whiteness of the bird's wings, the silence of snow.

The swan swoons. Death is near. The white bird darkens. 'You'd rush upon me, darkly roaring, like a great black shadow with a sheeny stare to perce me rawly. And I'd frozen up and pray for thawe' (626.24). 'The' – the last sound of the dying swan, 'the lethest zswound' (214.10) of lethally wounded Leda. Remember me when I cross the Lethe - voice of Joyce from beyond the grave.

The last tear. 'She signs her final tear. Zee End' (28.27). 'To hide away the tear, the parted' (625.30). The 'the' of the departed. That's the end.

The last kiss. Like Arrah na Pogue, Nora of the Kiss, freeing her lover by means of a message which she gives him with a French kiss, ALP gives us the keys to her riddle. 'The keys to. Given'. (628.15). 'Jesus said to Peter: And I will give unto thee the keys of the kingdom of heaven' (Mt. 16,19). But *Finnegans Wake* is not in heaven, but in Hell. In St John's vision, 'an angel came down from heaven having the key of the bottomless pit' (Rev. 20.1).

The last laugh.

Finn, again! Take.
Bussoftlhee,
mememormee!
Till thousendsthee. (628.14)

...–, ...–, ...– ...– (The Morse code for 'V'; 'More. So'. 628.06). It stands for 'victory', and 'fuck you'.

The penisolate war of exiled Shem the Penman is over. Penis mightier than the sword. Isolde was reunited with Tristan. ('Pen' is the name of the female swan). The Peninsular War between Wellington and Napoleon, and other Tweedledums and Tweedledees can be re-enacted again. For the time being, as in the last sentence of Homer's *Odyssey*, a peace has been established between the two contending forces.

Like Sterne's *Sentimental Journey*, *Finnegans Wake* ends in the middle of a sentence. 'The affectionate largelooking tache of tch' (111.19) is like the TUNC page with the large Tau and Xi dominating the page. TUNC is a simple anagram of the missing word in *A Sentimental Journey*. The voyage on the sea of words, full of seamen, such as Sindbad the Sailor, Noah, and Odysseus. All returning home to their Penelopes. 'when all is zed and done, the penelopean patience of its last paraphe' (123.04).

After the Forty days of the Deluge, Noah's Ark lands on the top of a mountain. 'And it came to pass at the end of forty days that Noah opened the window of the ark' (Gen. 8.6.) and sent out the raven and the dove. 'Look, there are yours off, high on high! And cooshes, sweet good luck they're cawing you, Coole! You see, they're as white as the riven snae' (621.36). 'Afartodays, afear tonights, and me as with you in thadark' (622.15). 'Softmorning . . . Folty and folty all the nights' (619.20). Noah was sending messages in empty bottles of Guinness. 'carried in a caddy or screwed and corked' (624.01), 'with a bob, bob, bottledby' (624.02) and 'cast ashore' (623.30).

The first fragment of *Finnegans Wake* was about a 'waterproof monarch of all Ireland' (380.34), the 'pomp porteryark' (624.14), later forming the core of Book ii, Chapt. 3 (pp. 309-382) in which the Norwegian Captain is in charge of a ship carrying bottled Guinness and Phoenix Stout. Guinness' barges used to leave from Kingsbridge, and Joyce had Jack Yeats' canvass depicting such a barge on the Liffey, in his Parisian flat.

It is noteworthy that this chapter opens with an acrostic of Noman.

'It may not or maybe a no' (309.01).

The stout ship is also Noah's Ark, where Noah brews beer and distills whiskey by arclight ('pa's malt had Jhem or Shen brewed by arclight', 3.13). Having taken one too many, he is sprawled across the Ark, exposing his nakedness. His alterego, HCE, is stretched across Dublin, from Howth to Chapelizod, the Wellington monument in the Park being his protruding member. (Both Noah's Ark and the Phoenix Park are also zoos). The comatose Noah is assaulted by his sons, and he curses Ham: 'And Noah awoke from his wine and knew what his younger son had done unto him' (Gen. 9,24). Something similar happened between HCE and three soldiers in the Park, though the nature of the crime is as obscure as in *Genesis*. Other important encounters between a father figure and a young man in *Finnegans Wake* are the blinding of the drunken Cyclops by Ulysses-Noman and the shooting of the bare-arsed Russian Bear/General by the Irish private Buckley at the Crimea. This crime was precipitated by the General using a sod of turf to wipe himself and not realising that 'sod' was a metonym for Ireland, The Old Sod. All these encounters suggest sodomy. Joyce links 'arse' with 'Erse' and Ireland with Sodom. 'Sod's brood, be me fear!' (4.06): God's blood, soda bread, and the breed of sodomites. Noman/Noah-man is also a pun on 'to know a man' in the biblical sense.

In the year of Joyce's birth, 1882, another crime was committed in the park, the Phoenix Park murders, in which Lord Cavendish and his Under-Secretary were assassinated by the Invincibles. At the trial one of the Invincibles was referred to as 'No. 1', i.e. no-one, another Noman.

'*No man*, said the Nolan . . .' were the first words of Joyce to be printed, in *The Day of the Rabblement*, and that word which 'always sounded strangely', 'gnomon', appears at the beginning of the first story in *Dubliners*. (The first word of Homer's *Odyssey* was *andra*, man.)

It was Odysseus who called himself no-one, Noman (*outis*) in the Cyclops chapter – an episode particularly dear to Joyce's heart. When the drunken Cyclops was blinded by Odysseus with a burning pole driven into his eye, the giant roared so much that other Cyclopes came up to see what was happening. – What the hell is

238

going on? Is somebody trying by treachery to murder you? – It's Noman's treachery that is killing me, screamed the giant. – Well, then, if nobody is harming you there is little we can do.

Odysseus then escaped from the blocked cave by hiding under a black ram, slipping through the giant's fingers when the Cyclops was letting his sheep out to graze, one by one. A sort of blindman's bluff. 'Beerman's bluff was what begun it' (422.31). Another 'beerman' is Finnegan, full of beer, stretched on a bier, bluffing his death.

There is an Irish parallel to this story. Finn MacCool got trapped in a cave of Goll, a one-eyed giant. Finn plunged a hot spit into the sleeping eye of the giant and escaped by putting a skin from a goat on himself and mingling with the giant's herd being let out.

The same motif of deceiving the blind old father by a furry disguise is Jacob fooling the dying Isaac by putting on a goatskin, to make his blind father believe that this is his firstborn, Ezau, ready to receive his blessing.

Another no-man was Jesus, half-God, half-man, also known as The Lamb. He slipped out from a cave too. When his disciples came back to the cave where he was buried, he was gone. 'He is not here, for he is risen' (Mt. 28.5). And in the *Acts of the Apostles* we read: 'when we had opened, we found *no man* within' (Acts 5,23). But the Noman of the *Wake* is a black-sheep, or rather half-man, half-goat. A pun on the god Pan. A fauny-man, a funny man. *Finnegans Wake* is a fairytale with the furry tail and the furry head of the hairwigged Earwicker. He falls and rises. What did the earwig say when it fell off the wall again? – Earwigo again.

Finnegans Wake is full of 'punns and reedles' (239.35). The answer to the central riddle of the *Wake*, Shem's riddle, when is a man not a man, is easy, – when he is a noman.

Joyce divided the name of Ulysses into *outis* (Noman) and Zeus. If Homer could make a pun on Odysseus's name, Joyce, our 'homerole poet' (445.32) could do the same with the name of Shem.

Shem in Hebrew means name, or God's name. As Hebrew reads backwards, *nomen* (name) gives *nemon*. *Nemo* in Latin means Noman.

Noman holds the key to the *Wake*. In Rev. 5.3 'No man . . . was able to open the book', and in the words of Noman Jesus: 'I will give unto thee the keys . . . then he charged his disciples that they should tell to no man' (Mat. 16.20).

Shem's riddle, with its solution hidden within Shem's name is modelled on the most famous riddle of all times, the riddle of the Sphinx . . . 'riddle a rede from the sphinxish pairc' (324.06), the Sphinx of the Phoenix Park. 'There is on earth a thing which has four legs, two legs, and three legs, and one voice'. The answer, provided by Oedipus, was – man: in infancy on all four, with a stick in the old age, and on two in between. The answer was hidden in Oedipus's own name: *oida* (I know) and *dipous* (biped, man), i.e. 'I know that the answer is man', 'know-man'. As Sophocles put it: 'The riddling Sphinx caused us to turn our eyes to what lay at our feet'.

The first key appears in the title.

FIN(d) NEG. ANSWA = KE(y).

The key word to Joyce's work. Like an abominable no-man, he says no to everything, to his country, to his church, to his family – Stephen's and Satan's *non serviam*.

'In the best manner of Shem', Joyce wrote to Miss Weaver, 'I developed painful dissertation, punctuated by sighs, excuses, compliments, hypotheses, explanations, silences = no, non, nein'.

Finnegans Wake follows in the wake of the blackshape' (608.21) of *Ulysses*, Noman the Black Sheep. Joyce believed that *Odyssey* was a Phoenician epic. 'The Phoenican wakes' (608.32). *Finnegans Wake* is Phoenician Fake. It slips through our fingers like water.

Let's play with the stream.

JOYCE AND THE FOLK IMAGINATION

Maureen Murphy

Joyceans generally agree that John V Kelleher's essay 'The Destruction of Da Derga's Hostel and 'The Dead" was a brilliant *tour de force* as well as the beginning of a new direction in Joycean scholarship, one that offered early Irish literary sources as a complement to those cited from classical European literature. Kelleher's essay was as important for his observations about how Joyce used his sources as it was for the correspondences that he identified:

> Everyone of course knows that Joyce was fond of weaving into his work parallels with myth, saga and epic. It is, however, a mistake to assume, when such a parallel is identified, that it must be complete. It rarely is. Even *Ulysses* does not reflect the entirety of the *Odyssey*. In *Finnegans Wake* wonders can be done with a mere hint of resemblance.
>
> Usually Joyce is content with a few salient indications as, for example, in the well-known sketch-parody of

Dante's *Divine Comedy* in 'Grace'. 'The Dead' and Bruiden Da Derga similarly is suggestive rather than explicit.[1]

Kelleher's student Maria Tymoczko has continued the investigation of Joyce's use of Early Irish sources, arguing that the *Lebor Gabála*, the Book of Invasions, offers a structural basis for *Ulysses*, one that, for example, adds Celtic resonance to the Cyclops elements in Joyce's portrait of the Citizen. Tymoczko has observed that Joyce, as well as the early compilers of the text, conflated two of the early mythological races: the short, dark, crude *Fir Bolg*, a race conquered by the *Tuatha De Danann* at the first Battle of Moytura, and the demonic Fomorians whom some, like Giraldus Cambrensis, reckoned to be a giant race. Led by Balor of the Evil Eye, whose gaze could destroy his enemy, the Fomorians too were defeated by the *Tuatha De Danann* at another, the second, Battle of Moytura. Tymoczko explains that the Citizen's character – at once crude and chaotic – embraces elements of both the *Fir Bolgs* and the Fomorians. He is both an ordinary person based on the figure of Michael Cusack and a gigantic figure based on Balor of the Evil Eye.[2]

Kelleher and Tymoczko's works invite comparisons between Joyce's work and yet another Irish source, for the Irish folktale is another analogue for the Cyclops chapter of *Ulysses*. Critics are sometimes reluctant to take folklore in Joyce seriously because of the attitude expressed in the well-known passages in 'The Day of the Rabblement', in the John Alphonsus Mulrennen passage at the end of *A Portrait of the Artist as a Young Man* and in his review of Lady Gregory's *Poets and Dreamers*.

Joyce's attitude toward folklore in these passages was in part influenced by his hostility to the Anglo-Irish literary establishment's mining and refining of the tradition and to the nativism of the Gaelic Leaguers who romanticise the Irish speakers of the West of Ireland. His particular dislike of Yeats' 'Cathleen Ni Houlihan' prompted 'The Day of the Rabblement' and Joyce's later parody in the figure of Old Gummy Granny. This dislike may reflect the fact that the play was celebrated both by the Irish Literary Theatre and the Gaelic League at what was the high point of their association, common interest, and mutual admiration that would be the casualties of the trouble over *Playboy of the Western World*.[3] In addition to his own aesthetic reasons, Joyce disliked the Irish language revival, believing it to be too insular. He resisted being overwhelmed by it and the entire wave of cultural nationalism that characterised the Dublin of his day.[4]

Richard Ellmann tells us that Joyce had a change of heart about the West of Ireland after a bout of rheumatic fever during the summer of 1907 and points to the difference between the portrayal of the peasant in *Stephen Hero* where he is the clownish figure one finds in the pages of Samuel Lover's *Handy Andy* and the shrewd countryman who plays his part for the city visitor in *Portrait*.[5] It would take Myles na gCopaleen's *Béal Bocht* to do justice to that encounter but it begins with the deromanticising figure of John Alphonsus Mulrennan.

Ellmann's argument offers another reason to look at folklore and its peasant conservator in Joyce; however, there are still other reasons to examine Joyce's use of folklore: its content, process and function. Folklore in its expression as the folktale is both the most ancient and, so far, the most enduring form of imaginative literature. It also provides the matrix for much great literature.

A folkloric reading of the Cyclops chapter of *Ulysses* offers some interesting correspondence between the action in Cyclops and that in the Irish version of the Polyphemus or 'Ogre Blinded' tale, a story that was in wide circulation well before Homer's time. In his paper 'The Gaelic Storyteller', JH Delargy called the Irish form of the tale, 'a distinct western, perhaps a Celtic 'ecotype', quite distinct from the version in the *Odyssey*.'[6] One characteristic of the 'Irish Ogre Blinded' (AT 1137) is that it is frequently combined with another tale called 'Old Robber Relates Three Adventures' (AT 953). Its listing in the combined form in Seán O'Suilleabháin and Reidar Th Christiansen's *The Types of the Irish Folktale* (1963) indicates that it was distributed in oral and printed versions all over Ireland.

Among the printed versions is 'The Black Thief and the Knight of the Glen' that appeared in *The Royal Hibernian Tales*, a chapbook that circulated in 1825, though the tale itself is much older. William Makepeace Thackeray picked up a copy in Galway and passed a few rainy days reading the tales. He praised the collection in general and 'The Black Thief' in particular, judging it 'worthy of the Arabian Nights', and reproducing much of the story in his *Irish Sketch Book* (1842).[7]

The story begins with a frame story that describes a card game between a woman and her stepsons. She plays with an enchanted deck and sets the sons an impossible task when they lose. The sons meet the Black Thief who tries to help them accomplish the task. When they fail and face death, the Black Thief offers to save the sons by telling three stories that describe greater threats of death than the sons face. The first story is full of transformations. The second is like the Cyclops episode in the *Odyssey* with its motifs of the one-eyed giant and the clever hero who disguises himself by wrapping himself in an animal's skin. The last and best story is the one that offers the most interesting correspondences to *Ulysses*.

In the third story, the Black Thief finds a woman crying with a child. She explains that a one-eyed giant who lives on human flesh has demanded that she give him a pie made from the child. The Black Thief saves the child by suggesting the ruse of putting only the finger of the child in a pie that is otherwise made of swine. In helping the woman and child, the Black Thief is trapped in the ogre's castle. When the ogre returns he hides among the dead bodies on the floor. The ogre arrives and calls for his dinner. Suspicious about the meat, he is given the child's finger and is satisfied. Still hungry, the ogre reaches among the bodies and cuts off part of the Black Thief's buttocks to be roasted. When the ogre falls asleep, the Black Thief takes the ogre's spit, reddens it in the fire, runs the spit through the ogre's eye and escapes.

The blinded ogre pursues the Black Thief by throwing a ring with a kind of homing device at him. The ring falls on the Black Thief's toe and the ogre leaps in his direction. The Black Thief cuts off his toe and throws it into the pond. The ogre follows it into the pond and is drowned.

When the Black Thief finishes the story, the King who holds the stepsons recognises that he himself was the child saved by the Black Thief. He releases the stepsons and rewards the Black Thief.

The correspondence between the folktale and its 'Black Thief and the Knight of Glin' form and the action in Cyclops begins too with a frame story. In Cyclops, a nameless narrator reports what happens in Barney Kiernan's pub. Bloom arrives to meet Martin Cunningham so that together they can go to see Mrs Dignam. Like the Black Thief, Bloom is going to aid a woman in distress concerned for the well-being of her child (children) and Bloom too will use a ruse of sorts, for he has figured out a technicality that will save Paddy Dignam's insurance for the widow and children.

Later in the episode, Bloom's cleverness causes hostility when the loungers at Barney Kiernan's believe that Bloom has picked the winner of the Gold Cup race: 'the only man in Dublin has it. A dark horse. He's a bloody dark horse himself, says Joe' (*U*, 329). It's not Bloom's winnings but his failure to stand his round of drinks that makes Bloom a black thief in their eyes; and Bloom, blind to the charge that he is hoarding his winnings, is truly a dark horse when one observes that the Irish word for blind also carries the meaning of dark.

In the folktale, the villain of the story is a one-eyed giant who lives on human flesh. Joyce's Cyclops is not a man-eating ogre; however, both the Citizen/Cyclops as well as lesser ogres like the nameless narrator destroy others with their invective (citizen) and by malice (narrator). As the Black Thief delivers the princes from death by telling his three stories, so too Bloom uses words about peace, love and justice to counter the destructive talk in the cave of Kiernan's pub.[8]

The one-eyed giant and the Citizen bring our heroes into proximity with the dead. The Black Thief lies among the corpses on the floor of the ogre's castle, while Bloom holds forth in Barney Kiernan's pub in the parish of St Michan's, a church well known in Dublin folklore for the condition of the corpses in its vaults.

Another hazard to the heroes is the chance that they may lose their backsides in their efforts. The Black Thief loses part of his buttocks to the one-eyed giant and Bloom is conscious of a similar risk. We're told that the Citizen's dog Garryowen 'for a fact (he) ate a good part of the breeches off a constabulary man in Santry that came round one time with a blue paper about a licence (*U*, 290)'. Bloom keeps an eye on Garryowen as he comes and goes. Later when he escapes on the car with Martin Cunningham, the Citizen unleashes Garryowen in pursuit.

Bloom keeps his distance from Garryowen but not from the conversation about flayed backsides. When the subject turns to caning as a form of discipline in the British Navy, Bloom accepts the nature of the punishment, further enraging the Citizen who regards flogging as yet another example of British inhumanity. He describes how 'the master of arms comes along with a long cane and he draws out and he flogs the bloody backside off the poor lad till he yells melia murder' (*U*, 323) and then follows the parody of the Credo, 'They believe in the rod, the scourger almighty . . . ' (*U*, 323).

The central motif in the Cyclops chapter of the *Odyssey* and the central motif in the third episode of 'The Black Thief' is the blinding of the ogre with a sharpened, flaming stake. Bloom too blinds the Cyclops/Citizen as well as the lesser ogres among the bar flies at Barney Kiernan's. Flourishing his cigar, Joyce's form of the reddened spit, Bloom punctures ignorance with facts (sometimes) and hate with love.[9] Ellmann enlarged on Joyce's invention to suggest its significance not only for the mock-heroic: the mighty spear juxtaposed with the tupenny cigar, but also for its ennoblement of the mock heroic: Bloom can demonstrate the qualities of man by word of mouth as effectively as Ulysses does by the thrust of his spear.[10] Nearly twenty years later, Ellmann returned to the scene to remark about the I/eye pun, 'Bloom with his advocacy of love tries to put out the Citizen's cyclopean "I"'.[11] There are not only eyes but also winks, nods and peeps indicating the ability of character to see what is there (Bloom), to see what is not there (Bergan sees Dignam's ghost) or not to see at all (the Citizen).

The final correspondence is the ogre's thrown object sent to destroy the fleeing hero. When Martin Cunningham hustles Bloom out of Kiernan's pub, the Citizen – almost as an afterthought – goes to the door in pursuit. His enchanted ring is a Jacobs biscuit tin with Irish scenes and Celtic designs; the homing device is Garryowen, dispatched to tear Bloom apart and, perhaps, to return the quarry to his master. The sun in his eyes, the Citizen is momentarily blinded like the Cyclops. Instead of a material ring, there is a seismic ring which records the extent of the destruction to the city of Dublin, to the Green Street Courthouse and its environs caused by the force of the Citizen's assault.

As the ogre in the folktale dives into the water and drowns, so too the Citizen is ultimately defeated by Bloom's getaway. In the folktale's denouement, the action shifts back to the frame story and to the recognition of the Black Thief as hero and of his reward. The Cyclops episode closes with Bloom's reward, a parody of Elijah's ascension to heaven where Bloom – Ben Bloom Elijah – is rewarded for bringing light to the Gentiles.

Turning from content to structure, or from the tale to its telling, the narrative method of the Irish folktale offers some interesting parallels to the narrative method in the Cyclops chapter. Some critics have identified two narrative voices in the episode. David Hayman characterised Narrator 1 as a mean-spirited sponger who relates the action and Narrator 2 as the voice of parodic interruption.[12] Richard Ellman identified Narrator 1 as Thersites and Narrator 2 as *Paugloss*.[13]

Other commentators have described the two narrative strands with other theories. For example, Mary Beth Pringle's 'Funfersum: Dialogue as Meta-functional Technique in the 'Cyclops' Episode of *Ulysses*' reviews the two narrator theories and concludes that Joyce's method offers 'apparently naturalistic readings of events in Barney Kiernan's and then subtly blurs the 'real' and the 'unreal' narrative strands'.[14] She further distinguishes between the style of the narrative strands: the former involving 'dialogue and advancing the action' and the latter involving parody passages that 'restate, illustrate, expand and comment upon' the action.[15]

The narrative method of the Irish folktale offers another way of considering what Joyce was doing with the narrative voices that critics have found in the episode. In traditional Irish storytelling, the action is interrupted at intervals by 'runs', rhetorical passages the function of which, according to Delargy in '*The Gaelic*

Storyteller, is 'to impress the listener, and the more corrupt and unintelligible they are the greater the effect; but they serve also as a resting place for the storyteller in the recital of long, intricate tales'.[16] Runs, a feature of the long hero tales and of *märchen* or international folktale types, often describe heroic action like setting out for a journey, the hero's dress or weapons, or a battle. They are the sign of the virtuoso storyteller, and the relationship of runs to the oral narrative is very like that of improvisation to melody which distinguishes the accomplished jazz musician.

Students of epic structure have devised a theory of formulaic composition which argues that oral epics were not memorised but were recreated with each telling. Kevin O'Nolan has applied that theory to early Irish literature and to the folktale, concluding that the long formula tends to be specific to a particular context while the short formula is detachable from the context.[17]

O'Nolan identified two kinds of long formulae in the Irish heroic folktale: those involving travel, combat, challenges and obligations, and those involving ordinary activity. O'Nolan's distinction if applied to the Cyclops chapter would allow one to consider that the material attributed to the second narrator – the parodic and the mock-heroic passages – functions the way that runs function in the Irish folktale. There are runs which describe in mock-heroic language the ordinary goings on in Barney Kier nan's pub: entrances, exits, rounds of drinks, and there are those that treat a number of themes parodically.

There are two types of parodic run. The first includes imitations of business and technical writing: a legal contract between Moses Herzog and Michael E Geraghty, a Report of the Society for Psychical Research, and Bloom's physiological treatise. There are burlesques of a parliamentary debate, of a civil court proceeding and of newspaper articles: a fight reported in the argot of an English sportswriter of the time, an arboreal wedding and a description of the visit of the Alaki of Abeakuta which was taken directly from an account in the *Freeman's Journal* for June 2, 1904. Finally, there are literary parodies: the catalogue of food from *The Vision of Mac Conglinne*, James Clarence Mangan's 'Prince Alfrid's Itinerary through Ireland' and – on the last page of the episode –

the second chapter of the Second Book of Kings.

The second group of these parodic runs is made up of those which satirise the Catholic, Gaelic, nationalist cultural hegemony of Dublin in 1904. Most of these runs involve the figure of the Citizen, the Cyclops of the episode who was based on Michael Cusack (1847-1906).

Joyce's caricature of Cusack retains his sobriquet, 'Citizen', his abrasive personality and some of his physical features: body build, full beard, even a 'frank-eyed look' – at least according to a 1906 photograph. Joyce elevates Cusack to Cuchulain in a parody of the heroic style pioneered by Standish James O'Grady, a style that replicates the alliterative style that is a feature of both Irish heroic literature and the Irish folktale.[18]

The burlesque moves from the description of the Citizen to the Citizen's actions. He is certainly among the faithful who participate in the ecclesiastical ceremony that takes place when the procession, led by Father O'Flynn, appears murmuring a litany of Joycean saints to Barney Kiernan's pub. Later, the force of the Citizen's biscuit-tin missile, a throw that befits the man who won the sixteen pound and the forty-two pound shotputs in 1875, rocks Dublin.

All that is good fun. Burlesque turns to satire, however, where Joyce portrays the Citizen as representing the worst aspects of Irish cultural institutions like the Gaelic League and the Gaelic Athletic Association; nationalism is inflated to chauvinism, to racism, distorting Cusack's character grotesquely. He wasn't a Gaelic League convert; he was a native speaker from Clare. While difficult and abrasive, he was not a bigot. Indeed, while Cusack was associated with the GAA, Protestants and Unionists were welcome. Cusack's vision of what the GAA was about was a kind of Home Rule for amateur athletics, one that would open amateur sports to all Irishmen – not just to 'gentlemen', and finally one that would support the revival of Gaelic Games – particularly hurling. In fact, the real Fenian in Cyclops is John Wyse Nolan whose name is a conflation of John Wyse Power and Jim Nolan, both of whom were active in the GAA (Power was a founding member) and both of whom had strong Republican sympathies.

Joyce's most extended and elaborate burlesque describes the death of the hero martyr, a figure that some critics have identified with Robert Emmet. 'The tear and the smile' reflects the mood of the crowd who are by turns cheerful, prayerful, sorrowful and grateful. Special delegations, including the Friends of the Emerald Isle led by a pocket-picking Papal Nuncio, witness the execution, which is death by hanging.

Hanging is a spectre that haunted the Irish folk imagination in the nineteenth century and even into the twentieth century.[19] For Joyce, the hanging, in 1882, of Myles Joyce, an Irish-speaker who did not understand the language of the court proceedings and could therefore not defend himself, became the symbol of 'the Irish nation at the bar of public opinion' in his 1907 essay 'L'Irlanda alla Sbarra', in *Il Piccolo della Sera* (*CW*, 198). Later, in *Portrait*, Joyce associated hanging with his vision of hell. When Stephen emerges from the Belvedere Chapel, he sees the schoolboys' coats hanging 'like gibbeted malefactors, headless and dripping and shapeless' (*P*, 124). Hanging is one of the horrors of Nighttown, and there is plenty of chat about hanging in Barney Kiernan's pub when Alfie Bergan produces Rumbold the Hangman's letter.

Joyce's satire in the execution scene turns on the relationship between the hero and his beloved on the one hand, and the hero and the Irish people on the other. Ultimately, he is betrayed by both. The blushing bride runs off – without delay – with her Oxford suitor, and the crowd betrays his memory.[20]

These betrayals are an aspect of a wider preoccupation with betrayal that occurs not only in Cyclops but in all of *Ulysses*, as it demonstrates how Joyce fused his own anxiety about betrayal with his art.

Writing to his brother Stanislaus on September 24, 1905 Joyce said:

Give me for Christ's sake a pen and ink
bottle and some peace of mind and then,
by the crucified Jaysus, if I don't
sharpen that little pen and dip it into

fermented ink and write tiny little
sentences about the people who betrayed
me, send me to hell. After all there are
many ways of betraying people (*Letters* II, 110).

Bloom also fuses personal and national betrayal: Boylan betrays
Bloom (as Mulligan betrays Stephen) and Castle spies betray the
men of '98 and Robert Emmet.[21] In Sirens, Bloom broods about
Boylan as he listens to Ben Dollard sing 'The Croppy Boy', the
ballad that describes the betrayal of a '98 rebel. In some versions
of the song the informer betrays his family simultaneously with his
country:

As I was going up Wexford Street
My own first cousin I chanced to meet
My own first cousin did me betray
And for one bare guinea swore my life away.

The version of 'The Croppy Boy' that Joyce used in *Ulysses*, the
version contributed by James McBurney of Belfast under the *nom
de plume* Carrol Malone to *The Nation* in 1845, describes a betrayal
that Joyce would have found irresistible: the betrayal of a young
rebel by a sham priest who hears the boy's confession before the
youth goes to Wexford to replace his father and his brother, both
of whom have died in the Rebellion. When the boy finishes his
confession, the priest reveals that he is in fact a yeoman captain
and the boy is hanged as a rebel.

'The Croppy Boy' was a favourite song in Joyce's own reper-
toire. Richard Ellmann described the song as one that Joyce sang
during musical evenings at the Sheehys', because Joyce believed
that the song showed his light tenor voice to advantage (*JJ*, 53).
In later years Joyce remembered the song well enough to write it
out in a 1934 letter to Georgio with advice about how to sing the
song.

The song was the battle charger of the great
Irish light bass William Ludwig. The

present generation does not know it.
It is a pure and noble musical poem, profoundly
sincere and dramatic. When you sing it,
be sure and hold the balance equal between the
captain and the young man. The last stanza
is sung on a solemn and impersonal note.
The effect of this stanza, when rendered by a
voice like yours, is electrifying. A far cry
from 'The Two Grenadiers' and 'The Volga Boat
Song'! This is not a patriotic song like
'The Wearing of the Green'. You could sing
it just as well at Sheffield as at Cork.
Study every word of it and you will make it a
masterpiece (*Letters*, III, 335).[22]

Joyce's letter suggests that the theme of the betrayed rebel had a universal significance for him.

Of all the '98 betrayers, the one who appears by name in *Ulysses* is Francis Higgins, the Sham Squire. Bloom has no '98 literature in his magpie's library; however, there was a copy of William Fitzgerald's *The Sham Squire and the Informers of 1798* among Joyce's library of 600 books left in Trieste when he moved to Paris in 1920. Higgins, a Dublin Castle agent, became proprietor of the *Freeman's Journal* in 1788. He managed the network of informers who operated at all levels of the United Irishmen, one of whom, Francis Magan, betrayed Lord Edward Fitzgerald.

Appropriately enough, the first reference to Higgins appears in Aeolus, where the fickleness of the wind is a good symbol for a double dealer. When Professor McHugh announces the arrival of the *Freeman* editor, saying, 'Here comes the Sham Squire' (*U*, 126), he playfully connects not only Crawford with Higgins but *The Freeman's Journal* with Dublin Castle.

Bloom thinks of the Sham Squire in Wandering Rocks in connection with the betrayal of Lord Edward Fitzgerald. 'That ruffian, that Sham Squire, with his violet gloves, gave him away' (*U*, 241). Higgins' name is ironically slipped between the names of two genuine Irish heroes – Michael Dwyer and Henry Joy McCracken – in the Citizen's litany of Irish heroes in Cyclops, to suggest that the betrayers and the betrayed are inextricable bound in Irish history (*U*, 296).[23]

Higgins is the only '98 betrayer mentioned by name in *Ulysses*, but Joyce knew others. Writing to Stanislaus on November 6, 1906, Joyce referred to Leonard MacNally and Thomas Reynolds when he spoke of Oliver St. John Gogarty, the model for Buck Mulligan, 'Ireland's gay betrayer':

> As for OG I am waiting for the SF [Sinn Fein]
> policy to make headway in the hopes that
> he will join it for no doubt whatever
> exists in my mind but that, if he gets
> the chance and the moment comes,
> he will play the part of MacNally
> and Reynolds (*Letters*, III, 187).[24]

Joyce's link between personal and national betrayal was part of his belief that betrayal is a feature of history. In his 1907 essay 'Fenianism', he reasoned that the movement's organisational pattern was particularly suited to Irish character 'because it reduces to a minimum the possibility of betrayal' (*CW*, 189). Joyce explained the failure of the Fenian movement as a consequence of betrayal. 'And why this disintegration of a movement so well organized? Simply because in Ireland, just at the right moment an informer always appears' (*CW*, 190), words that will recall lines from *Portrait*: 'When you can make the next rebellion with hurley sticks, said Stephen, and want the indispensable informer, tell me (*P*, 202).

'The Home Rule Comet' (1910) repeated the charge. 'She [Ireland] has betrayed her heroes, always in the hour of need and always without gaining recompense' (*CW*, 212). Two years later in 'The Shade of Parnell' (1912), Joyce judged his hero Parnell's greatest nobility to be his struggle with the 'desolate certainty' that 'one of the disciples who dipped his hand in the same bowl with him would betray him' (*CW*, 228). Joyce shared that certainty of betrayal with his hero. Lines from his broadside 'Gas from a Burner' link banished artists with betrayed heroes:

This lovely land that always sent
Her writers and artists to banishment
And in a spirit of Irish fun
Betrayed her own leaders, one by one (*CW*, 243).

Joyce's biographers tell us that Joyce expected, even courted betrayals; however, there was an historical and cultural context for his personal behaviour.[25]

Joyce's obsession with betrayal resulted in his belief that Irish heroes and historical movements failed as a consequence of betrayal – particularly betrayal by the 'indispensible informer'; yet Joyce also had some awareness – about which he had less to say – of the use of failure in Irish history and its part in the development of a particular Irish mystique, the mystique of blood sacrifice.

Proinsias MacCana has identified the central Irish myth as the *puella senilis*, the woman who is literally as old as the hills yet endlessly restored to youth through union with her rightful mate.[26] Critics who have identified the hero/martyr of Cyclops as Robert Emmet have followed the belief that the 'blushing bride' is Sarah Curran, but the hero's murmur 'Sheila, my own' suggests a parody of that myth of ritual marriage between the King and the land, for one of the allegorical names for Ireland is Sheila ni Guaire.

By the nineteenth century, the restoration of the old woman was not accomplished 'through union with her rightful mate', but through the sacrifice of young men. The historical realities of the failures of '98 and 1803 helped create the mystique of blood sacrifice, a motivating force behind the Irish republicanism of the twentieth century. Joyce's satire of that ethos of dying for Ireland in the death of the hero/martyr in Cyclops includes a parody of the precious blood of the precious victim, an allusion to the celebration of blood sacrifice associated with both Christian martyrology and the heroes of 1916.

Joyce recognised the obsessive presence of the mystique of sacrifice in historical as well as in artistic terms. In his 1902 essay on James Clarence Mangan, he saw the degree to which it limited artistic development.

> Mangan is the type of his race. History encloses
> him so straitly that even his fiery moments
> do not set him free from it. He, too, cries out,
> in his life and in his mournful verses against
> the injustice of despoilers, but he never laments
> a deeper loss than the loss of plaids and ornaments.
> He inherits the latest and worst part of a legend
> upon which the line has never been drawn out
> and which divides itself as it moves down the cycle
> (*CW*, 81).

In writing his own history of his people, Joyce was obsessively concerned with betrayal, but his understanding of Irish history suggests that even if Irish heroes were not betrayed, they would be consumed by an historical mystique that demanded blood sacrifice. The result was that Joyce fled both his fraternal betrayers and the women who would hold him captive: his mother, Mother Church and Mother Ireland.

NOTES

1 John V Kelleher, 'The Destruction of Da Derga's Hostel' and 'The Dead', *The Review of Politics*, 27, 3 (July, 1965), p. 421.

2 Maria Tymoczko, 'Symbolic Structures in *Ulysses* from Early Irish Literature', *James Joyce Quarterly*, 21, 3 (Spring, 1984), pps. 222-223.

3 Richard Ellmann observed the change from denunciation to parody in his chapter on Joyce in *Eminent Domain* (New York: Oxford University Press, 1967), p. 40.

4 Joyce considered himself politically a nationalist but resisted its cultural limitations. In a 1906 letter to Stanislaus, he said:

For either Sinn Fein or Imperialism will conquer the present Ireland. If the Irish programme did not insist on the Irish language, I suppose I could call myself a nationalist. As it is, I am content to recognize myself as an exile, and, prophetically, a repudiated one. *Letters*, II, 187.

5 *Eminent Domain*, p. 46.

6 JH Delargy, 'The Gaelic Storyteller', *Proceedings of the British Academy*, 31 (1945), 36.

7 William Makepeace Thackeray, *Irish Sketch Book* (London: Smith, Elder, and Co., 1887), pp. 181-187. (1842).

8 Both the Black Thief and Bloom are versions of Scheherazade who escapes death by telling stories. In his analytic study of fairy tales, Bruno Bettleheim describes Scheherazade as having a strong super-ego and being willing to take risks to obey a moral obligation. This description would apply equally well to the Black Thief and to Bloom. Bruno Bettleheim, *The Uses of Enchantment* (New York: Vintage, 1977), p. 88.

9 Philip Herring reports that Joyce's Notebooks for *Ulysses* record the cigar invention to blind the Cyclops.

10 Richard Ellmann, *James Joyce*, (New York: Oxford University Press, 1959), p. 370.

11 Richard Ellmann, *The Consciousness of Joyce* (New York: Oxford University Press, 1977), p. 67.

12 David Hayman discussed the narrative structure of Cyclops in 'Cyclops', Clive Hart and David Hayman, eds., *James Joyces 'Ulysses'*, (Berkeley: UC Press, 1974), pp. 243-275.

13 Richard Ellmann, *Ulysses on the Liffey*, (New York: Oxford University Press, 1972), p. 109. Joyce provided Ellmann with the

Thersites figure; however Frank Budgen has reported Joyce's remark that Thersites genuinely admires Ulysses.

> You see "I" is really a great admirer of Bloom
> who was, besides a better man, is also more
> cunning, a better talker and more fertile in
> his expeditions. If you've read *Troilus and
> Cressida* you will see that of all the heroes
> Thersites respects only Ulysses. He admires
> Ulysses.

Frank Budgen, *James Joyce and the Making of 'Ulysses'*, (London: Oxford University Press, 1972), p. 169.

That is why Joyce pointed out to Budgen that when the narrator describes Bloom's discoursing saying:

> I declare to my antimacassar if you took up
> a straw from the bloody floor and if you
> said to Bloom: Look at, Bloom. Do you see
> that straw? That's a straw. I declare to
> my aunt he'd talk about it for an hour so
> he would talk and talk steady (*U*, 311).

That it is an expression of admiration for Bloom. Ellmann apparently did not appreciate this approval and characterised the Thersites/narrator as bent only on reduction.

14 Mary Beth Pringle, 'Funfersum: Dialogue as Metafictional Technique in the 'Cyclops' Episode of Ulysses', *James Joyce Quarterly*, 18, 4 (Summer, 1981), p. 399.

15 Pringle, p. 399.

16 Delargy, p. 35.

17 Kevin O'Nolan, 'The functioning of Long Formulae in Irish Heroic Folktales', in Bo Almquist, Séamus Ó Catháin, Pádraig Ó

Héalai, eds., *The Heroic Process* (Dublin: The Glendale Press, 1987), p. 473.

18 Philip Marcus, *Standish O'Grady*, (Bucknell University Press, 1970), p. 86. Joyce parodies the style of Standish James O'Grady whose retellings of Irish legends had done more than the work of any other author to create a romantic 'heroic' vision of the Celtic past.

19 The number of stories in nineteenth century popular literature that end with hanging is an example of the way that anxiety manifested itself in the popular literature of the time and suggests the link between the stories people tell and their needs, fears and desires.

20 Robert Emmet's beloved Sarah Curran married Captain Henry Sturgeon of the Royal Staff Corps in 1805.

21 According to the narrator of Cyclops, the Citizen is still another betrayer, for the Molly Maguires are after him for grabbing the holdings of an evicted tenant (322).

22 Another '98 song associated with William Ludwig was 'The Boys of Wexford' sung shrilly by squatting newsboys in Aelous (129). Bloom recalls the song's refrain as he listents to Ben Dollard sing the Siege of Ross stanza of 'The Croppy Boy' (285). Lines from 'The Boys of Wexford' appear again shouted by the navvy in Circe (451).

23 There are unrelated Higginses in Circe who share some of the unsavoury qualities of the Sham Squire. The mysterious man in the Macintosh identifies Bloom as 'Leopold M'Intosh, the notorious fire-raiser. His real name is Higgins' (485). While it is true enough that Bloom's maternal grandfather was Julius Higgins (682), Bloom, who is a bit of a Sham Squire himself in his relationship with Martha Clifford, attempts to deceive with the false name M'Intosh. Finally, the Higgins surname of the prostitute

Zoe associates the name with corruption.

24 Thomas Reynolds betrayed Wolfe Tone, his friend who was also related by marriage. He betrayed the Dublin leadership of the United Irishmen as well. Leonard MacNally not only betrayed his friends and his nation, he betrayed his profession when he informed on his clients. Friend and legal adviser to the United Irishmen, MacNally counseled the defense in almost every State trial from that of Hamilton Rowan to that of the Catholic Directory in 1811.

25 Mark Schechner's psychoanalytic study of Joyce, *Joyce in Nighttown*, argues that Stephen's theory about Shakespeare's treacherous brothers has parallels among the fraternal betrayers in Joyce's life and fiction and that Stephen's conclusion that Shakespeare's psychic wound was the source of his art is really the same strategy Joyce used. He transcended his anxiety with his art.

26 Proinsias MacCana, 'Women in Irish Mythology', *The Crane Bag* (Dublin: Blackwater Press, 1980), 4, 1, p. 7.

JOYCE'S
PRECURSORS

A Norman Jeffares

In Joyce's end is my beginning. You will remember that *Finnegans Wake* ends thus:

On shandymount Finn's body lies.

Shandymound? Echo of Sandymount? No, Tristram Shandymount. On *Tristram Shandy* Joyce mounted his style. 'I am trying', said he, 'to build many places of narrative with a single aesthetic purpose. Did you ever read Laurence Sterne?'

Joyce's question is the right kind of question to be asked in the dark. You get into the train of education and no sooner are you off than you are plunged into the dark tunnel of specialisation. But when you do emerge into the light how much there is to see. Did you ever read Laurence Sterne? If you reply by asking 'Was he on the syllabus?', you should get a firm answer. That is no way to consider Joyce, the builder of many places of narrative. As our train races past, we can see some of them in the broad sweep of country into which we have burst from the narrow confines of the tunnel.

An old and complex landscape we see, long-settled, but repaired, expanded, contracted; the styles of literary building alter over the years. We race through this landscape heading for the future when we may leave the train and build a place for ourselves, our own words ordered in the pattern of our own style.

Where did Joyce begin? 'Begin at the beginning', was the terse advice of the King in *Alice in Wonderland*, one of Lewis Carroll's memorable characters – and Carroll was one of Joyce's beginnings, Carroll equipped for the journey, Victorian style, with his portmanteau full of his portmanteau-words. But Joyce escaping from an Aquininian tunnel saw Homer's building first of all: the epic: the beginning of his beginning. Shall we discuss the *Odyssey* then? Ah, you say, you can see Mr Bloom as the wandering, eventually homecoming Ulysses; Gerty as lovely Nausicaa on the strand, sea shells sherry and sand-shoes alive o so alive-oh; and Molly blooming not fading no pensive prohibiting prohibitive Penelope she. What did Joyce really get from Homer? Take a prospect of Odysseyland, bring out your Claude glass before we leave it behind in our mad rush to modernism, post-modernism, structuralism, poststructuralism, deconstruction, post-deconstruction, post-post-post, the mileage posts pass by, you crane your neck to look back but it's difficult, we are moving so fast, so fast, so fast.

Isn't the structure what Joyce needed? All God's artists need a structure, but Joyce needed one more than most. Because he overflowed, because without a structure he would have run into the sands, built on them a Hindu temple ambling, seemingly out of any architectural control? No, but because he had a need to marry his imagination and his intellect, a greater need than that of most artists. And because he naturally turned to Homer, because like Homer he came from an oral tradition, because he was a storyteller, he needed form, he needed a skeleton beneath the surface skin of style. By modelling the skeleton of *Ulysses* upon that of the *Odyssey* he gained freedom – for what? He needed to hold himself to his purpose, to his grand overall design, to keep the natural exuberance of his creativity under control. Why? Ah, there's the nub of it.

Joyce was concerned with the stuff of life, the experience of it. He sought in part by wit and humour (those vital elements in him so often unduly neglected by the prolific professors) to illuminate the way our minds work, consciously *and* subconsciously.

This is not – as the literary histories or the critical textbooks at which we have peered in the artificial light of the carriage as we moved through the restrictive tunnel of prescribed reading may have told us – a twentieth century phenomenon, this exploration of the way the mind works at several levels. Jung Joyce was not early Freudened into self-examinification; he did it, to be sure, all on his oney-oh in Dublin's 'fair city'. But others built their places of narrative before Joyce and some of their building anticipated his way of doing it. And he knew that. It is my theme.

Very well, we will begin at the beginning, the epic, the long narrative poem in elevated style about superhuman heroes. From our train speeding through time we see that virtually no sooner was *Gilgamesh* recited in Sumeria (say about 2700 BC) than Homer was composing his primary epics, the *Iliad* and the *Odyssey* (about the eighth century BC) and *Beowulf* was beaten out with mugs of mead in some eighth-century AD alehouse, followed by the *Chanson de Roland* fabricated about 169 years before the French language and Anglo-Norman armour invaded Ireland.

The secondary, literary epic got going with Virgil's *Aeneid* (say, 30-20 BC), the process accelerating in the Renaissance with Dante's *Divine Comedy* (1307-21), Camoens's *The Lusiads* (1572), Tasso's *Jerusalem Liberata* (1575) and Milton's *Paradise Lost* (1667 – revised in 1674).

Then came tertiary epic: the translations by Dryden of the *Aeneid*, by Pope of the *Iliad* and the *Odyssey*. Perhaps we should have another label, that of Quaternary epic (sometimes to be thought of even as Quartan epic for it sometimes gives you the shivers) for the kind of poem known as mock-epic – Pope's *Rape of the Lock*, for example, and *The Dunciad*.

The novel, too, has learned from primary, secondary, tertiary and quaternary epic. Here the genre had barely begun when it began to mock itself. Fielding's *Shamela* parodies Richardson's *Pamela*; he refined his attack in his second attempt, the novel that is a novel as well as a parody, *Joseph Andrews*. In that novel he showed he had begun to learn from Homer the usefulness of a journey, as a structure to hold the action together. But only begun, for Joseph is a young simple soul, no Ulysses of the many middle-aged wiles, nor yet the tolerant decent Everyman Fielding wanted to create.

Fielding realised the novel needed status: he provided it in *Tom Jones* with its very conscious linkage to the epic; indeed it is the mock-epic at its best. He took Homer's voyage and modified it, moving it from the sea to the roads, giving it three parts: the country; the journey on the roads; the city. The tale is told with a fine enjoyment of the parallels between the actions of its non-heroic characters and the heroes of Homer. Though here a digression is demanded, for Homer was not above a bit of irreverence. When the goddesses have a row one calls another a bitchface – and what of the nightclub song that is prescribed by that paragon of hosts King Alcinous of Phaeacia when he sees Odysseus is sad, thinking of home with an exile's intense loneliness? The King tells the blind harpist to get cracking with something cheerful, and Demodocus tells the story – a ballad or short narrative – of Ares, god of war, having an affair with Aphrodite, goddess of love and beauty, the wife of Hephaestus, the lame blacksmith god. Hephaestus suspects them, and constructs a device, a metal net which closes on the adulterous lovers and traps them when they are in bed together. Once he is sure they are immobilised Hephaestus summons the other gods and goddesses to see the trapped couple, and they all stand round and have their sweet fill of laughter. After this Ares is released upon payment of recompense – a hefty fine – no doubt for 'alienation of affections'. The Victorians were perhaps right to translate this flippant cynical Tom Lehrer-ish song as The Lay of Ares and Aphrodite.

But back to the mainline out of the siding, and we see that Fielding used the epic structure because it gave him a model for the novel, a structure, a mould, a form into which he could pour his ideas. It suited written as opposed to oral composition, and yet, paradoxically, the form came from an oral tradition; for the *Iliad* and the *Odyssey* were recited, passed on through memory;

they have all the devices of such work: repetitions, stock descriptions, stock similes that gave the reciter a kind of mental breather (for reciting at length is no easy task) and must have allowed his audience, too, a moment to relax, munch an olive and snatch a gulp from a goatskin before the narrative got going again. You can almost hear them say to themselves 'Oh, it's the old eagle-descending-on-a-lamb simile again – did you get those olives in Hymettus? Very good. Have a swig of this, it's last year's Chian red'.

Fielding knew the value of the oral tradition. He tries to talk to his reader when he gives his literary views. He needed humour: it had its place in what he was creating: a story of a man growing up, having adventures, developing in character and winning his girl; all of this happening within a stylised framework, character neatly balanced by character, and the action moving fast all the time.

Like all great writers Fielding developed. His sexy girls were called Molly – a name, the OED remarks, occasionally applied to a prostitute. Molly Straddle, for instance, in Fielding's *Jonathan Wild* is certainly one. Here she is, complete with Irish connections. The situation is that Heartfree has been robbed of his money. When an apprentice comes in with a £500 note which a gentlewoman, who is looking at jewels in the shop, wishes to change, Heartfree recognises the number as being that of one of those stolen from him and tells Wild this.

> Wild . . . with the notable presence of mind, and unchanged complexion, so essential to a great character, advised him to proceed cautiously; and offered (as Mr Heartfree himself was, he said, too much flustered to examine the woman with sufficient art) to take her into a room in his house alone. He would, he said, personate the master of the shop, would pretend to show her some jewels, and would undertake to get sufficient information out of her to secure the rogues, and most probably all their booty. This proposal was readily and thankfully accepted by Heartfree. Wild went immediately upstairs into the room appointed, whither the apprentice, according to appoint-

ment, conducted the lady.

The apprentice was ordered downstairs the moment the lady entered the room; and Wild, having shut the door, approached her with great ferocity in his looks, and began to expatiate on the complicated baseness of the crime she had been guilty of; but though he uttered many good lessons of morality, as we doubt whether from a particular reason they may work any very good effect on our reader, we shall omit his speech, and only mention his conclusion, which was by asking her what mercy she could not expect from him? Miss Straddle, for that was the young lady, who had had a good education, and had been more than once present at the Old Bailey, very confidently denied the whole charge, and said she had received the note from a friend. Wild then, raising his voice, told her she should be immediately committed, and she might depend on being convicted: 'but', added he, changing his tone, 'as I have a violent affection for thee, my dear Straddle, if you will follow my advice, I promise you on my honour to forgive you, nor shall you be ever called in question on this account'. – 'Why, what would you have me to do, Mr Wild?' replied the young lady, with a pleasanter aspect. 'You must know then', said Wild, 'the money you picked out of my pocket (nay, by G–d you did, and if you offer to flinch, you shall be convicted of it) I won at play of a fellow who it seems robbed my friend of it; you must, therefore, give an information on oath against one Thomas Fierce, and say that you received the note from him, and leave the rest to me. I am certain, Molly, you must be sensible of your obligations to me, who return good for evil to you in this manner'. The lady readily consented, and advanced to embrace Mr Wild who stepped a little back and cried, 'Hold, Molly; there are two other notes of £200 each to be accounted for – where are they?' The lady protested with the most solemn asseverations that she knew of no more; with which when Wild was not satisfied, she cried, 'I will stand search'. 'That you shall', answered Wild, 'and stand strip too'. He then proceeded to tumble and search her, but to no purpose, till at last she burst into tears, and declared she would tell the truth (as indeed she did); she then confessed that she had disposed of the one to Jack Swagger, a great favourite of the ladies, being an Irish gentleman, who had been clerk to an attorney, afterwards whipped out of a regiment of dragoons, and was then a Newgate solicitor, and bawdyhouse bully; and as for the other, she had laid it out that very morning in brocaded silks and Flanders lace.[1]

Wild's Molly Straddle was not so much a Molly as a gangster's Moll. Molly Seagrim is rather different. She is a forward piece of sixteen when she begins to impress the nearly-nineteen year-old Tom Jones. He casts 'eyes of affection' on her:

And this affection he had fixed on the girl long before he could bring himself to attempt the possession of her person: for though his constitution urged him greatly to this, his principles no less forcibly restrained him. To debauch a young woman, however low her condition was, appeared to him a very heinous crime; and the good-will he bore the father, with the compassion he had for his family, very strongly corroborated all such sober reflections; so that he once resolved to get the better of his inclinations, and he actually abstained three whole months without ever going to Seagrim's house, or seeing his daughter.

Now though Molly was, as we have said, generally thought a very fine girl, and in reality she was so, yet her beauty was not of the most amiable kind. It had indeed very little of feminine in it, and would at least have become a man as well as a woman; for, to say the truth, youth and florid health had a very considerable share in the composition.

Nor was her mind more effeminate than her person. As this was tall and robust, so was that bold and forward. So little had she of modesty, that Jones had more regard for her virtue than she herself. And as most probably she liked Tom as well as he liked her, so when she perceived his backwardness, she herself grew proportionately forward; and when she saw he had entirely deserted the house, she found means of throwing herself in his way, and behaved in such a manner, that the youth must have had very much, or very little of the hero, if her endeavours had proved unsuccessful. In a word, she soon triumphed over all the virtuous resolutions of Jones: for though she behaved at last with all decent reluctance, yet I rather choose to attribute the triumph to her, since, in fact, it was her design which succeeded.

In the conduct of this matter, Molly so well played her part, that Jones attributed the conquest entirely to himself, and considered the young woman as one who had yielded to the violent attacks of his passion. He likewise imputed her yielding, to the ungovernable force of her love towards him; and this the reader will allow to have been a very natural and probable supposition, as we have more than once mentioned the uncommon comelinesss of his person: and indeed he was one of the handsomest young fellows in the world.[2]

Perhaps in an age of female chauvinism we should ask why the term 'Yes-Man' is frequently in use. The Mollies of Fielding are Yes-women, and the supreme Yes-woman of literature will be Molly Bloom. 'And yes, I said, yes I will, Yes'. Fielding changed. His last work of fiction, *Amelia*, moves from models of primary epic to those of secondary. Virgil's story of Dido and Aeneas is paralleled by the amour of Booth and Miss Matthews in prison. It has, as Claude Rawson remarked,[3] 'a wry Joycean quality' about it. Booth is an older Tom Jones, and like Tom, his sexual sins reflect a generosity of spirit – matched by his wife Amelia who has all the tolerance of a Penelope.

Here we stop at the wayside halt called Ithaca. It's not Homer's Ithaca but one invented by a French author in which Odysseus has settled back into the routine of pre-Troydays, to the annoyance of his son Telemachus who wants to change the way they run the farm. Odysseus, in fact, has become just a bit of a bore and psychologically they are all ready for him to take off again. One morning he rhapsodises about the weather to his now less patient Penelope. 'Ah, dear', he says, 'do you remember on mornings like this we used to crush the grapes against the infant lips of Telemachus?' 'No, Odysseus', she replies with an edge in her voice, 'We have never had grapes on Ithaca. Some other island, some other woman, some other child . . .'

Back on our way again, we realise that in *Amelia* there is a deepening of feeling, of sensibility. Fielding no longer needs to undercut the portrayal of emotions with irony or mock-heroic mockery. The story becomes more serious, more complex. Booth's inner feelings are bursting to be fully explored, but somehow Fielding can only describe them from outside. As yet the mechanism for portraying inner ideas is not there. But cheer up, look out of the train window. The landscape is changing from Fielding's rustic England. There is Dr Smellfungus in view, the egregious Tobias Smollett who discovered and began the popularisation of the curative climate of the French Riviera. His *Travels* are full of reflections; they blend the rationalism of the eighteenth century with sharp Scottish intelligence. Here is Smollett recording his first glimpses of the Pont du Gard:

I would not willings pass for a false enthusiast in taste; but I cannot help observing, that from the first distant view of this noble monument, till we came near enough to see it perfectly, I felt the strongest emotions of impatience that I had ever known; and obliged our driver to put his mules to the full gallop, in the apprehension that it would be dark before we reached the place. I expected to find the building, in some measure, ruinous; but was agreeably disappointed to see it look as fresh as the bridge at Westminster. The climate is either so pure and dry, or the free-stone, with which it is built, so hard, that the very angles of them remain as acute as if they had been cut last year. Indeed, some large stones have dropped out of the arches; but the whole is admirably preserved, and presents the eye with a piece of architecture so unaffectedly elegant, so simple, and majestic, that I will defy the most phlegmatic and stupid spectator to behold it without admiration. It was raised in the Augustan age, by the Roman colony of Nîmes, to convey a stream of water between two mountains, for the use of that city. It stands over the river

Gardon, which is a beautiful pastoral stream, brawling among rocks, which form a number of pretty natural cascades, and overshadowed on each side with trees and shrubs, which greatly add to the rural beauties of the scene . . . If I lived at Nismes, or Avignon (which last city is within four short leagues of it), I should take pleasure in forming parties to come hither, in summer, to dine under one of the arches of the Pont du Garde, on a cold collation.[4]

There is practicality for you! Being a well educated eighteenth century Scot, Smollett tended to reflect rather than to indulge in reverie. And he did reflect the stream of consciousness in his last novel *The Expedition of Humphrey Clinker*. Here is Jenkins writing to Mary – not Molly, please note – Jones. But, by an interesting and revealing kink, the letter ends up by addressing Mary Jones as Molly. What would the Freudian critics make of that? After it I should not allude to the spelling, which is part of the pleasure of the letter, but draw your attention to its orthography:

Dear Mary,

The squire has been so kind as to rap my bit of nonsense under the kiver of his own sheet – O Mary Jones! Mary Jones! I have had trials and trembulation. God help me! I have been a vixen and a griffin these many days – sattin has had the power to temp me in the shape of van Ditton, the young squire's wally de shamble; but by God's grease he did not purvail – I thoft as how there was no harm in going to a play in Newcastle, with my hair dressed in the Parish fashion; and as for the trifle of paint, he said as how my complexion wanted rouch, and so I let him put it on with a little Spanish owl; but a mischievous mob of colliers, and such promiscous ribble rabble, that could bare no smut but their own, attacked us in the street, and called me *hoar* and *painted Issabel*, and splashed my ciofe, and spoiled me a complete set of blond lace triple ruffles, not a pin the worse for the ware. – They cost me seven good sillings to Lady Griskin's woman at London.

When I axed Mr Clinker what they meant by calling me Issabel, he put the byebill into my hand, and I read of van Issabel, a painted harlot, that was thrown out of a vindore, and the dogs came and licked her blood – But I am no harlot; and, with God's blessing, no dog shall have my poor blood to lick; Marry, Heaven forbid, amen! As for Ditton, after all his courting and his compliment, he stole away an Irishman's bride, and took a French leave of me and his master; but I vally not his going a farting; but I have had hanger on his account – Mistress scoulded like mad; thos I have the comfit that all the family took my part, and even Mr Clinker pleaded for me on his bended knee; thos, God he knows, he had raisins enuff to complain; but he's a good sole, abounding with Christian meekness, and one day will meet with his reward.

And now, dear Mary, we have got to Haddingborough, among the Scots, who are civil enuff for our money, thos I don't speak their lingo – But they should not go for to impose upon foreigners; for the bills on their houses say, they have different *easements* to let; and behold there is nurra geaks in the whole kingdom, nor anything for pore sarvants, but a barrel with a pair of tongs thrown across; and all the chairs in the family are emptied into this here barrel once a day; and at ten o'clock at night the whole cargo is flung out of a back windore that looks into some street or lane, and the maid calls *Gardy loo* to the passengers, which signifies, *Lord have mercy upon you!* and this is done every night in every house in Haddingborough; so you may guess, Mary Jones, what a sweet savour comes from such a number of profuming pans: But they say it is wholesome, and truly I believe it is; for being in the vapours, and thinking of Issabel and Mr Clinker, I was going into a fit of astericks, when this siss, saving your presence, took me by the nose so powerfully, that I sneezed three times, and found myself wonderfully refreshed; and this to be sure is the raisin why there are no fits in Haddingborough.

I was likewise made believe, that there was nothing to be had but *oat-meal* and *seeps-heads*; but if I hadn't been a fool, I mought have known there could be no *heads* without carcasses – This very blessed day I dined upon a delicate leg of Velsh mutton and cully-flower; and as for oat-meal, I leave that to the sarvants of the country, which are pore drudges, many of them without shoes or stockings – Mr Clinker tells me here is a great call of the gospel; but I wish, I wish some of our family be not fallen off from the rite way – O, if I was given to tail-baring, I have my own secrets to discover – There has been a deal of huggling and flurtation betwixt Mrs and an ould Scots officer called Kismycago. He looks for all the orld like the scarecrow that our gardener set up to frite away the sparrows; and what will come of it the Lord nows; but come what will, it shall never be said that I mentioned a syllabub of the matter – Remember me kindly to Saul and the kitten – I hope they got the horn-buck, and will put it to a good yuse, which is the constant prayer of,

> Dear Molly
> > Your living friend,
> > > WIN. JENKINS.[5]

We are coming near the very stream of consciousness and as we peer ahead we can see it dividing off Sterne from his contemporaries. His work seemed for a time a kind of genetic sport in the novel, because what Sterne was creating wasn't fully understood. Said Dr Johnson in 1776, 'Nothing odd will do long. *Tristram Shandy* did not last'.[6] An odd comment, that seems to us, and *it* hasn't lasted, for he was wrong, the old Cham; Sterne *has* lasted. He challenged the assumption that straight chronological order is the only structure for narrative fiction. His own structure was very carefully constructed, none the less.[7] What William James said in a *locus classicus* on consciousness[8] in his *Principles of Psychology* applies well to Sterne:

> Every definite image in the mind is steeped and dyed in the free water that flows around it. The significance, the value of the image is all in this halo or penumbra that surrounds

and escorts it . . .

> Consciousness does not appear to itself chopped up in bits. It is nothing jointed; it flows . . . let us call it the stream of thought, of consciousness, or of subjective life.

Consciousness, then, is not chopped up into divisions of time. How well Auden put it in *New Year Letter* when he said that all our intentions 'Mock the formal logic of the clock'. Sterne revolts against that formal logic in *Tristram Shandy*. At the moment of Tristram's conception Mr Shandy is interrupted by the clock striking. This may be what motivated Mr Shandy's intellectual interest in time. He is predetermined in his mind to give Uncle Toby a clear account of the matter by a 'metaphysical dissertation upon the subject of duration'. Here we meet another philosopher, for Mr Shandy, describing duration more fully and considering the succession of ideas, draws upon John Locke:

> In our computations of time, we are so used to minutes, hours, weeks and months – and of clocks (I wish there was not a clock in the Kingdom) to measure out their several portions to us . . . Now whether we observe it or not, continued my father, in every sound man's head there is a regular succession of ideas, of one sort or another, which follow each other in train.

In train? Imprisoned in space in our train we can the more easily, perhaps, understand imprisonment in time. It can be the routine of realists. Sir Roger Stevens, formerly an Ambassador in Sweden and Persia, when asked the difference between being a diplomat and the University Vice-Chancellor he subsequently became, said he felt imprisoned by his University diary, the routine of meetings of Council, of Senate, of Senate Business Committee, Honorary Degree Committee, and endless appointment committees, meetings of the Vice-Chancellors and Principals' Committee. As an Ambassador he rarely had engagements more than two or three weeks ahead in his diary. There was something inexorable, he thought, in the conventions of the University Calendar, in the way the time of the university's world had, realistically, to be arranged in the fixed routine of the terms that make up the academic year.

What Sterne was doing was reacting against realism and the realists; in his case against the rationale, the conventions of the world of the novel. He reacted by creating his own world, one of ideas and memories, of sensitivity, of mood. The Shandean world is not for the solemn. Dr Leavis, for instance, called it 'irresponsible and nasty trifling'. But it is an attempt, a brave one involving turning the novel inside out, to show that human life, a living, moving, changing thing, the mystery that it is, is *fixed* in a novel, an orthodox novel. Sterne had absorbed that classical sentence *Fixum restat in orbe nihil*. Writing when properly managed, he said, is but a different name for conversation. Here we realise he was born in Ireland, a land of oral culture. Dr Leavis was a product of a print-orientated culture. Ireland is a land of talkers. Wilde said of the Irish, 'We are the greatest talkers since the Greeks, too poetical to be poets, a nation of brilliant failures'. Here our diesel electric locomotive blows a fanfare on its airhorn.

Sterne knew what good conversation was. One thing leads to another. There may be no logical connection between them; there may be no *apparent* connection. But there is the stream of individual consciousness that carries on the flow of ideas and images. Sterne exploits it, for comic purposes, to shock the reader with surprises. (Joyce does the same). He seems to say to his readers, 'Your Worships, look, you appear to think logically, as if your mind is a machine; *but it is not*'. Locke had the idea of discrete elements capable of being arranged beside each other in space. But Sterne overflows, like Joyce. This may be the Irish mind at work, full of imaginative, oral exuberance. Why should this be so? Because conversation has to hold interest. It is the poor man's entertainment; it flourishes best when there are no other distractions. But why pick out the Irish? For the perennial contrast with the English, obviously. The late Professor Stanford maintained the difference between the English and the Irish was a matter of truth. The English tell you less than the truth, the Irish tell you more. Both are liars in their different ways. If you think of the decoration of the Book of Kells, the sheer exuberance of it, you will probably be reminded of the best kind of Irish talk, the kind of thing that Synge well understood when he puts 'a fine bit of talk' in the mouth of the tramp in *The Shadow of the Glen*. But after the verbal exuberance of the Renaissance, perhaps under the influence of the Puritans, the English tradition became instead one of restrained speech, reaching its crescendo of constraint in the clipped chat of the public school boys who ran the Empire with stiff upper lips closed tight in understatement. In the recent words of a Cabinet secretary, this is being economical with the truth. We Irish – as Berkeley might have said – are generous with it: it doesn't cost much. But the English are now catching up under the cultural pressure of working class attitudes of letting emotion rip at least once a week – in the pub, of course, on pay day – and under the subtler pressure of a not fully understood movement into an oral culture, of persons passive in the face of squarefaced screens, active in using the telephone rather than the letter, the luncheon rather than the memoir. Perhaps this oral culture will condone the seriousness of intellectual clowning; it is, after all, a form of exploration.

What Sterne does is to take Locke's ideas (as Joyce did Vico's) and clown with them. Here, in the fourth book of *Tristram Shandy*, he is playing with Locke's view that the association of ideas in the mind is a highly irrational process:

> I am this month one whole year older than I was this time twelve-month: and having got, as you may perceive, almost into the middle of my fourth volume – and no further than to my first day's life – 'tis demonstrative that I have 364 days' more life to write just now than when I set out; so that instead of advancing, as a common writer, in my work with what I have been doing at it – on the contrary, I am just thrown so many volumes back – was every day of my life to be as busy a day as this? – And why not? – and the transactions and opinions of it to take up as much description – And for what reason should they be cut short? As at this rate I should just live 364 times faster than I should write – It must follow, 'an' please your Worships, that the more I write, the more I shall have to

write – and consequently, the more your Worships read, the more your Worships will have to read.

Will this be good for your Worships' eyes? It will do well for mine; and, was it not that my opinions will be the death of me, I perceive I shall lead a fine life of it out of this selfsame life of mine; or, in other words, I shall lead a couple of fine lives together.

What Sterne does is to control the flowing of ideas; he comments freely on them. He *selects* the comic, the pathetic, the sentimental. His characters are eccentrics. Uncle Toby, a retired soldier, plays soldiers. Mr Shandy is full of theories. All this exuberance of creation comes from the countryside of Rabelais, of Burton; it re-emerges into view again in Thackeray and Thurber. Remember the latter's cartoon in which a man, accompanied by two women, comments to one, obviously a visitor, about a third woman crouching on a glass case, 'That's my first wife up there and this is the *present* Mrs Harris'. This has a logic of its own; it is zany; the mixture makes it supremely memorable. Mrs Shandy, however, could never remember:

> It was a consuming vexation to my father that my mother never asked the meaning of a thing she did not understand. That she is not a woman of science, my father would say, is her misfortune; but she might ask a question. My mother never did. In short, she went out of the world at last without knowing whether it turned round or stood still – my father had officiously told her above a thousand times which way it was, but she always forgot.

There is a different stream of consciousness to be observed: the linguistic one. Smollett, for instance, again ponders an example of it in the speech of Mrs Jones; it is full of meanings at different levels:

> Providinch hath bin pleased to make great halteration in the pasture of our affairs. We were yesterday three kiple chined, by the grease of God, in the holy bonds of matter-

money, and I now subscrive myself at your service . . .
Present my compliments to Mrs Gwyllim and I hope she
and I may live on dissent terms of civility.[9]

Here are ambiguities, fusions, telescoping of words and ideas,
incongruities and congeries, double meanings. This leads to the
telegram-style and the portmanteau word so beloved of Lewis Carroll. Sometimes this is based on visual detail. Pip in the opening
chapter of *Great Expectations* tells how he got his ideas of his dead
parents from seeing their tombstones:

> The shape of the letters on my father's, gave me an odd
> idea that he was a square, stout, dark man, with curly black
> hair. From the character and turn of the inscription, 'ALSO
> GEORGIANA, WIFE OF THE ABOVE', I drew a childish
> conclusion that my mother was freckled and sickly. To five
> little stone lozenges, each about a foot and a half long,
> which were arranged in a neat row beside their grave, and
> were sacred to the memory of five little brothers of mine
> . . . I am indebted for a belief I religiously entertained that
> they had all been born on their backs with their hands in
> their trouser pockets, and had never taken them out in this
> state of existence.

Thus runs the sharp insight of Dickens into a child's way of
thinking, into the flow of consciousness. He could recreate adults'
ways of remembering things too. Here is Jack Hopkins at Bob
Sawyer's party telling the story of the child that swallowed his sister's necklace:

> "Next day, child swallowed two beads; the day after
> that, he treated himself to three, and so on, till in a week's
> time he had got through the necklace – five-and-twenty
> beads in all. The sister, who was an industrious girl and
> seldom treated herself to a bit of finery, cried her eyes out
> at the loss of the necklace; looked high and low for it; but
> I needn't say, didn't find it. A few days afterwards, the
> family were at dinner – baked shoulder of mutton and

potatoes under it – the child, who wasn't hungry, was playing about the room, when suddenly there was heard the
devil of a noise, like a small hailstorm. 'Don't do that, my
boy', says the father. 'I ain't a-doin nothing', said the child.
'Well, don't do it again', said the father. There was a short
silence, and then the noise began again, worse than ever. 'If
you don't mind what I say, my boy', said the father, 'you'll
find yourself in bed, in something less than a pig's whisper'.
He gave the child a shake to make him obedient, and such
a rattling ensued as nobody ever heard before. 'Why,
dam'me, it's in the child', said the father, 'he's got the
croup in the wrong place!' 'No, I haven't, father', said the
child, beginning to cry, 'it's the necklace' I swallowed it,
father'. The father caught the child up, and ran with him to
the hospital, the beads in the boy's stomach rattling all the
way with the jolting; and the people looking up in the air,
and down in the cellars, to see where the unusual sound
came from. 'He's in the hospital now', said Jack Hopkins,
'and he makes such a devil of a noise when he walks about,
that they're obliged to muffle him in a watchman's coat, for
fear he should wake the patients'".

George Orwell has pointed out[10] the detail that he says only
Dickens would have noticed, such things as 'baked shoulder of
mutton and potatoes under it'.

We may be travelling fast but time is relative, so is speed; to
Alfred Jingle in *Pickwick Papers* the stage coach seemed every bit as
fast as our diesel electric, as he travelled past local landmarks:

'Terrible place – dangerous work – other day – five
children – mother – tall lady, eating sandwiches – forgot
the arch – crash – knock – children look around – mother's
head off – sandwich in her hand – no mouth to put in –
head of a family off – shocking, shocking! Looking at
Whitehall, sir? – fine place – little window – somebody
else's head off there, eh, sir? – he didn't keep a sharp look-
out enough either – eh, sir, eh?'[11]

You can find this kind of thing in Fenimore Cooper's *The Spy* (in the speech of Caesar the slave) and Melville's *Moby Dick* (where Ahab scans the sea 'What I've dared I've willed, and what I've willed I'll do . . . I now prophesy, I will dismember my dismemberer'). It is reminiscent of the selfcommunion in Stephen Dedalus' soliloquy on the sea shore, in some ways; but it goes back further, to 'Shakespeare's Llewellen or, if we want an Irish example, to Maria Edgeworth's *The Absentee*. Reflection; reverie; soliloquy: here, then, is Maria Edgeworth:

'It will do very well, never mind', repeated Petito, muttering to herself as she looked after the ladies whilst they ran downstairs 'I can't abide to dress any young lady who says never mind and it will do very well. That and her never talking to one confidentially or trusting one with the least bit of her secrets, is the thing I can't put up with from Miss Nugent; and Miss Broadhurst holding the pins to me, as much to say, do your business, Petito, and don't talk. Now that's so impertinent, as if one wasn't the same flesh and blood, and had not as good a right to talk of everything, and hear of everything, as themselves. And Mrs Broadhurst, too, cabinet counselling with my lady, and pursing up her city mouth, when I come in, and turning off the discourse to sniff, forsooth, as if I was an ignoramus, to think they closetted themselves to talk of snuff. Now, I think a lady of quality's woman has as good a right to be trusted with her lady's secrets as with her jewels: and if my Lady Clonbrony was a real lady of quality, she'd know that, and consider the one as much my paraphanalia as the other. So I shall tell my lady tonight as I always do when she vexes me, that I never lived in an Irish family before, and don't know the ways of it. Then she'll tell me she was born in Hoxfordshire; then I shall say with my saucy look 'Oh was you my lady? I always forget that you was an Englishwoman'. Then maybe she'll say, 'Forget! You forget yourself strangley, Petito'. Then I shall say with a great deal of dignity 'If your Ladyship thinks so, my Lady, I'd better go'. And I'd desire no better than that she should take me at my word, for my Lady Dashfort's is a much better place,

I'm told, and she's dying to have me I know.

Soliloquy, by *Reflection* out of *Reverie*. This horse is cantering beside our train, drawing attention to *Ironical Comedy*, a fast runner out of *Restoration Situation* by *Witty Dramatist*. And in the blood line there runs *Irish Talk*. Remember Yeats, who hated Locke, deliberately acting out his poems in imitation of Irving's Hamlet, of Irving and his plume of pride. 'Oh, well', said the policeman in Harold's Cross, disturbed by seeing the young man walking equally unconcerned over clean footpaths and muddy puddles, 'If it's only the poetry working in his head'. Here is the inner soliloquy becoming the outer, as drama demands.

There is a midway point – the diary. Fanny Burney soliloquises in hers. Who would have thought *her* a maidenly Molly Bloom? And a hundred years before Molly, too!

> Well, I am going to bed – Sweet dreams attend me – and may you sympathize with me. Heigh ho! I wonder when I shall return to London! – Not that we are very dull here – no, really – tolerably happy – I wish Kitty Cooke would write to me – I long to hear how my dear, dear, beloved Mr Crisp does. My papa always mentions him by the name of my Flame. Indeed he is not mistaken – himself is the only man on earth I prefer to him. Well – I must write a word more – only to end my paper – so! – that's done – and now good night to you.[12]

And what of Miss Bates? In *Emma* her stream of consciousness flows meanderingly round oxbow bends in mesmeric murmurings, in what Jane Austen permitted herself to call her 'incessant flow':

> "So very obliging of you! – No rain at all. Nothing to signify. I do not care for myself. Quite thick shoes. And Jane declares – Well!" (as soon as she was within the door), "well! This is brilliant indeed! This is admirable! Excellently contrived, upon my word. Nothing wanting. Could not have imagined it. So well lighted up! Jane, Jane, look! did you ever see anything –? Oh! Mr Weston, you

must really have had Aladdin's lamp. Good Mrs Stokes would not know her own room again. I saw her as I came in; she was standing in the entrance. 'Oh! Mrs Stokes would not know her own room again. I saw her as I came in; she was standing in the entrance. "Oh! Mrs Stokes', said I – but I had not time for more". She was now met by Mrs Weston. 'Very well, I thank you, ma'am. I hope you are quite well. Very happy to hear it. So afraid you might have a headache! seeing you passby so often, and knowing how much trouble you must have. Delighted to hear it indeed! – Ah! dear Mrs Elton, so obliged to you for the carriage; excellent time; Jane and I quite ready. Did not keep the horses a moment. Most comfortable carriage. Oh! and I am sure our thanks are due to you, Mrs Weston, on that score. Mrs Elton had most kindly sent Jane a note, or we should have been. But two such offers in one day! Never were such neighbours. I said to my mother, 'Upon my word, ma'am – 'Thank you, my mother is remarkably well. Gone to Mr Woodhouse's. I made her take her shawl – for the evenings are not warm – her large new shawl, Mrs Dixon's wedding present. So kind of her to think of my mother! Bought at Weymouth, you know; Mr Dixon's choice. There were three others, Jane says, which they hesitated about some time. Colonel Campbell rather preferred an olive. – My dear Jane, are you sure you did not wet your feet? It was but a drop or two, but I am so afraid; but Mr Frank Churchill was so extremely – and there was a mat to step upon. I shall never forget his extreme politeness. Oh! Mr Frank Churchill, I must tell you my mother's spectacles have never been in fault since; the rivet never came out again. My mother often talks of your good-nature; does not she, Jane? Do not we often talk of Mr Frank Churchill? Ah! here's Miss Woodhouse. Dear Miss Woodhouse, how do you do? Very well, I thank you, quite well. This is meeting quite in fairyland. Such a transformation! Must not compliment, I know" (eyeing Emma most complacently) – that would be rude; but upon my word, Miss Woodhouse, you do look – how do you like Jane's hair? You are a judge. She did it all herself. Quite wonderful how she does her hair! No hairdresser from London, I

think, could – Ah! Dr Hughes, I declare – and Mrs
Hughes. Must go and speak to Dr and Mrs Hughes for a
moment. How do you do? How do you do? Very well I
thank you. This is delightful, is not it? Where's dear Mr
Richard? Oh! there he is. Don't disturb him. Much better
employed talking to the young ladies. How do you do, Mr
Richard? I saw you the other day as you rode through the
town. Mrs Otway, I protest, and good Mr Otway, and Miss
Otway, and Miss Caroline. Such a host of friends! and Mr
George and Mr Arthur! How do you do? How do you all
do? Quite well, I am much obliged to you. Never better.
Don't I hear another carriage? Who can this be? – very
likely the worthy Coles. Upon my word, this is charming,
to be standing about among such friends! and such a noble
fire! I am quite roasted. No coffee, I thank you, for me;
never take coffee. A little tea, if you please, sir, by-and-by;
no hurry. Oh! here it comes. Everything is so good!"[13]

The question of the relationship of soliloquy and reverie is
raised in any contemplation of George Moore's now unduly
neglected writing. His development is in some ways akin to that of
Joyce.[14] After his career as Zola's richochet with *Esther Waters* and
A Mummer's Wife came his career as an Irish writer. His short
stories in *The Untilled Field* explore the sordid, the dreary, the
static in the countryside of the west of Ireland, whereas Joyce
drew upon what seemed to him the paralysis, the decay of Dublin
in the east.

Moore next created the melodic line, wanting to avoid transitions, interpolated retrospects, struggling movements from one
consciousness to another. And an audience is much less conscious
of these when listening to a story told orally. 'I often', he
remarked, 'tell my stories better than I write them'. The presence
of the storyteller carries the story along; he skips obstacles without
the listener perceiving the skips and bounds. The equivalent in
Moore's career to Joyce's *A Portrait of the Artist as a Young Man* is
The Lake, where Moore's capacity to blend imaginative reverie with
thought is magnificently achieved. Father Gogarty is affected by
his beautiful surroundings. Here is the first version of 1905:

The earth and sky were enfolding in one tender harmony of rose and blue, the blue shading down to gray, and the lake floated amid vague shores, vaguely as a dream floats through sleep. The swallows were flying high, quivering overhead in the blue air. There was a sense of security and persuasion and loveliness in the evening.

And here is the rewritten version of 1921:

And he watched the earth and sky enfolded in one tender harmony of rose and blue – blue fading to grey, and the lake afloat amid vague shores, receding like a dream through sleep.

After his superb evocations, the more effective as he worked on them, cutting them to simpler patterns, came his parallel to *Ulysses*, a *Portrait of Himself as Impotent Sigfried*, or to give it its proper title, *Hail and Farewell*. Like Joyce after him, Moore needed a model; but he chose Wagner rather than Homer. He was writing out of established success; though a landlord, he was hardly of the establishment, as his portraits in *A Drama in Muslin* and his vain efforts to be invited to Dublin Castle – in his preparation for writing that devastating exposé of the marriage market – clearly, and most amusingly, demonstrate. *Enfant terrible* he remained. But his Dublin is very different from Joyce's; *Hail and Farewell* moves among the figures of the literary movement that Joyce affected to despise. Moore had, by landlord's standards, to live on very little money indeed when beginning his writing career; shortage of money has been the spur that urged on many Irish writers – the list is long. Farquhar, Goldsmith, Sheridan, Wilde, Shaw and Yeats, for example, had to make their way in the world by writing. And so indeed had Joyce, more than any of them. None of the other families had to burn the wood of staircases in the fireplace of rented houses. But Moore's Dublin in *Hail and Farewell* is decidedly not short of funds; though Moore mocks and satirises, he does this at a social level different from Joyce's, and from a position of success.

After finishing *Hail and Farewell* Moore had, in every sense, exhausted Dublin. There followed his *Finnegans Wake* in *The Brook Kerith*, his movement into historical phantasy matched by the contemplation of *Heloise and Abelard*, all conveying the flow of thought easily, convincingly, in their stylised narrative.

But *The Lake* is *the* novel of Moore to leave with you – here is narrative, reflection, speech; the flow of inner and outer consciousness. This is not only the stream of consciousness but the fountain of human creativity:

> His thoughts melted into nothingness, and when he awoke from his reverie he was thinking that Norah Glynn had come into his life like a fountain, shedding living water upon it, awakening it. And taking pleasure in the simile, he said, "A fountain better than anything else expresses this natural woman", controlled, no doubt, by a law, but one hidden from him. "A fountain springs out of earth into air; it sings a tune that cannot be caught and written down in notes; the rising and falling water is full of iridescent colour, and to the wilting roses the fountain must seem not a natural thing, but a spirit, and I, too, think of her as a spirit". And his thoughts falling away again he became vaguely but intensely conscious of all the beauty and grace and the enchantment of the senses that appeared to him in the name of Nora Glynn.

The stream of consciousness uses the imperfect rather than the past tense: the author aims often at the continuous present; it is a tense, incidentally, peculiar to Irish, whose writers 'do be' using it continuously, and it is one of which Irish writers in English are well aware. It becomes a matter of montage, then. Moore achieved flow by adding 'and', Joyce by removing it. Why? Because he strives to represent a piece of objectivity through what can be called montage, because his art is to create reality through artifice, through trying to unite art and life. He was well aware of Bergson's views – Bergson is Bitchson in *Finnegans Wake* and so each moment in *Ulysses* necessarily is unique. Always passing the stream of life, says Bloom; and (as though he had read that *locus classicus* of William James: 'every definite image in the mind is steeped and dyed in the free water that flows around it'. Perhaps Joyce remembered James' *Principles of Psychology*?) 'How can you own water really? It's always flowing in a stream, never the same, which is the stream of life we trace?'

The idea was taken over into literary criticism by a reviewer, May Sinclair, who was reviewing Dorothy Richardson's novels in 1918. *Pointed Roofs* (1915) has in the accepted sense, no plot, no tragedy, no comedy, no love interest, no catastrophe – only Miriam Henderson who lives, experiences, reacts to the stimuli of others and the world of things – life to her is 'an incessant shower of innumerable atoms'. What does it all add up to? A governess in a school in Germany returns to England, is disappointed in love. Dorothy Richardson creates in her an over-sensible woman to whom the world exists as material for her sensibility to assimilate. How does one select? This is something that Virginia Woolf's characters search for: the paring down of experience. She puts it thus in *Orlando*:

But Time, unfortunately, though it makes animals and vegetables bloom and fade with amazing punctuality, has no such simple effect on the mind of man. The mind of man, moreover, works with equal strangeness upon the body of time. An hour, once it lodges in the queer element of the human spirit, may be stretched to fifty or a hundred times its clock length; on the other hand, an hour may be accurately represented on the timepiece of the mind by one second. This extraordinary discrepancy between time on the clock and time in the mind is less known than it should be and deserves fuller investigation.

Time is the crux as well as the multiplicity:

And indeed it cannot be decried that the most successful practitioners of the art of life – somehow continue to syn-chronise the 60 or 70 different times which beat simul-taneously in every normal human system so that when 11 strikes all the rest chime in unison. Now as she stood with her hand on the door of her motor car – the present again struck her on the head 11 times she was violently assaulted. 'Confound it all' she cried, for it is a great shock to the nervous system hearing a clock strike.

And talking of hearing the clock about to strike, I should leave you with two points to consider about Joyce, and, especially, about his predecessors. He and Édouard Dujardin did not invent the stream of consciousness, nor the monology of the interiors – the interior monologue. Joyce paid tribute to Dujardin's *Les Lauriers sont Coupes* (a short novel published in 1887 in which a young man rambles on in the present tense) and Dujardin's own rambling shambling definition is worth considering:

The internal monologue, in its nature on the order of poetry, is that unheard and unspoken speech by which a character expresses his inmost thoughts (those lying nearest the unconscious) without regard to logical organisations – that is, in their original state – by means of direct sentences reduced to the syntactic minimum, and in such a way as to give the impression of reproducing the thoughts just as they come into the mind.

This is worth considering because the interior monologue is *unheard*, *unspoken*. And the artist reduces it to the syntactic minimum. Joyce cut out 'and'. And the telegram-style, the portmanteau words of Lewis Carroll and earlier writers achieved this out of a Victorian attitude, not a modernist one. Art is not a matter of time.

The second point is that the poets knew about it too. Once the inhibitions of the eighteenth century were shed (perhaps more through Coleridge's ideas than is often thought) Browning's dramatic monologues are 'heard' by convention. They too demand elliptic syntax. And Coleridge paved the way in 'Frost at Midnight' which shows the range of the romantic mind:

The Frost performs its secret ministry,
Unhelped by any wind. The owlets's cry
Came loud – and hark, again! loud as before.

The inmates of my cottage, all at rest,
Have left me to that solitude, which suits
Abstruser musings: save that at my side
My cradled infant slumbers peacefully.
'Tis calm indeed! so calm, that it disturbs
And vexes meditation with its strange
And extreme silentness. Sea, hill, and wood,
This populous village! Sea, and hill, and wood,
With all the numberless goings-on of life,
Inaudible as dreams! the thin blue flame
Lies on my low-burnt fire, and quivers not;
Only that film, which fluttered on the grate,
Still flutters there, the sole unquiet thing.
Methinks, its motion in this hush of Nature
Gives it dim sympathies with me who live.
Making it a companionable form,
Whose puny flaps and freaks the idling spirit
By its own moods interprets, everywhere
Echo or mirror seeking of itself,
And makes a toy of Thought.

The theme, like our train, has reached its terminus. Now I offer you a return ticket, to return you to thoughts of that great writer washed by the lapping waters, to the Shandymount of Joyce, to Laurence Sterne, the greatest of Joyce's precursors.

NOTES

1 Henry Fielding, *Jonathan Wild*, II, v.

2 Henry Fielding, *Tom Jones*, IV, vi.

3 CJ Rawson, *Henry Fielding* (1968), p. 8.

4 Tobias Smollett, *Travels through France and Italy*, text from *The Miscellaneous Works* (1800) V, p. 312.

5 Tobias Smollett, *The Expedition of Humphry Clinker*, text from *The Miscellaneous Works* (1800) VI, pp. 237-9.

6 See, in this connection, Peter Quennell, *Samuel Johnson his Friends and Enemies*, (1972) pp. 214-16.

7 In this he resembles David Hume, who in his *A Treatise of Human Nature: Being an Attempt to introduce the experimental Method of Reasoning into Moral Subjects* (1739) regarded human personality as a 'bundle of perceptions' and put his views elegantly in a carefully constructed style: elegance and neatness were to allow his writing to command 'the Attention of the World' with its ironic scepticism, its presentation of personal identity as a mere legend, perceptions 'in perpetual flux and movement'.

8 I first met this in Melvin Friedman, *Stream of Consciousness. A Study in literary method* (1955), a stimulating book which prompted me to reread several of the texts from which quotations are made subsequently. Two other useful studies of the stream of consciousness are *The Stream of Consciousness in the Modern Novel*, ed. Robert Humphrey (1958) and *The Stream of Consciousness: scientific investigations in the flow of human experience*, ed., Kenneth F Pope (1975).

9 Tobias Smollett, *The Expedition of Humphry Clinker*, text from *The Miscellaneous Works* (1800) VI, pp. 383-4.

10 See his *Critical Essays* (1946), p. 46.

11 Jingle's telegram-style has to be translated by Job in 'the final snit' of the couple in Chapter LIII. Jingle, when Perker points out that Mr Pickwick by – 'corresponding with Jingle's creditor, releasing his clothes from the pawnbrokers, relieving him in prison, and paying for his passage' has 'already lost upwards of fifty pounds'. Jingle hastily rebuffs this. 'Not lost. Pay it all – stick to business – cash up – every farthing. Yellow fever, perhaps can't help that – if – ' Job translates: 'He means to say that if he is not carried off by fever, he will pay the money back again. If he lives, he will, Mr Pickwick'.

12 When Fanny Burney was being courted by the chevalier Alexander-Jean-Baptiste Piochard d'Arblay in the first seven months of 1793 – they married on 28 July of that year – her accounts of their relationship convey her hesitant reactions with great charm. Here is her account of her feelings on 10 April 1793:

> *Tuesday* [9 April] nothing passed whatsoever; but *Wednesday April* 10th., I received early a Note from Mrs. Lock, to invite me to Dine, though mentioning an Engagement for the Evening, but preferring Dinner to nothing, & adding 'And poor M. D'Arblay will be quite delighted'. This amazed me – but was too open to alarm me, & I resolved to go. I expected M^c de Ronchrolle would be there, & mentioned that for my inducement here.
>
> And now comes an account of the sweetest Hour or two that ever – I fear – will fall to my lot. I dare hope no repetition, circumstanced as I am every way! – more than passed now would distress & disturb – less, perhaps, now, would be uninteresting & flat. – To this Morning, just as it passed, I look back with unmixt pleasure.
>
> I had begged the Carriage to take me to Portland Place, & to bring me home early, as Mrs. Lock was engaged for the Evening. My Father had consented; his indisposition still preventing his using the Horses for himself.
>
> About one o'clock, while I was with my Father in the

study, Sarah came flying from the Parlour, exclaiming 'Sister Fanny, here's M. D'Arblay!' –

I did not affect being much grieved! – but I fear I was less calm than my Father knew how to account for: however, I had no time for such investigation; & hurried to the Parlour with what speed I could –

My mother had flown the premises, into the next Room; & Sarah did not re-appear: I found him therefore alone: & the moment he had enquired after my Health, he would have begun – without an instant's procrastination, upon a subject I had entreated him to leave out of our discourse.

I made an immediate check – & most truly in earnest – as he could not but see – my firm wish & plan being to avoid all further engagement or tie or entanglement, till I had settled my own doubts for HIM, & seen more of probabilities for myself. He resisted me gently, but not importunately, &, though he looked disappointed, looked, also, too just to attribute my averseness to any thing that ought to offend him.

Less than a week later she is considerably less hesitant in confiding her feelings to her sister Susanna Elizabeth Phillips in the blend of journal and letter that recorded, minuted down the tension and excitement created in Fanny by d'Arblay's courtship:

My Father came in very gravely, & full of reserve & thought. M. d'A. not aware how little this was his custom, used every effort to inspire the gaiety with which his own mind was teeming; & my dear Father, never insensible to such exertions, was soon brought round to appear more like himself; &, in a short time, his amiable Nature took the reins from his fears & his prejudices, & they entered into literary discussions with all the animation & interest of old friends. My Father then produced sundry of his most choice literary curiosities, & particularly Italian, when he found that language familiar to his Guest. His fine Editions of Ariosto, Dante, Petrarch & Tasso, were appreciated with delight. Then came forth the select Prints, &c, & then the collection of French Classics, which gave birth to disquisitions, interrogatories, anecdotes, & literary contentions, of the gayest & most entertaining nature: – while, though not a word passed between us, I received, by every opportunity, des regards si touchans, si heureux! – Ah, my dearest Susanna! – with a Mind thus formed to meet mine – would my dearest Father listen ONLY TO HIMSELF, how blest would be my lot! –

Extracts from Fanny Burney, *Journals and Letters* ed. Joyce Henslow, 2 vols 1972, pp. 59 and 81.

13 Jane Austen, *Emma* (1876) Chapter XXXVIII.

14 Melvin Friedman, *op. cit.*, pp. 37-41, points out various experiments in Moore's *Mildred Lawson* (in *Celibates* [1895]) and *Mike Fletcher* (1889), remarking that Moore said of *Ave Atque Vale* that 'my nonsense thoughts amuse me; I follow my thoughts as a child follows butterflies' (*Memoirs of my Dead Life* (1911) p. 3). He regards Moore as an anticipator of the stream of consciousness, citing his appreciation of his friend Dujardin's *Les Lauriens Sont Coupe's* (1887), where he thought Dujardin had 'discovered the form, the archetypal form, the most original in our time; but the psychology is a little "naturalist"' (see *Letters from George Moore to Eduoard Dujardin, 1886 – 1922* (1929), p. 40). Another letter to Dujardin, (8 November 1930) is cited as a metaphorical definition of interior monologue, in terms of Moore's own procedures: 'When the novel stops going into the wings to ring down the curtain we begin to hear exquisite music. The cage is open and the birds (our thoughts) sing in free verse'. See Dujardin, *Le Monologue Interieur* (1931) p. 79.

POUND'S JOYCE, ELIOT'S JOYCE

Denis Donoghue

I should declare an interest, before acting upon it. It may appear that by referring to Joyce, Pound and Eliot as if in the same breath, I am taking for granted the Modernism they are commonly supposed to exemplify. Or at least that I am content to see these writers in the context of 'the modern movement in literature' or some such designation. In fact, I no longer find the notion of Modernism at all useful: even in regard to certain work in music, painting, sculpture and literature, I don't see what is to be gained by bringing into one context such disparate artists as Mallarmé, Kafka, Rilke, Matisse, Picasso, Schoenberg, Webern, Eliot, Proust, Pound, Joyce, Yeats, Brancusi, Lawrence and Conrad. You may say: 'why then have you not included James and Hardy, unless you think that they, living in the years of a conventionally assumed Modernism, were somehow not of the modernist persuasion?' To which I would reply: 'I could well have included not only these but Stevens and Frost and Faulkner, making the notion of Modernism even less useful than ever'. These artists are interesting only in their differences, one from another. If we posit any quality they are deemed to share, or an historical predicament to which their work is supposed to be a response, we find that the quality, like the predicament, is so tenuous as to be useless. If there was a predicament, why did several major artists give no sign of suffering from it?

Even if we take up a smaller question: the history of modern poetry in English can be recited in any one of several rival versions. If you 'start' with Hopkins, as FR Leavis did in *New Bearings in English Poetry*, you can indicate a trajectory of forms and interests governing the poems of Eliot, Pound, Empson and a few other poets. If you start with Emerson and Whitman, you can describe a different motive, which may indeed include reference to Eliot and Pound but which will culminate in Olson and the Black Mountain poets. If you deem Pound to be the crucial figure, as Hugh Kenner does in *The Pound Era*, you claim privilege for the poetic interests which Pound made available to the Objectivists and to William Carlos Williams and Marianne Moore. If you take Eliot as the exemplary modern poet, you prescribe for him certain interests derived however circuitously from Tennyson, Arnold, Pater, the French Symbolists and Laforgue, with Whitman as a largely suppressed figure in the American background. And if you are Philip Larkin, you brush these affiliations aside as errors of judgement, and edit the *New Oxford Book of Twentieth Century Verse* on the assumption that Hardy is the greatest modern poet and that the genuine tradition of modern poetry respects the forms of poetry which he, rather than Eliot or Pound or Hopkins, made available. Meanwhile, what do we do with Yeats, unless like the Eliot of *After Strange Gods* we regard Yeats as not only a freak of nature but an Irish freak, a thing apart. At this point I suspect the whole project. Or rather: I become convinced that if we construe the history – assuming that is *has* a history – of modern poetry in one way rather than another, we do so for reasons not literary but political and ideological.

In some desperation I offer this thought: a writer is modern if he or she despises, fears or otherwise rejects Bernard Shaw. The only quality I find in common among the writers I normally called modern is contempt for Shaw, Wells, Chesterton, Belloc,

Bennett. I would add Ibsen but for the fact that Joyce revered him.

My theme is not, therefore, the work of Joyce, but the use to which Pound put it, and the quite different use to which Eliot put it. I take it for granted that in the management of modern litera-ture Eliot and Pound were the most compelling impresarios; and that they differed in every respect the possession of enemies in common.

II

When Pound settled in London, he found only two writers of any interest: Yeats and Hueffer. They were as different as they could well be. Yeats seemed to Pound a poet of Romantic disposition, much charmed with 'the associations that hang near words'; a Sym-bolist, still a pupil of Arthur Symons, an Impressionist, a subjec-tivist, wrapped in the glamour of old affinities and associations. A major poet, nonetheless. Hueffer seemed to Pound the true inheritor of the nineteenth century French novel, adept of Stendhal and Flaubert, devoted to the proposition – Pound's –that poetry should be at least as well written as prose. Hueffer wanted to get things right by getting them straight. He looked hard at objects and turned them into images by keeping his feelings well away from the process. An objectivist before Objectivism, an imagist before Imagism, he produced images which Pound praised as 'hard' without bothering to say precisely what makes one image hard and another so soft as to constitute only an impression. Perhaps that was a sufficiently recognised difference. Not that Hueffer was impeccable. When Pound wanted to show the kind of thing a poet shouldn't write, he picked a phrase, 'dim lands of peace'. It happened to be in a poem by Hueffer, though Pound didn't name the offender. The offence was that the words 'of peace' weakened the image. You could say 'dim lands' because some lands are dim, including perhaps the ones you're looking at or thinking of. But if you say 'dim lands of peace', you reduce the force of the image to a conceptual meaning: peace is the only quality the dim lands are allowed to have. As a proto-Imagist

Hueffer should have trusted his eyes and his mind enough to do the work of apprehension: concepts were a lesser day's work. Still, Pound admired Hueffer, perhaps more in principle than in any practice. It was an achievement, the most telling thing, to carry forward the French novel in English. Hueffer might not be as great a writer as Yeats, but he was working in the right way.

The juxtaposition of Yeats and Hueffer was congenial to a mind – Pound's – that liked to set values in opposition. He did it again in setting up an opposition between Petrarch and Cavalcanti. It was a disaster, Pound thought, that Shakespeare and other Elizabethan writers incorporated Petrarch's Italian rather than Cavalcanti's: the result was that certain values, alive in Chaucer's English, didn't survive to become the basis of a common style in the seventeenth century and thereafter. These values – lucidity, the direct apprehension of objects, the line of intelligence which traces the shortest distance between two perceptions – were lost to the language, and had to be recovered now by the discovery that the French still retained them.

Another version of the same opposition was provoked, in Pound's *Gaudier-Brzeska*, by his sense of two ways of the mind, and correspondingly two ways of dealing with matter. In one way, you could let your mind receive impressions from matter, and await these impressions in a spirit largely passive: trusting to luck. In another, you could direct a force of energy, intellectual concentration, upon an object, stabilising the object for the duration of your attention. This is what Pound meant by lucidity, the ability not only to 'see', but to remove the smudges that commonly make the seeing of an object a mere approximation.[1]

These versions of the opposition are like, but not indentical with, the distinction which Adrian Stokes made, in the vocabulary of sculpture, between modelling and carving. In modelling, the sculptor takes the material he uses as if it were raw, characterless, and arbitrary: any clay will do. The art of modelling is one of imposition; the sculptor imposes his vision of form upon matter which offers little or no resistance; it has no particular rights. In carving, the material is deemed to have nearly every right, because it contains or imprisons a form, latent or implicit, which it is the responsibility of the sculptor to release. He carves away the obstacles. When we look at a sculpture by, say, Barbara Hepworth, we don't feel that she has imposed her own feelings, her subjective rhythms, upon matter which she deems neutral. We feel that she has sensed, in the apparently raw material, rhythms internal to the matrix: the desire to release those rhythms is her supreme impulse. This version of the opposition isn't exactly the same as the other ones, if only because it's invidious; it's a far more severe distinction than the one between Yeats and Hueffer, even though Pound approved of Hueffer's way more than of Yeats'. But it's not seriously misleading.

In the end, Hueffer – at this stage called Ford Madox Ford – disappointed Pound, as he has disappointed many readers in the meantime. *The Good Soldier* is a remarkable achievement in one of the great French ways of fiction. The Tietjens novels are good, if not every bit as good, in the same way. But Ford dissipated his extraordinary talent; he wrote too much, wrote carelessly, and ended up, for Pound, as a representative victim of neglect. That is the way he figures – 'the stylist' – in Pound's 'Hugh Selwyn Mauberley'. In the end, too, he was displaced by Joyce, whom Pound regarded as an artist working in Ford's way but doing it more authoritatively.

Pound first heard of Joyce from Yeats, on the strength of a poem – 'I Hear an Army' – which Yeats recognised as an imitation of one of his early poems. Writing off to Joyce, Pound started one of his typically generous acts of nurturing. Over a few years, with *Dubliners*, *Portrait*, and several of the chapters of *Ulysses*, Joyce showed Pound that a wonderfully lithe, inventive, joyous prose was possible. Some chapters of *Ulysses* bored him, but no matter; the whole achievement was irrefutable. He was doubtful about *Work in Progress*, and by the time *Finnegans Wake* appeared in 1939, Pound had come to feel that Joyce had wandered or dozed off into a world where, perception being impossible, the resultant pages were a waste of genius. Nothing but a cure for the clap, he said, would justify such a production. Not that Pound was angry about it. He was always patient, but not woundedly patient or long-suffering, when his friends did something foolish or tedious. When Eliot started turning himself into a sage or an archbishop, Pound shook his head in dismay, but it didn't make any difference to his celebration of a superb poet. Besides, Joyce couldn't have expected Pound to be interested in a night-book, a 'Book of the Dead', in which no line traces the shortest distance between two points of light.

Pound was loyal and affectionate to his friends, even when he though they had gone daft. After *Work in Progress*, he continued to think Joyce a master, but he looked to Wyndham Lewis for the prose of lucidity and power. The fact that Lewis' relation to the objects of his attention was more regularly punitive than respectful did not cost Pound a pang: he had his own desire to denounce and to punish. In fact, had he known it, he was always closer to Lewis' art than to Joyce's. Sometimes he recognised this. When he came to feel that his own art and Joyce's were miles apart, he rationalised the difference by deciding that the real Joyce was the young, fragile, desire-ridden poet of *Chamber Music*: the rest was genius.

III

Eliot and Pound were as different as two poets could reasonably be, subject to the consideration that in every fundamental sense their differences didn't matter. In what Pound had to say, Eliot rarely took any interest; he was interested in the new ways Pound disclosed of saying anything. The short version of this is that Eliot was only interested in Pound's techniques and never in the causes he made the techniques serve. He was happy to see Pound saying whatever seemed worth saying, but he didn't feel obliged to enlist under Pound's flag. In the dreadful matter of the Rome broadcasts and the anti-Semitism, Eliot was appalled – as his letters to Robert Fitzgerald, when published, will show – but by then he had decided that Pound was demented. A magnificent poet, the best of all craftsmen, but politically and perhaps morally a simpleton.

Joyce was another matter. Mostly, he had the wit to mind his own business. In causes which sent other men into acrimony, he retained a Swiss neutrality and got on with his work. Now that we know more about his library and the interests it seems to declare, we are encouraged to think that he had political attitudes and that they were mainly socialist or anarchist. The notion is implausible. Among the modern writers, Joyce was the one who found it easiest to contain his anger, so long as the provocation was merely public or large-scale: only the domestic worries set him shouting and drinking. I think Eliot admired in Joyce, first, the writer who quietly went about his business; all the more so because Eliot himself kept intervening in nearly every public issue that came along.

But two considerations were especially important in Eliot's sense of Joyce. The first was that Joyce, a bad Catholic – no Catholic at all, if he had his way – was in every respect formed by a Catholic upbringing. Schooled in old Aquinas and even older Aristotle, he was, in Eliot's eyes, the most 'ethically orthodox' of the modern writers. In the strangely sick chapter of *After Strange Gods* in which Eliot reflects upon the alleged cruelty, or at least the streak of cruelty, in modern fiction, offering examples from Lawrence, Mansfield and Joyce, it is Joyce who comes out most honourably. The other writers are presented as morally destitute, forgivable only because they know not what they do. The Joyce of 'The Dead' knows exactly what he is doing, and is all the wiser, the more generous, for knowing it. Joyce, then, was one of Eliot's examples to illustrate the merit of being born and growing up in a living tradition, the orthodoxy which continues to exert its saving influence even against the wilfulness of an erring soul.

The second consideration is that Joyce recognised the necessity of bringing to bear upon chaos and heterogeneity the critical force of an adversary order. When Eliot first read the chapters of *Ulysses*, in the order in which Pound arranged for their publication, he saw at once that Joyce was a remarkable writer. This was the writer Eliot started foisting upon Virginia and Leonard Woolf, with little effect at first. When he began to see how the whole book was organised, he realised that the counterpointing of the *Odyssey* and *Ulysses*, the opposing of like to nearly-like, allowed Joyce to include in the modern story pretty nearly anything that occurred to him and to resort to the *Odyssey* for the idea of order, if not for order itself. It is often maintained that Eliot's review of

Ulysses gives a most unhelpful account of the book: in particular, that his reference to the vast anarchy and futility of contemporary history is merely a lurid flourish, a blatant claim for the sensibility he and Joyce shared and practised against the allegedly terrible conditions that made the exercise of it so crucial. Richard Poirier is not alone in denouncing Eliot for this claim to bear the burden of what Frost sarcastically called 'the larger excruciations', a phrase rich with the irony which Poirier notably endorses. That the early twentieth century, even in the years after the War and the Treaty of Versailles was unprecendentedly dreadful seemed to Frost, and not only to him, a ludicrous claim, sheer vanity. Frost felt that the times were neither right nor wrong; they were, as always, whatever you made of them. Eliot, on the other hand, insisted that the times were hideous unless they could somehow be controlled: they could only be controlled by seeing each event in the light of a larger perspective. This did not necessarily or always entail browbeating the present with the past; though where else but in the past and its records could one find evidence, images, symbols of order and authority? The distinction between 'the narrative method' of fiction and 'the mythical method' is Eliot's way of pursuing what he saw as a moral and therefore a formal predicament. In the narrative method, which is more generally called realism, the novelist writes as if the particular event he imagined occupied the entire space of apprehension: each event was merely itself. Or it was imagined as if it could merely lead to another event of the same kind in a line commonly called a plot. In the mythical method, any event might be imagined, but it would be imagined as if it were to be understood within a certain perspective: it is not merely what it appears to be, with the impoverished destiny of leading to more of the same kind. At worst, each event is the farcical or the humiliating or the bathetic correlative of another event, something that already participates in the order from which it derives its value. A story tells what happened; a myth tells the kind of thing that happens all the time, human life being what it is. More specifically: a myth, as Northrop Frye observes in *The Great Code*, tells the members of a society what it is good for them to know; it is the civic form of narrative. In a grim time, it is all the more necessary, and formally a consolation, to see the dreadful rigmarole as, even yet, a repetition; part of nature, part history, and therefore doubly part of us.

What Eliot admired in *Ulysses*, and what he incorporated in *The Waste Land* in the figure of Tiresias, was the operation of a futher discrimination of events than the events themselves could provide. The search, in *The Waste Land* and 'Ash-Wednesday', for what Leavis called 'an inclusive consciousness' is Eliot's attempt at the mythical method. In the review of *Ulysses* he claimed that Joyce invented it, and that it was an invention of Einsteinian magnitude for literature. The first adumbration of the method, he credited to Yeats. I have always assumed that he meant the procedure, in such a poem as 'A Woman Homer Sung', by which a modern object of attention and an earlier or mythical form of the same character are brought together; the unnamed Maud Gonne, the named Helen of Troy. Augustine Martin has argued that Yeats had arrived at this procedure many years before 'A Woman Homer Sung', specifically in the early stories of *The Secret Rose* and especially in 'The Adoration of the Magi', a story Joyce virtually knew by heart. If so, all the better; though it would surprise me to learn that Eliot read *The Secret Rose*. Generally, Yeats' poems tend to set up oppositions from within their own terms: when he imagined one form of life, he tended to imagine another, equal and opposite, and to set them at odds. It is unusual for him to confront some value which he has invented with another value which he has not. That he does this earlier and more often than I have recognised, I am grateful to learn.

In Joyce, as in Yeats, the relation between the particular object or event and its correlative precursor is open to a certain latitude. The modern instance need not be shamed in the sight of the other; though that is often the case. In Yeats, two forms or styles of glory are often brought into companionship. In Joyce, the range of tones is far wider. All that is required, for Eliot's reading of *Ulysses* to find in the book the grand significance he ascribes to it, is that the multitudinous sundry of its materials have been mastered; and mastered with Joyce's extraordinarily unanxious power of command. The comic force of the book is found to consist not

– or not merely – in the geniality of its comings-and-goings, its particularly gorgeous way of being ordinary, but in the unruffled, uncomplaining serenity with which Joyce's imagination entertains its humdrum or bizarre materials. If such heterogeneity can be made to flourish in a book; if such contingencies, the apparent detritus of history and culture, can be coaxed by Joyce's several styles to dance to his beat; then any achievement of order is possible. Eliot wanted to believe that it was indeed possible; wanted to sustain himself in the desperate conviction that life need not be merely one-damned-thing-after-another. In *The Waste Land* his recourse to a vaguely suggested myth of the Grail was his 'mythical method' at large in local detail, an allusion, a quotation, would serve the same purpose. If the implied moral of the story, in *Ulysses*, is 'be not afraid', the justification for this extravagance is that the mind exerts authority over any human remnant merely by adverting to it. Or so Joyce implies. In the abysmal light of the Holocaust it is impossible to believe him: there are acts and events before which the human imagination, as Hannah Arendt maintained in *The Origins of Totalitarianism*, stands abject and defeated. But the comedy of *Ulysses* encourages us to feel that the authority vested in the range and differentiation of its styles is sufficient to reconcile us to the world. This is what Eliot learned from the book and turned to his similar-and-yet different purpose in *The Waste Land*; that he could gain access to other orders by quoting them, alluding to them in choice fragments. It is not necessary for the reader to spot the quotations or know where they come from; it is enough that he sense that they come from elsewhere, and that he feel the residual semblance of their authority. Fragments of an otherwise gone time, they are still here to the extent to which any mind pays attention to them and feels the weight of them.

But I should not give the impression, by talking of mastery, that Joyce envisages the mind as a unitary power always in possession of itself: it is not a machine, an engine or an artefact safely removed from the flow of the experience it encounters and transforms. The orders which Eliot found in *Ulysses* are not prototypes of the Christian doctrines and dogmas to which he submitted himself a few years later. Reference to *Hamlet* is sufficient to correct any exorbitance in this regard which might have been given by referring to Aristotle and Aquinas. The only orders which Eliot found consolingly active in *Ulysses*, I think, were the provisional patterns, drawn as equably from drama, opera, pantomime and popular lore as from Homer, Shakespeare, and the New Testament. The consolation arises from the assurance that the mind need not capitulate to its experience. A provisional order is good enough for such assurance, even though in the end Eliot came to believe that it was not enough. William Empson once remarked that it doesn't even help living, to stop living in order to understand. The *ambulando* method is the only one we can practise, getting on with our lives. Those who resent Eliot's talk of control and authority, in his review of *Ulysses*, seem to think that for him, even in 1923, the authority had to be doctrinal, a fixed structure upon which one could rely. There is no evidence for this: even in *The Waste Land*, the authorities invoked are provisional, opportune for the local intimations they are called upon to provide but, beyond that, myths rather than doctrines.

IIII

Which Joyce is Joyce is a question hardly more tangible than FH Bradley's more famous one: which is the real Julius Caesar? There are as many Joyces as there are readers who read his books. If I urge upon you 'my' Joyce, it is in the hope of persuading you at least to include something of that Joyce in your own. In the same cause I would say that Joyce's art is closer to Eliot's than to Pound's, and that Pound eventually recognised this without rancour. The reason for saying this is that Pound's values, as a poet, were appeased chiefly by instances of a visual or quasi-visual imagination. He had, so far as I can divine, no epistemological misgiving. He never doubted the evidence of his eyes in their relation to his mind: seeing was believing. He didn't share, or suffer from, the Bradleyan or Bergsonian scruple. It was enough for him to see, in the literature he for that reason cared about, that it was possible to deploy intelligence in the form of language. The best paradigm of intelligence was the concentration of mind upon an object worth paying attention to: worth, because of its bearing upon personal or civic life. In his reading of *Dubliners*, *Portrait*, and the early chapters of *Ulysses*, Pound was convinced that Joyce was in the great tradition of Stendhal, Flaubert and James. The apparent stability of an object, arrested by a concentrated mind paying attention to it, was the basis of the only order Pound cared about. The *Cantos* records his search for instances of such intelligence, in the records of history, philosophy and government. *Sunt lumina* . . . The reason why Pound disapproved of the scatological passages in *Ulysses* was not squeamishness; it was that excrement and the act of discharging it weren't worth looking at; they could be taken for granted. *Finnegans Wake* was a waste of Joyce's genius because you couldn't see anything in it; besides, dreams were not interesting, the conscious mind in abeyance being either a nuisance or a scandal.

It may be asked: 'what about the ineluctable modality of the visible?' Wasn't Joyce's imagination, and not only in *Dubliners*, just as powerfully visual as Pound's or any other writer's. Let us see, starting with the famous opening of the Proteus chapter:-

Ineluctable modality of the visible: at least that if no more, thought through my eyes. Signatures of all things I am here to read, seaspawn and seawrack, the nearing tide, that rusty boot. Snotgreen, bluesilver, rust: coloured signs. Limits of the diaphane. But he adds: in bodies. Then he was aware of them bodies before of them coloured. How? By knocking his sconce against them, sure. Go easy. Bald he was and a millionaire, *maestro di color che sanno*. Limit of the diaphane in. Why in? Diaphane, adiaphane. If you can put your five fingers through it, it is a gate, if not a door. Shut your eyes and see.

Stephen closed his eyes to hear his boots crush crackling wrack and shells. You are walking through it howsomever. I am, a stride at a time. A very short space of time through very short times of space. Five, six: the *nacheinander*.

Exactly: and that is the ineluctable modality of the audible. (U: 3. I-13)

What is notable in this passage is the ease of movement from the modality of the visible to the modality of the audible. 'That rusty boot' is the only phrase which testifies to a distinctly visual form of apprehension. Defoe might have written it in *Robinson Crusoe*, a book that could not accommodate one word of the surrounding paragraph. Even the first phrase, 'ineluctable modality of the visible', is not a token of anything seen, or even a theory of vision: it is the sort of phrase a young man would remember from his reading, in English translation, of the *Summa* of Aquinas. It goes along, indeed, with signatures and the reading of them. But what intervenes between the object and the mind that sees it is language; and the words are heard in the mind's ear and spoken and caressed in the speaking. 'I am getting on nicely in the dark', Stephen says to himself a few moments later, as well he might. In the quoted passage, it begins to appear, nothing except the rusty boot is really seen; instead, phrases are remembered, called up, mulled over. Ineluctable modality of the visible: five words in one phrase, in syllables numbering respectively five, four, two, one and three, the whole a murmuring of 'l's' – ineluctable, modality, visible.

It was Eliot, not Pound, who responded to the auditory imagination at work in *Ulysses*, and made a point of it in a shrewd comparison of Milton and Joyce, two artists blind or nearly blind whose minds were filled with echoes. Memory, in Joyce, is mainly of things heard, things people said, old songs, stories told and listened to, arias from Italian opera, Ben Dollard's singing of *The Croppy Boy*, Dan Dawson's speech, the Dead March from *Saul*, 'Apologise/Pull Out His Eyes'. The kinship of Joyce and Eliot as writers is sufficiently acknowledged by remarking that in both, the auditory imagination predominates. It is well-established, since Kenner's *The Invisible Poet*, that Eliot more than any of his contemporaries practised a style of incantation. He was remarkably susceptible to writers of a similar bearing, even when there were many considerations urging him to reject them. Think of his susceptibility to Poe, Tennyson, Swinburne; to the nonsense poets, especially Lear and Carroll; to music, especially the music heard so deeply that it is not heard at all but 'you are the music while the music lasts'. In his poetry, the most irrefutable moments are words and phrases reaching into silence; staying in one's mind as if their meaning were the least part of them.

The kinship of Eliot and Joyce also accounts, I believe, for some of the most tendentious accounts which have recently been given of Modernism. Some of these show a political animus which is obvious: a denunciation of Eliot for his alleged élitism, his anti-Semitism, his Christianity, the appropriation of High Modernism through its stigmata – difficulty, complexity, allusiveness. The difficulty of *Ulysses* and *The Waste Land* is seen as being of the same kind; as distinct from that of the *Cantos* or *Paterson*. To read these latter works, it is claimed, we only need to know the bits of foreign language, and who the various characters are. The difficulties of *Paterson*, as of the *Cantos*, are on the surface. The difficulties of *Ulysses* and *The Waste Land*, it is maintained, are inherent in their mode of organisation: the problem is not what is there, but what is it doing there.

The political argument is sometimes, but not necessarily, Marxist. In *Fables of Aggression*, Fredric Jameson argues that the characteristic works of High Modernism are the early writings of Eliot and Joyce; these poems and fictions exhibit 'strategies of inwardness' to convert the paraphernalia of an alienated world into private gestures and styles. If this is true of Eliot and Joyce, their connexion with Pater becomes clearer than ever; acknowledged by Joyce, suppressed on the whole by Eliot. The purpose of art, requiring *ascesis* and concentration, to use Pater's terms, is to convert or transmute the sundry of mere appearances into moments of exquisite intensity. The intensity is deemed to make up for the transience of the experience, and for the lyric doom and penury between one such moment and another. The process is just as clear in Eliot's Prufrock and Joyce's Stephen of *Portrait* and *Stephen Hero* as in Pater's Marius.

As a Marxist, Jameson finds these strategies of inwardness repugnant, for obvious reason: if a mind can so transmute the degraded and alienated bits-and-pieces of common experience, there is no incentive to rush out and change the world. A revolutionary programme is nullified if everyone can so transform his mere contingency into the rich inwardness of a Stephen

Dedalus; or even of a Prufrock, since Prufrock's self-irony is a vivid experience in its own right. Rather than allow these strategies of inwardness to sustain a self which should otherwise depend entirely upon the sociality of political revolution and a new community, Jameson sponsors any form of objectivity, even one like Wyndham Lewis' of the Right. Lewis' sentences, as Jameson shows in *Fables of Aggression* never connive with their referents: his syntax deploys his clauses as elaborate engines of cognition, upon which no uninvited emotion may obtrude. The comparison which Jameson makes between *The Childermass* and *Ulysses* shows that while Lewis' sentences keep themselves strictly apart from the activities they administer, Joyce's allow for the reconciliation of materials however disparate in the mind they seem merely to suffuse. The heterogeneity of the materials makes all the stronger the self they inhabit. To Jameson, this amounts to a scandal, and it makes Joyce's art bourgeois liberal, a comfort to conservative readers since they appear to be reading a radical book yet find their sense of self endorsed at every point.[2]

That Joyce's strategy is a scandal not only to Marxists is clear from a recent essay by the psychoanalytical critic Leo Bersani ('Against *Ulysses*': *Raritan*, VIII, 2 Fall 1988, pp. I-32). Bersani resents the fact that *Ulysses* is still thought to be a radical or subversive work despite 'the traditional view of human identity' which it implicitly defends. The book is such that readers have the impression of knowing Bloom, Stephen, Molly and Gerty, no matter what agitations are going on from page to page. The fact that the narrative presents or quotes these characters upon levels of reality which they themselves would be incapable of articulating only strengthens our sense of their existence: we seem to have, as Bersani says, 'the essence of a character independently of his or her point of view'. But the most acute scandal, to Bersani, is the claim which *Ulysses* seems both to make and to justify, that the serene and perhaps redemptive management of its cultural acquisitions is entirely feasible. The anxiety which *Ulysses* struggles to transcend is that of disconnectedness; but Joyce's authority in the book is such that the anxiety and the disconnectedness are indeed felt to be transcended:

Where *Ulysses* really leads us is to Joyce's mind; it illuminates his cultural consciousness. At the end of the reader's exegetical travails lies the promise of an Assumption, of being raised up and identified with the idea of *culture* made *man*. Joyce incarnates the enormous authority of sublimation in our culture – of sublimation viewed not as a nonspecific eroticising of cultural interests but as the appeasement and even transcendence of anxiety. (p. 29).

Bersani wants the reader to stay unhappy, or at least to give up the mundane satisfaction of assuming his identity and his ability to cope somehow with the deliverances of a culture over which, in any large sense, he exerts no control. For that reason, Bersani points to *Bouvard et Pécuchet* as a more genuinely *avant-garde* fiction than *Ulysses*; because in Flaubert's novel the only thing the mind can do with the mass of human knowledge which the book incorporates is to 'submit all of it to the same, tirelessly repeated stylistic operation' (p.22). No power or mastery over this mass of materials is claimed: it is an interminable repetition of the same.

But Bersani's resentment, which I don't object to taking as a measure of his scruple, arises from his sense of a conspiracy at large between art, which pretends to be subversive, and networks of power which art in the end does nothing to disturb. Art should at least delay the process, probably inevitable, by which every expressive resource is enlisted in the current system of hegemony. I don't disagree with this. I am constantly struck by the assimilating and becalming power of social institutions, their skill in what I once called the domestication of outrage. Foucault was probably right to maintain that the exercise of power in modern society is anonymous; it does not reside in a person or even in a corporation, it is rather an endless circuit of energy and force. Foucault has been rebuked for causing low spirits, or for making apathy respectable: 'nothing to be done', as *Waiting for Godot* says.

These resentments, complaints, and apathies are fixated upon knowledge and the control of knowledge. The reason why modern literary theory is obsessed with the seeming epistemological claims of language is that knowledge, the act of knowing, is still deemed to be the essentially human act. Politics is the control and administration of knowledge. But suppose we were to read a book – *Ulysses*, again – in which memory, not knowledge, is the operative term: memory voluntary and involuntary, according diversely to Proust and Bergson. Would it make a difference? What seems to me extraordinary in Joyce is his willingness to let experience issue from memory and imagination, rather than from knowledge. He remembers and forgets and remembers again and incorporates his memories as sounds, and recovers chiefly as sounds the weight and diversity of cultural possessions.

It would be wrong to describe Joyce's mind as a switchboard. That would entail repeating Yeats' error, when he thought of Joyce and indeed of Pound as helpless before the contents of their minds: naturalists, who could merely transcribe whatever happened to lodge in their minds. It would be even more seriously wrong to claim that by removing the reader's attention from knowledge to memory, resentment such as Bersani's and Jameson's would evaporate. A sense of identity, of selfhood, could just as easily be maintained by the acoustic flow of memories as by the attraction of every experience toward a personal centre. Most of the events in *Ulysses*, including the painful ones, are occasions gone except for the inescapable remembrance of them: Bloom's father's suicide, his son Rudi, Stephen's guilt about his mother. Bloom's stunned fixation upon Molly's afternoon conjunction with Blazes Boylan is a catastrophe of memory. I would go further, toward *Finnegans Wake*: what is a pun but a word spoken with the sense of its having once been another word, a cousin once removed but still in the same family?

The Joyce I am trying to describe is, I would claim, in accordance with Eliot's rather than with Pound's; especially the Eliot who spoke of words resorted to with a sense of their reaching down and back to deepest unconscious origins and bringing up to the surface experiences beyond any known intention.

NOTES

1 There are two opposed ways of thinking of a man: firstly, you may think of him as that toward which perception moves, as the toy of circumstance, as the plastic substance *receiving* impressions; secondly, you may think of him as directing a certain fluid force against circumstance, as *conceiving* instead of merely reflecting and observing. One does not claim that one way is better than the other, one notes a diversity of the temperament. The two camps always exist. In the 'eighties there were symbolists opposed to impressionists, now you have vorticism, which is, roughly speaking, expressionism, neo-cubism, and imagism gathered together in one camp and futurism in the other. Futurism is descended from impressionism. It is, in so far as it is an art movement, a kind of accelerated impressionism. It is a spreading, or surface art, as opposed to vorticism, which is intensive.

Gaudier. Brzeska: a Memoir by Ezra Pound, A New Directions Book, Second Edition, 1970, pp. 89/70.

2 In Lewis, however, it is not the unification but rather the dispersal of subjectivity which is aimed at. Homogeneity of tone is neither desired nor achieved, and the successive transformations of the individual characters undermine the visual status of any individual metamorphosis and betray its origins in verbal cliché.

The status of the individual subject in Lewis cannot ultimately be described, let alone understood, unless we replace it in that peculiar narrative situation in which it is fixed and from which it depends: what we have hitherto termed the agon, the relational or dialogical axis of which "characters" become the merest poles. It is clear, for instance, not merely that the "relationship" between Bloom and Stephen has nothing structurally in common with the team of Pullman and Satters, but even more significantly that in Joyce each of the two major characters retains a monadic unity which has vanished from Lewis' tandem treatment of his couple.

What remains of this last in Wyndham Lewis' narrative system may perhaps best be conveyed by a juxtaposition of the metamorphoses of the heroes of *The Childermass* with the superficially analogous moments in *Ulysses*, where the Nighttown section releases Mr Bloom to an equally delirious and premeditated acting out of his most marginal daytime fantasies and private thoughts: "Under an arch of triumph Bloom appears bareheaded, in a crimson velvet mantle trimmed with ermine, bearing Saint Edward's staff . . . Bloom with asses' ears seats himself in the pillory with crossed arms, his feet protruding . . . A charming soubrette with dauby cheeks, mustard hair and large male hands and nose, leering mouth . . . Pigeonbreasted, bottleshouldered, padded, in nondescript juvenile grey and black striped suit, too small for him, white tennis shoes, bordered stockings with turnover tops, and a red school cap with badge . . . " etc. It would not be wrong, but too simple, to observe that, far from dissolving the personality into its external determinations, as Lewis' transformations do, the Joycean phantasmagoria serves to reconfirm the unity of the psyche, and to reinvent that depth-psychological perspective from which these various private fantasies spring. What is more significant in the present context is the way in which, in Joyce, the "visions" are organized with a view towards unity of tone and staged with a well-nigh sensory and hallucinatory intensity.

Fables of Aggression: Wyndham Lewis, a Modernist Fascist by Frederic Jameson, University of California Press, 1979, pp. 57/8.

J O Y C E ' S
H U M A N I S M

Brendan Kennelly

The kind of humanism I discern in Joyce is possible only to a psyche that is largely unsupported, vigilant in its scrutiny of self-development, consciously experimental. No matter how 'normal' or 'abnormal' a writer's life may seem, all his days are essentially an experiment in living. In the case of Joyce, this experiment was conducted in such a way that his art became his life: he ruthlessly used his life as fodder for his imagination. The choice stated in Yeats' lives –

The intellect of man is forced to choose
Perfection of the life or of the work

– would not have presented a difficulty for Joyce. His despairs, his degradations, most of them conscious, his extraordinary bravery, his unconcealed selfishness, his vicious wilfulness, his blithe exploitation of his brother, his manic toying with language, the bravado of his distortions, the sense that his work is the product of a cosmic solitude, the happy arrogance implied in his natural anarchy, his attitude to drink – all these run with a natural pride in the human river that *is* Joyce. Alessandro Francini Bruni puts the case well about the particular matter of Joyce's drinking:

> One day when he was drunker than usual, I said to him sharply, "My old Bacchus, have you gone mad?" He answered meekly as an unweened calf, "No, I am developing myself".

Allowing always for the possibility of that mockery, both of himself and of others, Joyce's words are 'I am *developing* myself'. Not;

> 'I am exhausting myself, I am sickening myself, I am creating poison, assailing my body and mind and senses, I am deliberately immersing myself in the most fabulous form of futility that I know – but – "I am *developing* myself".

What frightened others was a source of education for Joyce. He *was* developing himself, as he never ceased to do.

I want to suggest that Joyce did indeed develop himself to the point where he had the detachment of enternity in time – or as close to that detachment as it is possible to get. His experiment in human-ness makes one more human to contemplate.

We all know the famous cloud-image of detachment, of indifference, in Joyce. It may seem odd to say that the object of this conscious experiment in self-development is a form of indifference, but how can the ice know it is water until it lets the sun caress it to the point of melting?

What *is* indifference? What does it make possible?

Joycean indifference is the opposite of what we may call the popular notion or idea of indifference, which is simply a couldn't-careless attitude. Joycean indifference is different, not only from that sort of indifference, but from its opposite – urgent commitment. Joyce's indifference has to do with his own sense of the complexity of his life, and therefore of his art. It has to do with what Joyce

recognised as *necessity* and with how he grappled in art with what he envisioned, either by choice or compulsion, in life. Simone Weil, a Jewish girl whose writings always remind me of Joyce – though she writes as a believer, while Joyce believed in nothing, not even, as has been said, in the bread he was eating – Simone Weil, out of her *believing* heart, so close in many ways to Joyce's *un*believing heart, has this to say about necessity;
(Emphasis is mine);

> *Necessity* is an enemy for man as long as he thinks in the first person. To tell the truth, he has *with necessity the three sorts of relationship* which he has with men. In fantasy, or by the exercise of social power, it seems to be his slave. In adversities, privations, grief, sufferings, but above all in affliction, it seems an absolute and brutal master. In methodical action there is a point of equilibrium where *necessity*, by its conditional character, presents man at once with obstacles and with means in relation to the partial ends which he pursues and wherein there *is a sort of equality between a man's will and universal necessity* . . . one must try to achieve this point of equilibrium as often as possible.

> . . . The bitterest reproach that men make of this *necessity* is its absolute *indifference* to moral values. Righteous men and criminals receive an equal share of the benefits of the sun and of the rain; the righteous and the criminals equally suffer sunstroke, and drowning in floods. It is precisely this *indifference* which the Christ invites us to look upon and to imitate as the very expression of the perfection of our heavenly Father. To imitate this *indifference* is simply to consent to it, that is, to accept the existence of all that exists, including the evil, excepting only that portion of evil which we have the possibility, and the obligation, of preventing. By this simple work the Christ annexed all Stoic thought, and by the same token all of Heraclitus and Plato.

> No one could ever prove that such an absurdity as consent to necessity could be possible. We can only recognize it. There are in fact souls which consent to it.

Necessity is an enemy for man as long as he thinks in the first person . . .

There is a sort of *equality* between a man's *will* and universal necessity . . .

One must try to achieve this point of equilibrium as often as possible . . .

The bitterest reproach that men make of this *necessity* is its absolute *indifference* to moral values . . .

It is precisely this *indifference* which the Christ invites us to look upon and to *imitate* . . .

To *imitate* this *indifference* is simply to *consent* to it, that is, to accept the existence of all that exists, including the evil . . .

I always find it difficult, even though I recognise it is necessary, as I read Joyce's work, to bear in mind the *quality* of his indifference, and the *quality* of the imaginative *equilibrium* he achieved between necessity and indifference. For, when I do bear this in mind, I seem to understand the *distance* he achieves from human feeling, the high, icy clarity of his perspective on feeling, the better to re-create it in words. Because of this achieved equilibrium between necessity and indifference, he writes like a man who is both a million miles away from the object of his scrutiny and also so close to it that he appears to have a Keatsian capacity for flowing into it, and through it, and out of it again. He presents, therefore, from that cosmic distance and with that felt immediacy, the *reality* of human emotions, that is, not only what people feel, but what they *feel* they feel. The presentation, in 'A Painful Case', of what Mr Duffy *feels* he feels, and therefore feels (for a while) is a case in point. This feeling *of* the feeling of loneliness is the creation of that special indifference:

She *seemed* to be near him in the darkness. At moments he *seemed* to feel her voice touch his ear, her hand touch his.

He stood still to listen. Why had he withheld life from her? Why had he sentenced her to death? He *felt* his moral nature falling to pieces.

When he gained the crest of the Magazine Hill he halted and looked along the river towards Dublin, the lights of which burned redly and hospitably in the cold night. He looked down the slope and, at the base, in the shadow of the wall of the Park, he saw some human figures lying. Those venal and furtive loves filled him with despair. He gnawed the rectitude of his life; he *felt* that he had been outcast from life's feast. One human being had *seemed* to love him and he had denied her life and happiness: he had sentenced her to ignominy, a death of shame. He knew that the prostrate creatures down by the wall were watching him and wished him gone. No one wanted him; he was outcast from life's feast. He turned his eyes to the grey gleaming river, winding along towards Dublin. Beyond the river he saw a goods train winding out of Kingsbridge Station, like a worm with a fiery head winding through the darkness, obstinately and laboriously. It passed slowly out of sight; but still he heard in his ears the laborious drone of the engine reiterating the syllables of her name.

He turned back the way he had come, the rhythm of the engine pounding in his ears. He began to *doubt the reality* of *what memory told him*. He halted under a tree and allowed the rhythm to die away. He could *not feel* her near him in the darkness nor her voice touch his ear. He waited for some minutes listening. He could hear nothing: the night was *perfectly silent*. He listened again: *perfectly silent. He* felt *that he was alone.*

Joyce, the narrator, does *not* say, 'his moral nature was falling to pieces' or 'he was outcast from life's feast' or 'he was alone' but 'he felt' these states.

The hallmark of *Dubliners* is the cruel precision with which is revealed the failure of many of the characters to know what they are *not* feeling. In 'A Painful Case', it's as if the narrator were God looking down on this severed monster of a man, a dull compendium of interesting quotations, terrified of connection with a woman, terrified of living, who, because of the way he has diligently *not* lived, the committed rituals of his non-existence, the civilised prowling in the suburbs of self, feels that he feels these things. Viewed in this light, the ending of 'A Painful Case' becomes more bleak and savage and, I would say, more deeply, authentically human.

The problem for me this morning is to try to get at the roots of Joyce's terrifying ability to get at the true humanity of his characters, his pitiless revelations of their hearts' habitual poverty.

No writer will remain interesting to another human being unless, at the back of his work, there is the sense that he (the writer) is in *contact* with his own humanity. What others call authority is articulate contact with self.

The first thing to say about Joyce is that he was a non-believer (I shall use that term).

He was very proud.

He had no respect for money and power.

He rejected the consolations of belief.

He was, as one of his friends said, a genuine negator.

He was a hard drinker, practically all the time.

He had bad eyes – like Milton, like Homer (we are told), like O'Casey, like Raftery.

Joyce was a non-believer.

People get upset about this.

A friend of Joyce, an Italian, is the man who calls Joyce a negator. He then says –

> Joyce . . . doesn't blaspheme because the Irish don't have our ambition in that exercise. He doesn't destroy and he doesn't rebuild. *He does worse; he denies*. He moves further and further even from Christ the Man. *I feel sorry for him because I love him*, because I would like to see him happy, and because happiness cannot be found in our talents, in the approval of the world, or in the masterpieces that we create. Happiness can be found only in the teachings of Jesus, over whose last words, "Eli, Eli, lamma sabactani," I

have seen Joyce cry secret tears.

'I felt sorry for him because I love him, because I would like to see him happy.' That is a very decent feeling on the part of Bruni. It is also a complete waste.

Joyce was emptying his heart and mind and soul of the warm friendliness and support of belief. He rejected that warmth, that especial creative support, and sought instead the loneliness and mystery and rich potential of language itself, in the beginning was the Word, and he sought also an *unsupported* perspective on the casual loneliness of men and women. He wanted *a* way, *a* truth, and *a* life.

It is this *unsupported* quality in Joyce that some people seem to find hard to take, even to be afraid of: so, like Bruni, they feel they should love him. (Yet Joyce was not unsupported, not totally, not even in his mind: he had Nora; he lived with Nora, he *listened* to Nora).

Yet in so far as it is possible to live the unsupported spiritual life, the unscaffolded spiritual life, Joyce did live it. It is this quality of non-belief, of unsupported spirit-life, that drew the following comment from Professor Curtius, a German critic, in 1929, in *Neue Schweitzer Rundschau*. The Italian I quoted, Bruni, is full of intelligent, futile concern. Curtius, on the other hand, writes out of fear. The fear is as pointless as the concern.

> Joyce's work . . . springs from a revolt of the spirit and leads to the destruction of the world. With implacable logic he presents in his walpurgisnight, amid larvae and lemurs, a vision of the end of the world. *A metaphysical nihilism is the substance of Joyce's work*. The world, macro- and microcosm, is founded upon the void . . . All this wealth of philosophical and theological knowledge, this power of psychological and aesthetic analysis, this culture of a mind schooled in all the literatures of the world, all these gifts serve but to spend themselves, to refute themselves in a world-conflagration, a flaming welter of metallic iridescence. What is left? An odour of ashes, the horror of death, sorrow of apostasy, pangs of remorse – Agenbite

of Inwit.

The fear of 'metaphysical nihilism' underlying that statement is as futile as the concern, 'I feel sorry for him because I love him', underlying Bruni's prayer for Joyce. Both men have failed to grasp the nature of Joyce's indifference – the distance that makes him so immediate, the immediacy that justifies and clarifies the distance.

Both men are upset by the lonely strength of that indifference which the faith of one man and the fear of the other cannot tolerate in the unsupported Joyce.

Also, and most importantly, Joyce was brutally clear in his mind about two things that have a confusing and weakening effect on most of us – money and power.

Joyce's contempt for money is possible only to the prince of mockers. I know this is a complex problem – money is a part of the reality of all our lives, a nagging, hassling, bedevilling part, at times – but Joyce, in that amoral indifference of his, fought off, as far as possible, the claims that money makes. The sad truth is, often, that people do not make money; money makes people. This is terrifying. The question is – how *independent* are we of money? Is the quality of our work dependent (to what extent?) on the nature and extent of that *independence*? The usual justification for selling out, gradually, to money is family – because family is good.

So the indulgence in the traditional decency of the prostitution is justified by the need to support the virtue. As the years wear on, the distinction is blurred – and the prostitution *becomes* the virtue.

As far as I can see, we are all, more or less, guilty of this.

Joyce, because of his amoral indifference, is not. On the whole, he is not. I think that God has one thing in common with great writers – he has no morals. Joyce's attitude to power is similar. For example, his attitude to politics – to political conformity – is quite consistent with his attitude to money. 'Material victory is the death of spiritual predominance.'

As an artist I attach no importance to political conformity.

Consider: Renaissance Italy gave us the greatest artists. The Talmud says at one point, 'We Jews are like the olive: we give our best when we are being crushed, when we are collapsing under the burden of our foliage.' Material victory is the death of spiritual predominance. Today we see in the Greeks of antiquity the most cultured nation. Had the Greek state not perished, what would have become of the Greeks? Colonizers and merchants. As an artist I am against every state. Of course I must recognize it, since indeed in all my dealings I come into contact with its institutions. The state is concentric, man is eccentric. Thence arises an eternal struggle. The monk, the bachelor, and the anarchist are in the same category. Naturally I can't approve of the act of the revolutionary who tosses a bomb in a theater to destroy the king and his children. On the other hand, have those states behaved any better which drowned the world in a blood-bath?

Joycean indifference *has* to result in this attitude to political conformity, to the State. God is a shout in the street; Joyce does not believe in the bread he is eating; he is against every state – what is there room for? What is there left?

A great deal.

For a start, there is fascinating human rubbish, mesmeric triviality, a great deal of dirt. Borges says Joyce is 'wondrously paltry'. It is a splendid phrase.

It is possible to see *Ulysses* as an epic of bric-a-brac trivia, a colossal presentation of smallnesses – the evidence available to the non-believing, indifferent mind and eye. To put it another way, and to use one of Joyce's favourite words, it is 'human'. During the war years, Joyce was working in Zurich on *Ulysses*. In the evenings, he liked to sit and talk and drink wine, light gold Fendant, a strong Valois wine. Georges Borach recorded much of Joyce's conversation. In this extract from Borach's note-book, Joyce is talking about the *human-ness* of various works of literature.

The most beautiful, all-embracing theme is that of the *Odyssey*. It is greater, more *human* than that of *Hamlet, Don Quixote*, Dante, *Faust*. The rejuvenation of Old Faust has an unpleasant effect upon me. Dante tires one quickly; it is as if one were to look at the sun. The most beautiful, most human traits are contained in the *Odyssey*. I was twelve years old when we dealt with the Trojan War at school; only the *Odyssey* stuck in my memory. I want to be candid; at twelve I like the mysticism in Ulysses. When I was writing *Dubliners*, I first wished to choose the title *Ulysses in Dublin*, but gave up the idea. In Rome, when I had finished about half of *Portrait*, I realized that the Odyssey had to be the sequel, and I began to write *Ulysses*.

Why was I always returning to this theme? . . . I find the subject of Odysseus the most *human* in world literature. Odysseus didn't want to go off to Troy; he knew that the official reason for the war, the dissemination of the culture of Hellas, was only a pretext for the Greek merchants, who were seeking new markets. When the recruiting officers arrived, he happened to be plowing. He pretended to be mad. Thereupon they place his little two-year-old in the furrow. In front of the child he halts the plow. Observe the beauty of the motifs: the only man in Hellas who is against the war, and the father. Before Troy the heroes shed their lifeblood in vain. They wish to raise the siege. Odysseus opposes the idea. The strategem of the wooden horse. After Troy there is no further talk of Achilles, Menelaus, Agamemnon. Only one man is not done with; his heroic career has hardly begun: Odysseus. Then the motif of wandering. Scylla and Charybdis – what a splendid parable! Odysseus is also a great musician; he wishes to, and must, listen; he has himself tied to the mast. The motif of the artist, who will lay down his life rather than renounce his interest. Then the delicious humor of Polyphemus . . .
On Naxos the fifty-year-old, perhaps baldheaded, with Ariadne, a girl who is hardly seventeen. What a trait of generosity at the interview with Ajax in the nether world, and many other beautiful touches. I am almost afraid to

treat such a theme; it's overwhelming.

The most beautiful, all-embracing, *human* theme.

The first point Joyce makes in relation to his own love of the *human-ness* of the Odyssey is this: 'I want to be candid'.

The word 'candid' comes from the Latin *candidus*, meaning 'white' or 'glistening'. I think of that, always, in relation to Joyce – a candid style, a white, glistening style.

It is amazingly apt.

'Candid' also means pure, clear, stainless, innocent, free from bias, impartial, just, frank, open, straightforward, sincere in what one says. All that, and more.

'I want to be candid'.

This is Joyce's achieved artistic morality, having shed the dead moralities of his youth. This new morality is a morality of candour. The candid heart speaks for itself.

This matter of candour is, and always has been, an extremely complex problem for writers. It is connected with style. How to be candid, spiritually *direct*? 'The poet *never* speaks *directly*,' says Yeats, 'There is *always* a phantasmagoria.'

Immediately, we are into the paradoxical situation in which candour is made possible through a film, a set of *dramatis personae*, a machinery of *oratio obliqua*, a set of voices mouthing acceptable contradictions, a chorus of complexity.

Yeats, mostly, achieved directness by being indirect.

His candour comes to us through masks. He is, nonetheless, in the terms I'm trying to describe, a *candid* poet. But Yeats' candour has, as it were, to be gathered from all the sources, the voices, the personae, the masks.

For Patrick Kavanagh, *in*directness is tedious; almost, in his terms, a lie. Masks are boring. There is no need for masks, Kavanagh would say. He writes:

> The poet has nothing to conceal. There is no skeleton in his cupboard. Hence his confidence. The average man, by which I mean the man who will not accept his fate and be as God made him, is always afraid that he will be found out. He is living a lie. The poet is honest. Poetry is honesty.

> The problem that confronts me here
> Is to be eloquent, yet sincere . . .

Of these three writers – Joyce, Yeats, Kavanagh – Yeats, who *may* be the greatest, is the one who most gives the impression of having something to conceal.

Does Joyce achieve total candour?

Well, I don't know. Indifference makes possible a savage, disciplined interest. I would say that Joyce's white, glistening style, his impartial, just style, shows a mind that in turn reflects the soul's wish to be candid.

I have not read the recent book about Nora Barnacle, but there is little doubt in my mind that, in this matter of candour, Nora is the most important single external factor. And from the moment they met, she inspired in Joyce this passion for being candid. There is a book entitled *Nora Barnacle Joyce* by Padraic O'Laoi, published by Kennys of Galway, which has a lovely description of the evening Joyce and Nora Barnacle went out walking in Dublin, in the direction of Ringsend. This walk with Nora is one of the crucial moments in Joyce's moral-artistic life.

There is something about the man-woman sexual relationship (especially, ironically enough, in marriage) which tends to prevent full candour, and therefore full honesty. Frequently in Joyce, it is marriage (*not* Dublin) which is the centre of the paralysis of the universe, and of the penis. So often, in Joyce, marriage is an intimate abyss, a chasm of familiarity.

Worst of all is the desperation fostered by familiarity. The deepest sadness has to do with the unexpressed aspects of marriage – hence the lies of silence, the anonymous humiliations, little Chandler's 'cheeks suffused with shame', Gabriel Conroy's ludicrous encounter with his own lust and its failure, before the remembered passion of a dead boy. Such attitudes, such moments, such pathetic concealments, seem to me to have appeared to Joyce to be the very *nature* of paralysis, the very opposite of that spiritual, sexual, emotional *fluency* that is the bedrock of his relationship with Nora and the essence of his style as a writer.

> As they strolled towards Ringsend they were very open with each other. Joyce questioned Nora in much detail about her family, her early life and friends in Galway, with particular attention to her boyfriends there and her romances. He was like an explorer discovering some new river. He wended his way step by step back to the source of her life and explored all the tributaries that formed the main stream of her life. On his side Joyce was open and honest with Nora and gave her in much detail the story of his family and life . . .

> They were both interested in each other's sexuality as their later letters reveal. And soon they engaged in a little love play. In this Nora took a positive role and aroused Joyce without any prompting from him. Later he recalled that encounter at Ringsend as "a sacrament which left in me a final sense of sorrow" and again "the recollection of it fills me with amazed joy" . . .

> . . . Their love matured over the summer of 1904. Again and again Nora had to listen to a detailed account of his sexual history; his encounters with prostitutes and perverts . . .

> One quality above all others attracted her to Joyce – it was *his absolute candour*. He opened his soul to her in its entirety

and never attempted to hide from her even his most secret thoughts.

Thinking about this situation and its implications, it is possible to appreciate why Joyce's brother, Stanislaus, refers to Joyce as 'a genius of character'. (This is the opposite of the often-heard Irish phrase 'A genius of a character' which is merely a matter of colourful over-simplification). Joyce, in his brother's eyes, is 'a genius of character'. Why? It is interesting that where Padraic O'Laoi talks about Joyce's candour in love, Stanislaus talks about Joyce's candour in hatred – about his extraordinary moral courage – his shocking ability to be scurrilously truthful:

> Jim is a genius of character. When I say 'genius' I say just the least little bit in the world more than I believe; yet remembering his youth and that I sleep with him, I say it. Scientists have been called great scientists because they have measured the distances of the unseen stars and yet scientists who have watched the movements in matter scarcely perceptible to the mechanically aided senses have been esteemed as great; and Jim is, perhaps, a genius, though his mind is minutely analytic. He has, above all, a proud, wilful, vicious selfishness, out of which by times now he writes a poem or an epiphany, now commits the meanness of whim and appetite, which was at first protestant egoism, and had, perhaps, some desperateness in it, but which is now well-rooted – or developed? – in his nature . . . He has extraordinary moral courage . . . His great passion is a fierce scorn of what he calls the 'rabblement' – a tiger-like, insatiable hatred. He has a distinguished appearance and bearing and many graces: musical singing and especially speaking voice (a tenor), a good undeveloped talent in music, and witty conversation. He has a distressing habit of saying quietly to those with whom he is familiar the most shocking things about himself and others, and moreover, of selecting the most shocking times for saying them, not because they are shocking merely, but because they are true.

To give you a sense of the full nature and impact of this candour, however, let me turn to *Ulysses*. The most obvious choice is Molly's soliloquy. But Joyce's candour is not confined to sex – he brings it to bear on all aspects of human experience, from birth to death. He brings that scientific capacity for minute analysis as well as total sensuous openness to bear on experience. He makes us understand that our own capacity for experiencing practically anything is, in fact, shockingly limited. It's not that we go dream-like or zombie-like through reality – it's just that we half-do, or quarter-do, most things. We half-listen, half-speak, half-taste, half-pay attention, half-reflect, half-remember. When Eliot says 'Mankind cannot bear very much reality' he is talking, I believe, about the shoddiness, the shadowy cheapness, we enforce on our senses, on our minds, on our hearts, by our lack of candour with ourselves and others. This failure to fully experience normal realities – like talking or eating or smelling or brooding or excreting or laughing or good vicious gossiping or using words – is part of that paralysis so ruthlessly scrutinised by Joyce. The unfinished sentences in 'The Sisters' are as much paralysis as the paralysis of the old priest. We are all aware of the paralysis of language in our universities, among our politicians, on radio and television. Near the end of the twentieth century we still have not learned the vital lesson – in, say, literary criticism – of Joyce's candour. Or we don't re-learn it frequently enough.

I want to look at one passage from *Ulysses*. It has to do with eating. On the threshold of the Burton, Mr Bloom halts. Men are eating. He sees men eating. He smells men eating. He studies men eating. They are eating to get strength. They are eating flesh. They are chewing death. Joyce takes us into the mouths, into the busy teeth of these eaters. He makes us think of the casual orgies necessary for everyday life. He hints at eating in Irish history and mythology. He makes us conscious of eating-words in our normal conversation.

(Are you finding it difficult to swallow this discussion? Yes I am yes I am Yes!) He tells us about eating and prayer; do Catholics eat God?; we know that eating and elemental violence are inseparable; we know that, equally, eating and 'good conversation' are said to go together – but in the end, it is the brutality that is most emphasised.

It may well be that we cannot afford to pay too much attention to what we do – do not dwell too long on anything. What is needed is sufficient attention to make us feel we know something, or have experienced it. But no writer I know experiences normal, or so-called normal, reality the way Joyce does. The intensity of his scrutiny of the casual simply stops the mind. Mr Bloom is at the door of the Burton. The Burton is packed with hungry men. We walk straight into a normal orgy, the almost unbearable grotesqueness of this ordinary activity:

Men, men, men.

Perched on high stools by the bar, hats shoved back, at the tables calling for more bread no charge, swilling, wolfing gobfuls of sloppy food, their eyes bulging, wiping wetted moustaches. A pallid suetfaced young man polished his tumbler knife fork and spoon with his napkin. New set of microbes. A man with an infant's saucestained napkin tucked round him shovelled gurgling soup down his gullet. A man spitting back on his plate: halfmasticated gristle: no teeth to chewchewchew it. Chump chop from the grill. Bolting to get it over. Sad booser's eyes. Bitten off more than he can chew. Am I like that? See ourselves as others see us. Hungry man is an angry man. Working tooth and jaw. Don't! O! A bone! That last pagan king of Ireland Cormac in the schoolpoem choked himself at Sletty southward of the Boyne. Wonder what he was eating. Something galoptious. Saint Patrick converted him to Christianity. Couldn't swallow it all however.

– Roast beef and cabbage.

– One stew.

Smells of men. His gorge rose. Spaton sawdust, sweetish warmish cigarette smoke, reek of plug, spilt beer, men's beery piss, the stale of ferment.

Couldn't eat a morsel here. Fellow sharpening knife and fork, to eat all before him, old chap picking his tootles. Slight spasm, full, chewing the cud. Before and after. Grace after meals. Look on this picture then on that. Scoffing up stewgravy with sopping sippets of bread. Lick it off the plate, man! Get out of this.

That passage is remarkable for it orgiastic detail, the gruesome precision of its observation, the congested, civilised, ordered gluttony of the scene. The writing is mercilessly physical.

But even more remarkable is the fact that the entire activity is filtered through Bloom's consciousness – the man who sees what is happening before his eyes. He doesn't glimpse it, or half-see it, or quarter-see it. He stands there at the door of the Burton and he takes it in; he takes it in and he puts words on it, or Joyce puts words on it for him. And all the time the entire thing is part of Bloom's mental life – deliberate, deep, slow, meditative, marginalised, corrective, discriminating, sensual, fine, oily, sniffy. Bloom sniffs with his mind.

And his candid mind, inevitable as weather, is the focus and filter and analytical arena of it all.

'Am I like that? See ourselves as others see us. Hungry man is an angry man'.

'Couldn't eat a morsel here'.

'Get out of this'.

'Out. I hate dirty eaters'.

'Eat or be eaten. Kill. Kill'.

For all the implacable physicality of the writing, this is in fact a mental drama. Joyce creates a consciousness on which all things impinge, and even enter. Bloom is not made brisk and cocky with sustained purpose. He is made vulnerable, discriminating and reflective through being endlessly impinged on, entered into. He is battered by images, smells, impressions. His candid consciousness makes him a victim of the situation, while his full expression of that consciousness makes him a quiet master.

'Never know whose thought you're chewing'.

My argument is, or has been, that candour in Joyce comes from getting rid of a certain kind of inherited supportive morality. A vacuum is created, deepened by the rejection not only of belief, but of the very notion of belief. (This is impossible: language tells us that some people believe in nothing – they *do* believe in nothing). For the moment, though, I am suggesting that this non-belief creates a spiritual indifference which is the product of necessity. The mind is rid of the illusion of supportive nobilities and virtues and the way is cleared for the re-creation of the wondrously paltry – the real poetry of men and women – their human smallnesses. Yet the end result is that of a new dignity, coming from the denial of support, coming therefore from the candid heart and mind, the white, glistening style.

Even at a basic stylistic level, this candour brings great rewards. Listen, for example, to the opening words of a few short stories from *Dubliners*. Is there anything more candid than – 'There was no hope for him this time'. ('The Sisters')

'It was Joe Dillon who introduced the Wild West to us'. ('An Encounter')

'She sat at the window watching the evening invade the avenue'. ('Eveline')

'Mrs Mooney was a butcher's daughter'. ('The Boarding House')

'Mr James Duffy lived in Chapelizod because he wished to live as far as possible from the city of which he was a citizen and because he found all the other suburbs of Dublin mean, modern and pretentious.' ('A Painful Case')

'Two gentlemen who were in the lavatory at the time tried to lift him up; but he was quite helpless'. ('Grace')

'Lily, the caretaker's daughter, was literally run off her feet'. ('The Dead')

I have tried to define, or at least to describe, the presence in Joyce's style of a quality, a condition, a customary radiance, which I suggest comes directly from his character (his 'genius of character'), which he consciously developed over the years. That word 'human' which he repeats over and over, like a mantra, is what one has to grapple with. Joyce's humanity is among the bravest of the twentieth century, or indeed in the history of literature. That humanity has been recognised and admired by many, but no-one has paid tribute to Joyce's human-ness more beautifully than another blind poet, the South American Jorge Luis Borges, in his poem *Invocation to Joyce*.

I shall end with that poem:

> You, all the while,
> in cities of exile,
> in that exile that was
> your detested and chosen instrument,
> the weapon of your craft,
> erected your pathless labyrinths,
> infinitesimal and infinite,
> wondrously paltry,
> more populous than history.
> We shall die without sighting
> the twofold beast or the rose
> that are the center of your maze,
> but memory holds its talismans,
> its echoes of Virgil,
> and so in the streets of night
> your splendid hells survive,

so many of your cadences and metaphors,
the treasures of your darkness.
What does our cowardice matter if on this earth
there is one brave man,
what does sadness matter if in time past
somebody thought himself happy,
what does my lost generation matter,
that dim mirror,
if your books justify us?
I am the others. I am all those
who have been rescued by your pains and care.
I am those unknown to you and saved by you.'

JOYCE AND GOGARTY

ROYAL AND ANCIENT, TWO HANGERS-ON

Ulick O'Connor

One of the difficulties in writing about this subject is that both of the protagonists have become known to many readers as characters in fiction. Oliver St John Gogarty appears in *Ulysses* as Malachi St Jesus Mulligan, and James Joyce as Stephen Dedalus. For this reason people often assume that the characteristics of the relationships that are described in *Ulysses* existed in real life –which is not at all true if an overall view is to be taken. Therefore one will have to try and distinguish between the two writers.

Secondly I would like to make it clear at the start the categories that I place the two of them in. When we are talking about James Joyce we are talking about the major prose writer of the century. With his novel *Ulysses* he can be held to have affected the imaginative output of painters, writers and musicians of this century in a way that no other writer has done. He bestrides the creative universe of our time. He is in a category into which one might perhaps admit Yeats, Eliot, Garcia Lorca or Pirandello, Eugene O'Neill but few others. On the other hand, Oliver St John Gogarty – though I have no wish to diminish his contribution – was a fine lyric poet but not a major one, as Yeats was.

I would also like to make a reference to the nature of the Gogarty-Joyce friendship. As they appear in *Ulysses*, Gogarty of course is portrayed as having betrayed Stephen Dedalus. As a result it has become popular to assume that he and Joyce were enemies throughout their lives. But through conversations with Gogarty himself and from a look at certain episodes in Joyce's later years, a different picture emerges. Joyce when he died had at his bedside Gogarty's *Life of St. Patrick* and a Greek lexicon to interpret the quotations in it. A few years earlier, writing to Harriet Weaver, he describes a crash in which Oliver St. John Gogarty was involved, in which case he said that since both the occupants of the plane were unhurt he might make a joke about it. He was also glad to see that his friend Buck Mulligan was unharmed. It is quite clear from this that Joyce had mellowed as regards Gogarty. On one occasion about 1954, I was walking with Gogarty near Hume Street (where George Moore had once lived) and when the subject of Joyce came up, Gogarty turned to me with a very firm look in his eye and said:

A Portrait of the Artist is one of the most beautifully written books in English of this century.

Let us start off with the pair of them as they were in Dublin at the turn of the century. Both of them were students. Padraic Colum remembers them as engaged in an 'apostolate of irreverence', satirising Church and State with their outrageous poems and limericks. Gogarty was known by George Moore as the 'author of all the limericks that enabled us to live in Dublin' and had the reputation round the city as being the creator of many of the bawdy ballads and blasphemous parodies that were circulating in that tuneful town. He was also a very well known athlete, being Irish champion cyclist, and as well had saved three men from drowning in the Liffey. Altogether a twentieth century incarnation of a Regency buck, with his primrose waistcoat and handsome violet eyes. Joyce, who accompanied Gogarty on his city trips and was very much of the brood of mockers himself, had the same appetite for literature and poetry as Gogarty and a similar imaginative stance towards life. They met one day when Gogarty came up to Joyce on a tram and asked him if he wrote poems. Joyce rather coldly said yes. They began to meet afterwards in Gogarty's country home in Glasnevin. There under the trees in the afternoon with tea served by the Gogarty servants, the two young men would compose lyrics, Joyce tending more towards the Elizabethan and Gogarty towards the Cavalier poets. Two poems will give an indication of how they wrote.

> My love is in a light attire
> Among the apple-trees,
> Where the gay winds do most desire
> To run in companies.
>
> ● ● ● ● ● ●
>
> And where the sky's a pale blue cup
> Over the laughing land,
> My love goes lightly holding up
> Her dress with dainty hand.   (James Joyce)

> My love is dark, but she is fair,
> As dark as damask roses are,
> As dark as woodland lake water
> That mirrors every star.
>
> But, as the moon who shines by night,
> She wins the darker air
> To blend its beauty with her light,
> Till dark is doubly fair.   (Oliver Gogarty)

They both shared a young man's contempt for the literary movement that was taking place around them. Gogarty railed at the 'Celtic Chloroform' while Joyce was inclined to say that the Celts had contributed nothing but 'a whine to Europe' and disparaged Lady Gregory's 'dwarf dramas'.

Often they would give expression to their reaction against society by going to the brothel area of Dublin which was known as the Kips. Here Gogarty had a ready acquaintance with the Madams of the Place, which gave Joyce an easy entrance. Gogarty's wit and camaraderie enchanted the ladies but Joyce was often somewhat taciturn in their company, perhaps a little embarrassed. Often to relieve his embarrassment he would sing Gregorian hymns and Gogarty celebrated this in a Limerick.

> There was a young fellow called Joyce
> Who possesseth a sweet tenor voice
> He goes to the Kips
> With a psalm on his lips
> And biddeth the huers rejoice.

A ballad which Gogarty wrote about the area can give us a glimpse into his ability to capture without any of the roseate prism of the pre-Raphaelites, or the hearty attempts of Belloc to recreate the Paris of Villon, the atmosphere of the Dublin brothels. In Villonesque metre and rhyme Gogarty remembers the figures who came to the Hay Hotel. The Hay Hotel was a house in the outskirts of the Kips where gentlemen went afterwards to recover from the effects of their activities inside. It was called the Hay Hotel because there was hay in the window for the horses of the cabbies who waited outside.

THE HAY HOTEL

> There is a window stuffed with hay
> Like herbage in an oven cast;
> And there we came at break of day
> To soothe ourselved with light repast:
> And men who worked before the mast
> And drunken girls delectable:
> A future symbol of our past
> You'll, maybe, find the Hay Hotel.
>
> Where are the great Kip Bullies gone,
> The Bookies and outrageous Whores
> Whom we so gaily rode upon

THE ARTIST AND THE LABYRINTH

When youth was mine and youth was yours:
Tyrone Street of the crowded doors
And Faithful Place so infidel?
It matters little who explores
He'll only find the Hay Hotel.

Dick Lynam was a likely lad,
His back was straight; has he gone down?
And for a pal Jem Plant he had
Whose navel was like half a crown.
They were the talk of all Meck town;
And Norah Seymour loved them well;
Of all their haunts of lost renown
There's only left the Hay Hotel.

Fresh Nellie's gone and Mrs Mack
Mary Oblong's gone and Number Five,
Where you could get so good a back
And drinks were so superlative;
Of all their nights, O Man Alive!
There is not left any oyster shell
Where greens are gone the greys will thrive;
There's only left the Hay Hotel.

There's nothing left but ruin now
Where once the crazy cabfuls roared;
Where new-come sailors turned the prow
And Love-logged cattle-dealers snored:
The room where old Luke Irwin whored,
The stairs on which John Elwood fell:
Some things are better unencored:
There's only left the Hay Hotel.

Where is Piano Mary, say,
Who dwelt where Hell's Gates leave the street,
And all the tunes she used to play
Along your spine beneath the sheet?
She was a morsel passing sweet
And warmer than the gates of hell.
Who tunes her now between the feet?
Go ask them at the Hay Hotel.

JAMES JOYCE

Nay; never ask this week, fair Lord.
If, where they are now, all goes well,
So much depends on bed and board
They give them in the Hay Hotel.

When Joyce came to recreate his experiences in the Kips he
put them into his 'Nighttown' episode in *Ulysses*, one of the
seminal pieces of writing in modernday literature, in which he
splits time as Bergson had shown Proust and Pirandello how to
do. Here in this episode, which Joyce has written in film script
style, he allows the events of the day to reverberate through the
subconsciousness of the characters he has created in his novel. It is
almost as if Joyce had the chromosomes of the genes of the talking film in him, and being unable to create it, contented himself
with achieving on paper what a film could have done, had the
manner of making such a film existed at that time. The way the
scene appears in the novel reminds one of what Frederico Fellini
did with his *8½* in 1958 when he recreated on film the dreams of
his boyhood. But that was what Joyce was. His mind was bursting
out in every way in anticipation of some method by which he
could achieve the vision which he saw.

Joyce delighted in his friend Gogarty's outrageous behaviour
and his parodying of all that the respectable classes in the city held
sacred. When Gogarty went to Oxford in 1903 to study for the
Newdigate Medal he and Joyce wrote constant letters to one
another. We can see how close the friendship was from a letter
Joyce wrote to Gogarty and from Gogarty's letters back to Joyce.
The sad thing is that most of Joyce's letters were burnt in the fire
at Gogarty's country house, Renvyle, during the Civil War in 1923.
But we can see from Gogarty's letters and Joyce's that they were
soulmates. Gogarty talks to Joyce as 'Aengus of the Birds' and
called himself the Bard Gogarty. He even says to Joyce:

Oh Aengus of the Birds, sing sweetly so that the stones may
move and build a causeway to Oxford so that you may

come over.

He also sympathises with Joyce on a difficulty he has when, after an overvigorous episode in the Kips, Joyce found himself bearer of a subsequent affliction. Gogarty wrote:

I am glad to see that our Holy Mother has visited you with the Stigmata. I enclose a letter to a friend of mine, Dr. Walsh.

The enclosed letter read:

Dear Dr. Walsh: A friend of mine has an ambition to obtain employment as a water clock. Kindly restore his urethera to periodic function. The name of the tissue surrounding the injured part is James Joyce.
Oliver Gogarty.

When Gogarty came back to Dublin in the summer of 1904 his novel idea was to go out to a Martello tower outside Dublin and there to live with Joyce while his friend could write his masterpiece and he himself could write poetry. There is no doubt that he was very much taken with Joyce as his closest friend of the time and wanted to do everything to help him.

The best picture of their life there of course is in the opening of *Ulysses*:

Stately, plump Buck Mulligan came from the stairhead, bearing a bowl of lather on which a mirror and a razor lay crossed. A yellow dressing-gown, ungirdled, was sustained gently behind him by the mild morning air. He held the bowl aloft and intoned:

– *Introibo ad altare Dei.*

Halted, he peered down the dark winding stairs and called up coarsely:

– Come up, Kinch. Come up, you fearful jesuit.

• • • • • •

– The mockery of it, he said gaily. Your absurd name, an ancient Greek.

He pointed his finger in friendly jest and went over to the parapet, laughing to himself. Stephen Dedalus stepped up, followed him wearily halfway and sat down on the edge of the gunrest, watching him still as he propped his mirror on the parapet, dipped the brush in the bowl and lathered cheeks and neck.

Buck Mulligan's gay voice went on.

– My name is absurd too: Malachi Mulligan, two dactyls. But it has a Hellenic ring, hasn't it? Tripping and sunny like the buck himself. We must go to Athens. Will you come if I can get the aunt to fork out twenty quid?

He laid the brush aside and, laughing with delight, cried:

– Will he come? The jejune jesuit.

Ceasing, he began to shave with care.

– Tell me, Mulligan, Stephen said quietly.

– Yes, my love?

– How long is Haines going to stay in this tower?

Buck Mulligan showed a shaven cheek over his right shoulder.

– God, isn't he dreadful? he said frankly. A ponderous Saxon. He thinks you're not a gentleman. God, these bloody English. Bursting with money and indigestion. Because he comes from Oxford. You know, Dedalus, you have the real Oxford manner. He can't make you out. O, my name for you is the best: Kinch, the knife-blade.

Let us see the scene from Buck Mulligan's eye as Gogarty

writes in a letter to his friend GKA Bell in Oxford, describing how he refreshed the world under the sea by returning a lobster to it.

> I bought a lobster today alive, and when I put him in a little pool his marvellous colours reappeared freshly so that I resolved to restore him to the 'great sweet mother' and I took the twine off his claws and sent him seaward. I suppose they'll catch him again if he has not taken his experience to his ganglion. I am without him to supper now but perhaps it is better to have had him feed whatever little of the idea is in me with the beauty of his colouring than to supply my more transient need with the muscles inside his skeleton; Surely I'm not a Christian? No, the Galilean incidents around the lake: filling nets with fish and actually increasing other lakes prove that I have not imitated. My lobster is now wandering in the weird submarine moonlight which they say is emitted night and day by the animalcules at the sea-bottom and stretching his stiffened joints and (if he could) wondering has he been to Hades and gained a rebirth.

GKA Bell was a friend of his at Oxford and later was to become the Bishop of Chichester. He had hundreds of letters from Gogarty, which were about to be burnt when I saved them from the flames by visiting his widow in Chichester in 1959. I took photostats of all the letters, which is fortunate, as Bell's biographer burnt the originals later on. In these letters we can see very much what enjoyment Gogarty was getting from his friend and there are numerous references to Joyce in them. But after the first few weeks Joyce seems to have been misbehaving himself in some way so as to annoy Gogarty. And finally there is a reference to Joyce's leaving the tower.

> 'I have broken with Joyce', Gogarty writes to Bell on the 16th August 1904.

> His want of generosity became to me inexcusable. He lam-

pooned Yeats, *AE, Colum and others* to whom he was indebted. A desert was revealed which I did not think existed amid the seeming luxuriance of his soul.

Now the interesting thing about this is that it does seem to coincide with a pose that Joyce had adopted at that time after his return from Paris. He had dressed himself in a wide brimmed hat and cloak in imitation of the young Rimbaud and he may have adopted some of Rimbaud's habits as well. We know that Rimbaud as a young man made a virtue out of exercising ingratitude towards those who had helped him. (If you bought him a drink he was quite likely to spit at you).

It is also true that Joyce, finding himself in an unfriendly world and feeling with the sensitivity of the artist, had to make his own soul, so to speak, creating an atmosphere in which, by assuming a hostile manner, he was able to protect himself. Whatever it was, there was a breach between the two at this time. It might well have been healed except that Joyce, a few months later, went off to Trieste with his girl Nora and didn't return to Ireland for four or five years. Gogarty wrote many letters to him during his absence and it is quite clear from the letters that the two were on friendly terms.

In letters Gogarty poured out his soul to his friend and included very often his latest episode in the Rabelaisian ballads he was writing. These letters, which are at Cornell University, indicate the relationship between the two. But Joyce's own letters back to his brother Stannie indicate that he was becoming suspicious of Gogarty and to some extent resented him. I have to say that I think Stannie's evidence is suspect all the time because he was jealous of Gogarty. Well might Stanislaus be jealous, because if it hadn't been for him perhaps Joyce would have not made the impact on literature that he did. It was Stanislaus' unselfishness that helped to keep Joyce alive. He didn't want anybody else getting in on the act. But whatever the reason, it seems that between the pair of them they concocted a dislike of Gogarty.

One can see the difficulties that Joyce had in the relationship. He had decided to devote his life specifically to works of the imagination, to live in a world where the creative stance was the only justifiable one. It was in fact a priest-like vocation to his art. He could have seen Gogarty very well as somebody who wanted to have it both ways. Gogarty was undoubtedly a poet. But he remained on in Dublin, he became a successful surgeon, he married a rich woman and, in Joyce's eyes, he settled for an easy life. There was nothing specifically wrong for a poet in all this. After all William Carlos Williams was a doctor and Wallace Stephens was an insurance inspector, quite apart from the fact that TS Eliot was a bank clerk. But one can well see that Joyce, with his ascetic dedication to his art, would have looked on Gogarty to some extent as taking the easy way out. In addition there is no doubt that Joyce had a pathological obsession with betrayal – an almost voluptuous desire to be betrayed. He writes to Stanislaus in 1905 saying that Gogarty would betray Sinn Fein and Griffith as previous traitors such as Leonard MacNally and Reynolds had betrayed the national cause.

Now this is a grossly unfair prediction and, as it would turn out to be, untrue. Gogarty had joined Sinn Fein as a young student in Trinity when it was a small radical group and when membership could have affected his future prospects as a professional man in the capital city, very much for the worse. He was to remain a loyal supporter of Sinn Fein and Arthur Griffith throughout his life, and in the 1920-21 era of Irish War of Independence Gogarty played a not insignificant part in support of his friend Arthur Griffith and his other friend Michael Collins.

I think we can take Stannie's statement that Gogarty had said to him that he wanted to break Jim's spirit with drink as either inaccurate or untrue. From my knowledge of Gogarty, from my feeling for him as a biographical subject, I think it is quite uncharacteristic. It may possibly have been said in jest, but there was certainly no malice in it. Gogarty just wasn't that sort of person. Throughout his life he was an admirer and not a denigrator of talent. But Joyce, whether it was during the attempt to get *Dubliners* published in Dublin, or whether it was the publication of *Ulysses*, or in his confrontation with the British Consul in Zurich, or his insisting that the attack on the train on which his wife was travelling in Ireland in 1922 was a deliberate attack on him, always chose to see himself as the 'betrayed' – in the role of a St Sebastian. Beckett's clever phrase about Proust could have been well applied to his friend and mentor Joyce.

The stations of an inverted Calvary retain their original dimension, their crescendo, their tension towards a cross.

Joyce and Gogarty met for the last time in 1909, when Joyce returned for a holiday to Dublin from Trieste. He had been five years absent. Gogarty, who was now established as a young surgeon, hearing that Joyce was in town, sent him a note asking him to come and see him, proposing that they have lunch at the Dolphin together.

31 VII '09   15 Ely Place
                                                   Dublin

Dear Joyce,

Curiosis Cosgrave tells me you are in Dublin. Before trying to get you to come to lunch at Dolphin on Monday next at 1 o'c. I would like to have a word with you. My man will drive you across (if you are in). I leave town at 5 each evening; but there can be changes if you turn up.

He will call about 3.20. Do come if you can or will. I am looking forward to seeing you with pleasure. There are many things I would like to discuss and a plan or two to divert you. You have not yet plumbed all the depths of poetry; there is Broderick the Bard! of whom more anon.

Yours

O.G.

Joyce seems to have accepted this invitation, but before the date for lunch came around, Gogarty, finding himself involved in a surgical consultation, wrote and asked Joyce could he come on another date.

2 VIII '09

15 Ely Place
Dublin

Dear Joyce,

I find that at 1 o'c tomorrow there is a patient coming who cannot come at any other time. I will be glad if, in view of this, you will forgive a little postponement of the lunch. I will let you know.

Yours

O.G.

There are two accounts of their subsequent meeting, one Joyce's, the other Gogarty's. Gogarty has written that Joyce came along to Ely Place and, after sitting in the dining-room for some time, looked out of the window at the roses in the garden and said enigmatically, 'Is this your revenge?' After he had made this remark he left the house. This was the last Gogarty saw of his contrary friend.

Joyce gives a somewhat different account of the affair in a letter to Stanislaus dated 4 August 1909.

Gogarty met me in Merrion Square. I passed him. He ran after me and took me by the arm and made a long speech and was very confused. He asked me to go to his house. I went. He made me go in and rambled on. To everything, I said, 'You have your life. Leave me to mine.' He invited me to go down to Enniskerry in his motor and lunch with him and wife. I declined and was very quiet and sober. He offered me grog (?) wine, coffee, tea: but I took nothing. In the end he said, blushing, 'Well do you really want me to go to hell and be damned?' I said, 'I bear you no ill will. I believe you have some points of good nature. You and I of six years ago are both dead. But, I must write as I have felt.' He said, 'I don't care a damn what you say of me so long as it is literature.' I said, 'Do you mean that?' He said, "I do. Honest to Jaysus (sic). Now will you shake hands with me at least?' I said, 'I will; on that understanding.'

Joyce's account would appear to contain at least some omissions, if we look at it in relation to the evidence contained in the two letters referred to above. There is no reference to the fact that Gogarty had written to him or to the fact that he had seemingly accepted the invitation to lunch. It is probable that Joyce was, as usual, on the defensive when writing to his brother about Gogarty and was anxious to impress on him his obdurate resistance to the siren-lure of Dublin life. Whichever account is true, this was to be the last occasion on which the two writers met.

Joyce, of course, went on to write *A Portrait of the Artist as a Young Man* (1916) and later *Ulysses* (1922) and *Finnegans Wake* (1939). Gogarty became a very successful ear nose and throat surgeon, had a house in Dublin and a house in the country. Married to a rich wife, to all intents and purposes he could be said to have had a very comfortable existence. He continued to write poetry and two of his poems were included in *The Oxford Book of English Verse* edited by Sir Arthur Quiller-Couch. 'The Plum Tree by the House' and 'The Image-Maker'. One wonders how Joyce must have reacted to this.

In the 1920-21 period Gogarty was very much occupied with political affairs and was one of those who helped the IRA in their fight for freedom. He became a Senator of the new Irish State in 1922 and he involved himself along with Yeats in public affairs.

It was about this time that he began to have a reputation as a poet, apart from his social success as a brilliant conversationalist in the Dublin tradition of Wilde and Sheridan in the English salons of their time. By 1924 Yeats was referring to him as a true lyric poet and in 1936, when *The Oxford Book of Modern Verse* was published, Yeats went so far as to refer to him as 'one of the great lyric poets of our age'. There were other numerous tributes to Gogarty's poetic gifts and though Yeats undoubtedly overestimated him by including seventeen poems in *The Oxford Book of Modern*

Verse, there is no doubt that Gogarty was a true poet who has his place in Irish literature.

When *Ulysses* appeared in 1922 and Gogarty saw himself depicted as Mulligan, he was furious. It seemed to him a betrayal that Joyce should have written about him as he did. He snarled:

That bloody Joyce whom I kept in my youth has written a book you can read on all the lavatory walls of Dublin;

When Norah Hoult, wishing to place Gogarty as a character in one of her novels, gave him smoke-blue eyes, because, as she said, Joyce was always right about such things, Gogarty replied indignantly that this was not so. Augustus John, who was a close friend of Gogarty's, could never draw him out on the subject of Joyce. Likewise, when John went to sketch Joyce in Paris, he could get no response from his sitter when he brought up Gogarty's name. Another artist, Sean O'Sullivan, did elicit a comment from Joyce while he was engaged in painting him; he happened to mention that Gogarty was a successful surgeon in Dublin. 'God help anyone who gets into the hands of that fellow', is how Joyce received the information.

As late as 1938, when Philip Toynbee was visiting Gogarty in Ely Place, Dublin, he mentioned Joyce's name, and the only reply he got from his host was, 'James Joyce was not a gentleman'.

When he went to America in 1939, Gogarty created a sensation in certain literary circles by attacking those aspects of Joyce's work which he looked on as confused and lacking in artistic merit. Critics who praised the obscurities in Joyce's work, he regarded with contempt. On a brochure sent to me from New York in 1954, Gogarty had noted down his reactions to this type of criticism. The brochure dealt with a forthcoming 'study' of *Ulysses* and was heavily studded with neo-Freudian jargon. One matter that seemed particularly to irritate Gogarty was that he claimed Leopold Bloom had been 'converted into a new Messiah', a symbol of the 'Blossoming Earth'.

As I said at the outset of this piece, Joyce is a colossus in the world of literature and he towers over the other people of his time. But it is interesting to see that the approach which Gogarty took when he resorted to prose writing was similar to that which underlay Joyce's concept of the novel. It was thought by some writers in the twenties that Joyce may well have finished off the novel with his *Ulysses* because it broke all the rules of the preceding writers and also made new ones which seemed impossible to live up to. Joyce was not interested in plot. He was interested in the human condition primarily, without ennobling it in any way by invented fiction. He did create his characters but he harnessed them very much to fact.

And thus it is that one sees constantly in the approach of the major writers of the century a desire to harness themselves to the actual facts of their lives. It is clear from Proust's approach that he but very slightly distorted the actual events of his life in order to get the massive effect of the fourteen volumes in which he describes the events which overtake Swann. Proust was to say to Gide that the only thing necessary in a work like that was not to use the word 'I' too often. So it was that when Joyce came to write *Ulysses* we find that the actual events of 16 June 1904 form a framework for the characters who move through the book. Gogarty too when he went to write his autobiography in two works (*As I was going down Sackville Street* which he described as 'a phantasy in fact', and *Tumbling in the Hay*) uses facts in an imaginative form so that the events seems to be whirling round outside time and space although he is recalling the events and the characters of his boyhood and later years.

But when it comes to poetry it is interesting to compare both of them. Joyce is in my view, which is perhaps an unpopular one, a very fine poet, especially in, *Chamber Music*. There is no doubt that the last poem – which was called by Yeats 'a technical and emotional masterpiece' – is remarkable when one considers it was written as early as 1904. These stressed metres which had gone out of English poetry and which were to be revived when Hopkins' verse made its appearance ten years later, are now apparent in Joyce's writing. The half rhymes, the imagery, the plunge into the subconscious are all things which anticipate much later movements in English verse.

I hear an army charging upon the land
　　And the thunder of horses plunging, foam about their
　　knees.
Arrogant, in black armour, behind them stand,
　　Disdaining the reins, with fluttering whips, the
　　charioteers.

They cry unto the night their battlename:
　　I moan in sleep when I hear afar their whirling
　　laughter.
They cleave the gloom of dreams, a blinding flame,
　　Clanging, clanging upon the heart as upon an anvil.

They come shaking in triumph their long green hair:
　　They come out of the sea and run shouting by the
　　shore.
My heart, have you no wisdom thus to despair?
　　My love, my love, my love, why have you left me alone?

Joyce gave up poetry as his main creative outlet in 1904, and only returned to it from time to time. But when he did actually set about publishing the book of verse in 1915 it seemed that his adventures in prose had quite dulled his taste. When *Pomes Penyeach* came out in 1915, there were things in it which would have disgraced a fifteen year old schoolboy. For instance, a poem like 'She Weeps Over Rahoon' really makes one's blood curdle. One can only think that absence from his craft would have allowed him to use such phrases as 'grey moonrise', 'softly falling', 'sadly calling', 'sad heart'.

Rain on Rahoon falls softly, softly falling,
Where my dark lover lies.
Sad is his voice that calls me, sadly calling,
At grey moonrise.

Love, hear thou
How soft, how sad his voice is ever calling
Ever unanswered, and the dark rain falling
Then as now.

Dark too our hearts, O love, shall lie and cold
As his sad heart has lain
Under the moongrey nettles, the black mould
And muttering rain.

In fact it is interesting that apart from 'A Prayer', which is acceptable as a shot at a modern genre, the only really telling piece in the whole collection is 'Tilly', which was written in 1904 about the time of Joyce's mother's death and which, with 'I Hear an Army', gives an idea of the direction in which he might have gone if he had continued as a poet.

However, it was as a prose writer that Joyce entered into realms of the imagination, in a way that no poet of this century (with the exception of Yeats) ever managed to equal.

Gogarty, on the other hand, showed solid growth from his work as a young student. For instance his poem. 'The Image Maker', which he wrote in 1906 at the age of 25 (and which, as I have noted, appears in *The Oxford Book of English Verse*) shows his ability to deal with a complex idea in poetic form.

Hard is the stone, but harder still
The delicate performing will
That, guided by a dream alone,
Subdues and moulds the hardest stone,
Making the stubborn jade release
The emblem of eternal peace.

If but the will be firmly bent
No stuff resists the mind's intent;
The adamant abets his skill
And sternly aids the artist's will,
To clothe in perdurable pride
Beauty his transient eyes descried.

His remarkable gift of being able to reproduce classical metres under the discipline of Anglo-Saxon stress is illustrated by his use of the Sapphic form in 'Portrait With Background'.

Here your long limbs and your golden hair affright men,
Slaves are their souls, and instinctively they hate them,
Knowing full well that such charms can but invite men,
    Heroes to mate them.

Eyes of the green of the woods that maddened Tristram!
Fair skin and smooth as the rosy-footed dove's wing!
Who would not fight, if he saw you, against this
    Trammelling of Love's wing?

Aye; and bow down if he saw but half the vision,
I dare not call to the mind's eye, to adore you;
And be, if that great light shone with precision,
    Awe-struck before you.

Then there is 'Golden Stockings'!

Golden stockings you had on
In the meadow where you ran;
And your little knees together
Bobbed like pippins in the weather.
When the breezes rush and fight
For those dimples of delight,
And they dance from the pursuit,
And the leaf looks like the fruit.

I have many a sight in mind
That would last if I were blind;
Many verses I could write
That would bring me many a sight.
Now I only see but one,
See you running in the sun,
And the gold-dust coming up
From the trampled butter-cup.

'Ringsend', which he wrote in his later years, captures the quality
of the early brothel poems in a more general and universal way.

JAMES JOYCE

RINGSEND (After reading Tolstoy)

I will live in Ringsend
With a red-headed whore,
And the fanlight going in
Where it lights the hall-door;
And listen each night
For her querulous shout,
As at last she streels in
And the pubs empty out.
To soothe that wild breast
With my old-fangled songs,
Till she feels it redressed
From inordinate wrongs,
Imagined, outrageous,
Preposterous wrongs,
Till peace at last comes,
Shall be all I will do,
Where the little lamp blooms,
Like a rose in the stew;
And up the back garden
The sound comes to me
Of the lapsing, unsoilable,
Whispering sea.

But his masterpiece was undoubtedly 'Leda', which he wrote in the
mock heroic style, and combining the classical idea with an entirely
modern genre.

Though her Mother told her
    Not to go a-bathing,
Leda loved the river
    And she could not keep away:
Wading in its freshets
    When the noon was heavy;
Walking by the water
At the close of day.

● ● ● ● ● ●

What was it she called him:
    Goosey-goosey gander?
For she knew no better
    Way to call a swan:
And the bird responding,
    Seemed to understand her,
For he left his sailing
    For the bank to waddle on.

Apple blossoms under
    Hills of Lacedaemon,
With the snow beyond them
    In the still blue air,
To the swan who hid them
    With his wings asunder,
Than the breasts of Leda,
    Were not lovelier!

Of the tales that daughters,
    Tell their poor old mothers,
Which by all accounts are
    Often very odd:
Leda's was a story
    Stranger than all other.
What was there to say but:
    Glory be to God?

•　•　•　•　•

When the hyacinthine
    Eggs were in the basket,
Blue as at the whiteness
    Where a cloud begins;
Who would dream there lay there
    All that Trojan brightness;
Agamemnon murdered;
    And the mighty Twins?

I think Joyce would be especially delighted at this last verse, with its synthesis of the Trojan tale woven into the rhythms of a nursery rhyme – 'Goosey Goosey Gander'.

So that is how we must see them today. Gogarty a fine poet, Joyce a major figure, who has influenced every art in the evolution of the twentieth century.

In the end, Joyce, in his ascetic devotion to his art, may have given his life to express the insight that he had into the human condition. After *Finnegans Wake* was finished he seemed almost to turn over and die. Gogarty went on writing poetry until a comparatively late age. But there was something sad about the last years of Oliver Gogarty. He decided to be a full time writer only when he was almost in his sixties, and he left for the USA in 1939, feeling that he could make his living there by writing. Ironically, he became best known there as Buck Mulligan in *Ulysses*, and as the poet whom Yeats had praised in *The Oxford Book of Modern Verse*. He turned to journalism, forgetting perhaps that in doing so he would make it more difficult to bring to life the thing that he valued most, the material for his poetry.

I think that in his last years he must have felt he had not reached his full potential as a poet. Had he decided at an early age to devote himself entirely to his imaginative gift, he would have left more behind him. But perhaps this is to read into Gogarty something that wasn't part of his nature. He was essentially a Renaissance man. This is how Mario Rossi, the Italian critic, saw him: *L'uomo Universali*; a figure from Greece of the golden age, somebody who in his own words 'loved life and used it well' – which was from Gogarty's poem 'The Old Goose' published in '*An Offering of Swans*' (1924) – in order to find in life something worth expressing in his art.